PROPHETIC WORSHIP

BY
VIVIEN HIBBERT

Worship with Passion
Ps 27
Vivien Hibbert
2/2020

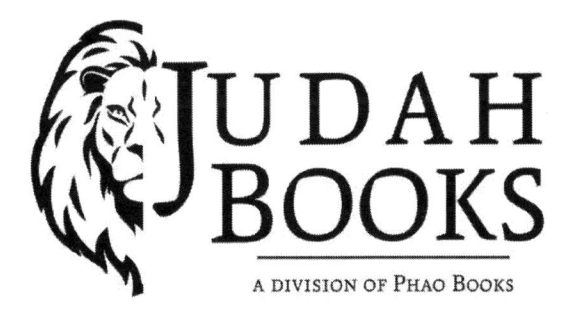

JUDAH BOOKS

A DIVISION OF PHAO BOOKS

PROPHETIC WORSHIP
Published by Judah Books a division of Phao Books

© 1999 Vivien Hibbert – Reprinted 2006, 2020

ALL RIGHTS RESERVED

No part of this publication may be reproduced, stored in a retrieval system, or transmitted in any form by any means—electronic, mechanical, photocopy, recording, or otherwise—without prior written permission of the publisher, except for brief quotations in critical reviews or articles. For further information or permission: contact Judah Books, 904 E. 12th St., Texarkana, AR 71854 or www.judah-books.com

ISBN 13: 978-0-9905345-3-2

Unless otherwise indicated, all scripture quotations are from the *Life Application Bible: New King James Version*. Copyright © 1988, 1989, 1990, 1991, 1993, 1996 by Tyndale House Publishers

Scripture quotations marked (AMP) are taken from The Amplified Bible, Copyright © 1987 by The Zondervan Corporation.

Scripture quotations marked (KJV) are taken from the King James Version.

Scripture quotations marked (Moffatt) are taken from A New Translation of The Bible Containing the Old and New Testaments, Copyright © 1922, 1924, 1925, 1926, 1935 by James Moffatt, Harper & Brothers Publishers, New York, NY.

Scripture quotations marked (NASV) are taken from New American Standard Version, Copyright © 1969, 1962, 1963, 1968, 1971, 1972, 1973, 1975, 1977 by The Lockman Foundation.

Scripture quotations marked (NEB) are taken from the New English Bible, Copyright © 1961, 1970 by Oxford University Press and Cambridge University Press.

Scripture quotations marked (NIV) are taken from the New International Version, Copyright © 1973, 1978, 1984 by International Bible Society.

Scripture quotations marked (NLT) are taken from the New Living Translation, Copyright © 1996, 2004, 2015 by Tyndale House Foundation, Inc., Carol Stream, Illinois 60188. Used by permission of Tyndale House. All rights reserved.

Scripture quotations marked (TPT) are taken from The Passion Translation®
Copyright © 2017, Broadstreet Publishing® Group, LLC.
Used by permission. All rights reserved. thePassionTranslation.com

Scripture quotations marked (WEY) are taken from the 1912 Weymouth New Testament. Public Domain.

TABLE OF CONTENTS

Foreword	5
Acknowledgments	7
Preface	11

PART ONE: AN INTRODUCTION TO PROPHETIC WORSHIP — 15

Ch. 1: What is Prophetic Worship?	17
Ch. 2: What is the Difference between Praise and Worship?	35
Ch. 3: The Foundation of Worship	45
Ch. 4: Understanding the Ancient Words for Praise and Worship	57

PART TWO: THE SCRIPTURAL PATTERN FOR PROPHETIC WORSHIP—2 COR. 3:18 — 73

Ch. 5: Worship is for Everyone	77
Ch. 6: Worship is the Place for Transparency	83
Ch. 7: Worship is Prophetic	91
Ch. 8: Worship is Transcendent	99
Ch. 9: Worship is Transforming	117
Ch. 10: Worship is Eternal	129
Ch. 11: Worship is Initiated by the Holy Spirit	137

PART THREE: PROPHETIC WORSHIP—A NEW EXEMPLAR — 145

Ch. 12: An Introduction to Breaking Worship Traditions — 147

Ch. 13: Redefining Praise and Worship — 157

Ch. 14: The Control of the Service — 165

Ch. 15: The Priesthood of All Believers — 169

Ch. 16: Time Limits in the Worship Service — 179

Ch. 17: The Emphasis and Priority of Worship — 187

Ch. 18: Transcending Denominational Barriers in Worship — 191

Ch. 19: The Impact of Culture on Worship — 201

Ch. 20: Music and Art in Worship — 217

Ch. 21: Recognizing the Prophetic Sound in Worship — 231

Ch. 22: The Maturity of Worshipers — 245

Ch. 23: Individual Experience vs. a Corporate Journey — 255

Ch. 24: Hearing the Voice of God in Worship — 261

Ch. 25: Conclusion — 281

Endnotes — 287
Bibliography — 297

Foreword

*Worship God! For the testimony of Jesus
is the spirit of prophecy.
Revelation 19:10b*

Why, one might ask, "Do we need another book on worship?" However, in the case of this book, one might ask a totally different question: "Why wasn't it written sooner?" I sense God desires to bring a greater unity to the Body of Christ in the realm of worship. Even though I believe this book is in the perfect timing of God, I admit to having not a little concern that such a comprehensive treatment on worship has not been written.

In the season in which we live, there are many ideas about worship. The reason for this is the great hunger, which the Holy Spirit has divinely imparted to the people of God. Because of this hunger, we either jump in over our heads where even angels fear to tread, or we get in just enough to get our feet wet. While maintaining a thoroughly biblical perspective, the contents of this book will produce an assurance in your heart that extravagant worship is not *risky*, but will be transforming and reviving to all.

The bottom line concerning worship is obedience to God. A life of obedience is the highest expression of worship. Though having said that, I emphatically believe what takes place in a sanctuary while His people are gathered is of greater importance than most believe. Worship is encountering God. Could it be that a sense of supernatural awe could be restored to the Church if, through worship, she pressed into God's presence? A *worship service* is simply His people gathered around His presence, worshiping in spirit and truth until they see or experience something which can only be explained as a "God-thing."

A need has arisen which can only be satisfied by one on whom rests the anointing of God. Vivien Hibbert is one anointed with tremendous insight into the kind of worship which changes lives, churches, and nations. I believe a mantle is upon her to proclaim the glorious truth about prophetic worship. She desires to bring fresh vision for worship to churches all over the world. She has pastored, so she has the understanding of a pastor's heart. While serving as Worship Director for the church I pastored, she truly brought scriptural understanding of prophetic worship and a release of God's presence in our midst. It is her heart's desire to see the glory of the Lord cover the earth as the waters cover the seas.

If followed, the truths expressed in this book will help develop and keep worship life-changing and fresh for any congregation. I know of no other book as comprehensive as this, concerning prophetic worship. Once you apprehend the heart of what God has shown Vivien, you will never again be satisfied with substituting a *song service* for a worship service.

Olen Griffing
Apostolic Elder, Gateway Church
Dallas, TX

Vivien Hibbert is beyond doubt the best teacher on the subject of prophetic worship. This book contains 'fresh manna' for true worshipers.

Dr. E. Charlotte Baker
Pastor, Teacher & Author

I highly recommend Prophetic Worship for those who want to hear the Lord among His people today. Vivien Hibbert articulates clearly the differences between traditional and prophetic worship. She has experience and understanding that can help the Church transcend horizontal worship and experience the presence of God.

LaMar Boschman
Dean of the International Worship Leader's Institute

ACKNOWLEDGMENTS

So many people have helped me write and rewrite this book. Huge thanks to each of these friends who have prayed, encouraged, pressed, pushed, and forced me to dig deeper as a writer and communicator. I may have thought I would drown, but each of you believed in this project and helped to bring it to birth. Each one of you deserves more praise than can fit into these three pages, but I will make an attempt at expressing my heart.

Gwen and Harvey – I don't know where I would be today without your kindness. I do know that this book would remain unpublished, and I might be involved in some secular endeavor. You found me disheartened and finished with ministry as I had known it; and you picked me up, inspired deep changes in my life, motivated me into setting out on a new course and put the tools into my hands to move forward. Time and again we dig out the "precious from the vile" together (Jer. 15:19). I owe you the greatest debt of all – friendship.

Waterwaze, Ashdown, AR – This is my home church where the truths of prophetic worship are embraced and promoted every week. We are on a remarkable journey together as we seek to worship God in spirit and truth. Thank you, Terry, Anna, and every member of this unique congregation. You are all so valuable in my life – you are champions in our wee "city of champions." Special thanks to Jill Dudley.

The Fellowship, Salt Lake City, UT – I will never forget your friendship through some of the most difficult days of my life. You have watered my soul again and again – thank you. You are another congregation that models prophetic worship for all generations. I am so grateful that we walk together – always.

New Beginnings, Chicago Park, CA – What an encouragement you are to me! I treasure your friendship and the commitment you have made to see this message reach the whole Body of Christ. To each one – thank you.

Whole Life Ministries and Pastor Sandra Kennedy, Augusta, GA – Another wonderful worshiping church where God's presence is honored above all else. Thank you for uncompromisingly hosting Jesus in your sanctuary, in your hearts and in your services.

Pastor/Apostle Olen and Syble – It was at Shady Grove in Grand Prairie, TX where we first watched the Lord taking us into deep realms of worship and supernatural encounters with His presence. It had happened before, of course, to countless believers over the course of time, but at Shady Grove we saw these encounters work effectively in a large and diverse congregation. It was your uncompromising hearts of worship and bold leadership that inspired us all to go into profound worship every week. None of us escaped those meetings unchanged. This book is my frail attempt to describe what we learned and make it available for the entire Body of Christ. You are my heroes.

Charlotte Baker — Although she died on September 16, 2014, Sister Baker's legacy continues to grow and bear fruit. She is the "mother" of so many who are a part of the current worship revival throughout the nations. More than any other, she faithfully dreamed, taught, birthed, and mentored prophetic worship before there was ever such a term. I am eternally grateful for her life and the secrets she unselfishly gave to all who were hungry for true worship.

For *all of the gracious friends who have prayed for me as I have labored to write this book* — I am forever grateful for your love, support, and practical help. You have been a rich blessing to me; thank you all.

To my precious friends in Colombia — thank you for your love and prayers. You are so dear to me. Colombia lives in my heart. What a joy to worship extravagantly in your nation. *Gustavo and Amparo* – I thank God for you. You are responsible for encouraging and equipping me to write this book. Muchas gracias.

Acknowledgements

Symposium, Pasadena; Karitos, Chicago; Dance Camp, Charlotte – three completely different worship conferences where I have worshiped, wept, learned, developed and imparted this message over the past 30 years. What wonderful worship companions you all are!

New Zealand Churches — It has been so many years since I have lived in my homeland, New Zealand, yet I never forget the friends, churches and worship times that laid a foundation for everything that is in this book. Aotearoa, you are forever in my heart.

Cindy, Jessica – I am so grateful for your willingness to help get this project over the finish line. You are treasured friends indeed. Your many skills have been a huge boost.

Thank you Lord that You draw us to Your face and invite us to contemplate Your wonders forever. You are the subject and reason for this book; Your presence is my single goal. May You alone be glorified.

*One thing I have desired of the Lord, That will I seek:
That I may dwell in the house of the Lord All the days of my life,
To behold the beauty of the Lord, And to inquire in His temple.
Psalm 27:4*

Preface

*"The great search of the human heart
is the search to discover the One
who is worthy of our worship."*

\- Sammy Tippit

The prayer of all those who have helped with this project is for this book to inspire worship in the hearts of every reader. Please look beyond the words on these pages. My desire is to express the heart of the Father as He longs for communion with His people. May you see His face. May the weight of His glory constrain you as you read these words. May something of eternity be opened to you, and may your hunger for God be increased and even overwhelm you.

> The [Holy] Spirit and the bride (the church, the true Christians) say, Come! And let him who is listening say, Come! And let everyone come who is thirsty [who is painfully conscious of his need of those things by which the soul is refreshed, supported and strengthened]; and whoever [earnestly] desires to do it, let him come, take, appropriate, *and* drink the water of Life without cost (Rev. 22:17, *AMP*).

Worship is the most fundamental activity of all mankind. It is born in the deepest longing of every heart—the desire to know and be known. All true worship is a delight to both God and man. It is God who initiates the call upon the heart to arise to new places of intimacy and maturity in Him. Because of this, He places within us a cry for more of Him. If the Church is to minister life to all the earth, then this cry must increase and be formed within us. The longing for true communion in worship must become our life and our breath. Worship is ultimately the key that unlocks our lives before the Lord.

At its very heart, worship is, and will always be, prophetic. Unfortunately, it has not been taught or treated as prophetic in many of our churches. We fail to glimpse the glories or plumb the depths of what God intends for us as worshipers. Because of this lack, we have missed the very nature and essence of God's heart as we meet Him in church services and private devotion.

The word *worship* is often misunderstood as is the word *revival*. Churches post signs outside their buildings that inform the community of their next *revival*. What they really mean is that special meetings are to be held at that location. Whether true revival occurs or not will depend on a sovereign act of God and the brokenness of His people.

This illustrates how we have reduced the meaning of *revival* to an event rather than an encounter with God. The same thing has happened to the word *worship*. We may say that we have "worship services" on Sundays, but whether worship really takes place is the underlying theme of this book.

To overcome this confusion in the terms *revival* and *worship*, many writers are forced to add adjectives such as *true, real, genuine,* or even *prophetic*. It would be the same as if I often said to you, "Let me give you some food," but all I ever gave you was a picture of food. If I wanted you to understand that there was really something to eat, I would have to indicate that the food on that particular occasion was *real*.

I have tried to clarify the meaning of *worship* through the title of this book. The term *prophetic worship* is not found in the Bible, but all worship is prophetic by biblical definition, because it involves an encounter with the presence of God and His voice among us. If God is not present, it is impossible to worship. Once His presence is known, it is impossible *not* to worship. I have used the word *prophetic,* because it is such an apt description of what takes place whenever we meet with the Lord. It is the description of His voice and communion among us. I am also trying to emphasize worship that is born in His presence rather than in age-old traditions that have lost their significance. It is my conviction that people who give themselves to worship are also giving themselves to the Spirit of prophecy. The reality of His presence and our communion with Him make worship prophetic. The problem with our definitions only arises when we stand outside His presence and refuse to commune with Him in the corporate worship setting. In that case, I would have to suggest that *true, real, genuine* or even *prophetic* worship is not taking place.

This book is a call to leaders, believers, and artists of every sort to seriously consider the priority and possibilities of worship in their lives and ministries. Worship is the primary ministry of the angels. It is the only ministry that will continue for believers when they enter heaven. It is the ministry that causes the likeness of Christ to be formed in every heart. It is the most noble of all earthly activities.

No matter how many instruments we have in our band or what level of excellence we achieve, *we will not have worship unless we have God's presence.* Take note of the plethora of skilled musicians and worship leaders in the Body of Christ today. Worship CDs are top sellers in Christian music stores and online. Exceptional new songs can be heard from every corner of the world and every denomination of the Church. Yet, it is not the music that causes worship. The music is simply the vehicle that true worship can ride upon. We must go *through* the songs into the presence of the Lord.

Let worship visit the arts and the arts visit worship again. It is time for all the arts to return, both to the Church and to their place in worship. Let the Church experience genuine revival so we might release prophetic artists to every nation and have prophetic worship in every denomination.

In order for worship to resume its rightful place in our hearts, we must all make a serious commitment to becoming students of His presence. We must return to the simplicity of loving Jesus and openly communing with Him in our services.

It is my desire that this book will point to Jesus and glorify Him. Ultimately, the truth of worship is found in Jesus Christ himself, not in the formats and traditions of our various denominations. A new movement is being born in the Church, made up of believers of all denominations, nations, and generations—a zealous and worshiping people that arise from the north, south, east, and west—prophetic worshipers who hunger and thirst for the presence of God and His transforming work in their hearts.

Let us pray with Moses, the most dangerous prayer of the Bible: "Show me Your glory." (Ex. 33:18)

There are shelves of excellent books written on worship. I have no desire to rewrite these volumes or repeat the concepts that have already been penned. However, it is in humility that I seek to add some further thoughts to this vast subject. It is a subject that could never be fully explored, even after a thousand lifetimes.

I bless you as you read and enter into prophetic worship.

Part One

An Introduction to Prophetic Worship

CHAPTER ONE

WHAT IS PROPHETIC WORSHIP?

> *"Worship is the submission*
> *of all our nature to God.*
> *It is the quickening of conscience by His holiness,*
> *the nourishment of mind with His truth,*
> *the purifying of imagination by His beauty,*
> *the opening of the heart to His love,*
> *the surrender of will to His purpose,*
> *and all this gathered up in adoration,*
> *the most selfless emotion of which our nature is capable,*
> *and, therefore, the chief remedy for that self-centeredness,*
> *which is our original sin and the source of all actual sin."*
> — William Temple

Prophetic worship is presence worship. It gives expression to our passion and communion with God. Prophetic worship is filled with God's voice and manifest presence as He responds to us. Whenever we recognize and make way for God's voice in our worship, we have prophetic worship. His participation in our worship is the "prophetic" component. This presence-filled worship can occur in our private devotion or in the worship expression of any church – anywhere – at any time. We just have to make way for God's voice and expression among us.

> *"Prophetic worship is presence worship."*

God's participation in worship should be the standard experience for every Believer and every Church on a daily basis. Unfortunately, this is so often not the case as we tend to shut God out of our lives just as the Israelites did thousands of years ago: *Then they said to Moses, "You speak with us, and we will hear, but let not God speak with us, lest we die."* (Ex. 20:19)

God desperately *wants* to be with us, speak with us, and reveal Himself to us, but we are like so many of His people throughout the ages, who have shied away from His presence all too often. We fill our worship with songs, prayers, readings, exhortations, dances and words until there is no room for God's response. We do all the talking. We have no thought that the God of Heaven and Earth would want to speak into our souls, whisper into our hearts, shout into our sanctuary, or roar into our nation...right there in the midst of our earnest worship offerings. For over two thousand years, we have come up with every excuse to program Him out of our worship services – all while our songs, music, dances and other expressions of praise have become more and more beautiful and creative.

We sing and dance for Him; we clap our hands and shout our praises; we lift our voices and bow down before Him. That is all so good...so excellent, but these things are only one part of worship. Once we have completed our songs and ministry to Him, we sit down and go on with our service – announcements, offerings, etc. We do not even realize that God is not finished with us. Worship is never complete when it only goes one way – just as love is not fulfilled when it is unanswered. Our ministry before Him is part one. His ministry and voice in response is the subject of this book – it is the prophetic part of worship. So many individuals and churches do not wait long enough for that response from God. Many do not realize that He longs to be involved in our worship. If only we would wait just a moment and linger in His presence. To "linger" means "to stay longer than is usual or expected...to be slow in parting...slow to speak or act."

I like those thoughts when we apply both of them to worship. If only we could plan to linger and wait on God as a consistent part of our worship – to make way for His voice and His response to our praise and stay longer than "normal", where we are slow to speak and where we are unhurried as we "hang out" with God. That doesn't mean we have to have agonizingly long worship...it just means that we cut out a few of the songs we planned to sing and make room for the Lord to sing a couple of His.

I am sure you have experienced services where the worship was dynamic and alive. God's presence was unmistakable. Every member of the congregation was basking in His glory, and suddenly the moment was cut off because the song was over, the time was up, or the worship leader did not recognize what to do with such glory. How our hearts ache whenever this happens.

We need to approach worship with the understanding that He has a plan and purpose for every service. He has a master scheme already prepared to bless us beyond anything we could ever imagine, and yet we shut Him out day after day, week after week, century after century. We give no thought to what He might want to say, do, or accomplish in the midst of worship. We need worship leaders who know how to enter His gates and open the doors to His courts. We need worship ministers, musicians, singers and dancers who know how to interact in the courts of the King and carry the voice of the Bride and the Bridegroom.

There will be times when He will come among us as King, Warrior, Healer, Shepherd, Restorer, Father, etc. The

> "We can meet with the Creator of the universe, interact with Him in His courts and hear His heart every time we step aside from our busy lives and enter his presence."

possibilities are infinite...endless and absolutely breathtaking. All it takes is worship ministers who know how to open these doors and draw God's people into Him.

We can meet with the Creator of the universe, interact with Him in His courts and hear His heart every time we step aside from our busy lives and enter his presence.

THE PRESENCE OF GOD IN WORSHIP

God asked Jeremiah a question for all the ages: *who is he who will devote himself to be close to me?' declares the Lord.* (Jer. 30:21b NIV).

God's Master plan for worship hinges on the fact that God longs for us to be close to Him. In other words, we are able to radically and remarkably host His presence as a part of our lives and our corporate meetings. There is nothing more magnificent in worship than this. He dwells or abides with us at all times (John 15:4-7) – His presence is a delightful constant in our personal lives and in our corporate meetings.

God's dwelling or abiding presence leads to the *expression* of His presence...or His *manifest presence*. This is what we are graced with in prophetic worship. When God reveals Himself, shows up, speaks, or displays Himself in some way – that is prophetic worship.

God has given us the Holy Spirit as an ever-abiding presence in our lives (1 John 4:13). His presence is a constant fact. As worshipers, we can always draw near to Him. However, He responds to our love and longing for Him with the manifesting of His presence in some way (Jn. 14:21; 17:24).

God's presence in worship is not a "hit or miss" occurrence – it should not be something that happens once or twice a year. This should be the "norm" in every worship service and every time we meet with Him. He desires that we break in on Him and that He would be invited to break in on us.

PROPHETIC WORSHIP IS FOR EVERYONE

Prophetic worship is not a style of worship – something to be preferred over another or something we can choose whether to include in our services. For example, some may prefer a liturgical service to a contemporary-style service or hymns instead of present-day choruses. Prophetic worship does not present a choice like that. You can have prophetic worship in any of those services – no matter the denomination or style of music – because God's voice and presence flow alongside and out of whatever we do in worship. Prophetic worship is God's response and participation within the worship conversation. Whether it is a conservative service or a radically innovative and contemporary service – we can still have prophetic worship because we ultimately want God's presence in every service.

Sing your hymns or your choruses and then listen for God's voice. Make way somewhere for Him to draw near and speak back to His people. Do not always dictate to him how this should be done. Trust Him to break into your service in a way that is respectful of your congregation's distinctive traditions and unique worship journey.

Therefore, prophetic worship is not a style of worship but a theology of worship that more accurately describes worship as it can be in every church and denomination.

Prophetic worship is not Pentecostal, Charismatic, Methodist, Anglican, Baptist, or any other tradition. It is Biblical worship. It is worship as God desires it. Prophetic worship has been laid out in the scriptures from the beginning; we have just not apprehended all that is available to us in worship and communion with the Lord. The people of God have limited the scope and meaning of *worship* by using this term to describe their particular Sunday service. Worship in both the Old and New Testament is meant to be interactive, bold, dynamic, supernatural, revelatory, and infused with the voice and presence of God.

> *"Worship in both the Old and New Testament is meant to be interactive, bold, dynamic, supernatural, revelatory, and infused with the voice and presence of God."*

It is worth noting that there is not a separate Bible for each denomination. The principles of prophetic worship are clear throughout the Word of God. Prophetic worship is equally relevant in a Baptist church as it is in a Presbyterian church or a Pentecostal church because this worship is about how we allow

God's presence to flow in our services. Every church believes in the presence of God and wants the presence of God. If we start there, then we are on our way to prophetic worship.

Bob Sorge explains it this way: "Prophetic worship is, quite simply, walking and talking with the Lord. Worship is an exchange—it is two-way communication."[1]

So many worship leaders are bound to their song list. If only we could see songs as a tool to get us into the presence of the Lord rather than the beginning and end of our worship experience. Once we make space for the Lord by lingering at the end of a song or waiting in His presence, He is so faithful to respond. We must see the song as the vehicle to carry the people to the Lord. Take the people *through* the song to the Lord. The song is not the worship – the song transports us to worship. That is why so many people get bored with certain songs – they are only focused on the song. But, if you go *through* the song to the face of God, you will never be bored. Focus on the face and presence of God – not just the music and how it makes you feel. Emphasize the heart of worship rather than the songs of worship.

After a recent *Karitos* conference in Chicago, several artists came together for an evening of worship. There were dancers, singers, musicians, painters, and poets. Because there were no time constraints, we were able to relax and allow the Holy Spirit to flow through each one of us. He became the conductor of a divine orchestra engaged in a conversation between Heaven and Earth. The various worshippers became instruments to highlight aspects of His voice as He flowed seamlessly from artist to artist. Sometimes He used the prophetic song to convey His message, or a dance, or a well-timed scripture reading and exhortation. Painters just seemed to have the perfect means to illustrate His message. All of the people flowed as one.

The particular thing that blessed me was the way so many people seemed to *get it* for the first time. There is no better means to communicate this message than experience. One time in this atmosphere and you will comprehend how Heaven and Earth flow together in the worship exchange. God is certainly not sitting passively by.

THERE IS NO AUDIENCE IN PROPHETIC WORSHIP

For years, I have heard it said that God is the "Audience of One." If that is the case, then we are performing for Him, and that is not right at all. I understand what people are trying to say – they are trying to get away from thinking of the congregation as the "audience." We want to give the Lord due reverence and are asking the people to get involved in their worship responsibilities. I get it.

As I have said, what we do in worship is just one part of the worship journey or conversation. There is another component that is the subject of this book – God's part. In worship there is no audience – only communing hearts. The Lord does not sit far away passively watching and listening to our worship. He is seated among us and enthroned in the praises of His people (Ps. 22:3); He desires to breathe into our hearts, speak into the service, and sing through the instruments. In many ways, He longs for His voice to be heard and His will to be inserted into our gathering. This is a life-changing thing for any church – every time we are together, He is with us (Matt. 18:20).

No doubt, every church already experiences His presence. Recognizing His presence is a key; then knowing what to do when we encounter Him is crucial. He is found in what we might have often considered "mundane" or "plain." Such things include our songs, the fellowship of believers, the kindness of friends and strangers, the authentic prayers of hungry hearts, the gifts of the Holy Spirit, the communion table, the dances of children and worshipers, the comforting words of pastors, the sounds of an instrument, and a thousand more intentional and unforeseen moments of our services. If only our spiritual eyes could see Him at work and flow more naturally with His divine design. It would truly be Heaven on Earth. Each of these things can become an instrument of God's voice and a part of the prophetic process if we allow God to flow. They are transformed from the routine to the divine through the reality of God's presence among us.

To be clear, what makes worship prophetic is His presence,

the manifesting of His glory, the life of His Spirit, and the sweetness of His voice among us. It is not the style, volume, length, or anything that *we* do in the worship that makes it prophetic. It is *God's response* and *participation* in the service that makes worship prophetic. We make way for Him – we open the gates for the King of glory.

THE PREMISE OF PROPHETIC WORSHIP

Throughout this book, I want to explore the idea that *worship is by definition prophetic in nature.* This is the premise and underlying theme of every chapter. Worship is prophetic because it flows from the presence and self-revelation of God. Worship is not possible until God reveals himself, but once He does, it is impossible *not* to worship Him. This thought will be repeated throughout the text, as it is a fundamental and pivotal concept of prophetic worship. Two great writers on worship concur.

"...worship is a natural response to an awareness of God's presence."[2]

"...worship is the human response to divine revelation, set in a dialogue pattern."[3]

The term *prophetic worship* is something of a misnomer as *true worship* has always been and always will be *prophetic*. No matter what style or form it takes, worship "in spirit and in truth" (John 4:24) is worship that is alive with the thoughts and voice of God. In a wider sense, God's voice will encompass the essence of the term *prophetic*. Through worship, we come into greater intimacy and knowledge of God.

We can praise Him without sensing or experiencing His presence, but without a God encounter, we cannot move into true worship. We worship face-to-face as we allow the Lord to respond and sing or speak back to us, to have His way among us and *uncover* Himself or make Himself known. This is the part that is so often missing – where we intentionally make space for the Lord to speak, sing or resound among us.

Some might think that we have not worshiped unless we have

gone on for several hours, or completed a liturgy, or fallen on the floor, or sung a hymn...or any other such thing. None of those things indicates we have worshiped. True worship involves the heart and God's presence. He has to be involved. It is not about what we do; it is about connection and communion with Him. It is not about our music – one style or another; it is about the authentic song from our heart and the place we make for the Lord among us. We can say:

- Prophetic worship is not necessarily spontaneous. However, the Lord does many things "suddenly." Being spontaneous is not what makes worship prophetic – His presence and voice makes worship prophetic.
- Prophetic worship is not necessarily emotional. Yet, the Lord often uses our emotions in worship. Being emotional is not what makes worship prophetic – His presence and voice makes worship prophetic.
- Prophetic worship is not necessarily long, but the Lord may often stays longer than we think is "normal."
- Prophetic worship is not necessarily loud. Yet, the Lord's voice sometimes roars like thunder or a trumpet.
- Prophetic worship is not necessarily extreme or unusual. However, the Lord is not constrained by our limitations of what is too extreme. He is known for being unusual according to our denominational or cultural norms.
- Prophetic worship is not necessarily filled with the arts. But the Lord is an artist and He expresses Himself artistically through His people.
- Prophetic worship is not necessarily filled with the gifts of the Spirit. But it may be as the Holy Spirit reveals the Father and the Son through these gifts.

He certainly does not aim to shock us, but by the same token, we are not involved in worship to make any of us comfortable. The goal is not to please any of our people but to honor God and see

His will done *on Earth as it is in Heaven*. Whenever we worship, we bring a little of Heaven into Earth. We gather in His name to glorify Him and worship in a way that is pleasing to Him, not necessarily in a way that satisfies us. You would never know that in many churches today. We seem to insist on worship that makes us comfortable and worship that suits our personal preferences rather than worship that is grounded in Biblical and theological truths.

PROPHETIC WORSHIP AND THE REVELATION OF GOD

In the first chapter of his letter to the Ephesians, Paul prayed, "That He may grant you a spirit of wisdom and revelation [of insight into mysteries and secrets] in the [deep and intimate] knowledge of Him, by having the eyes of your heart flooded with light, so that you can know *and* understand the hope to which He has called you, and how rich is His glorious inheritance in the saints (His set-apart ones)" (Eph. 1:17–18, *AMP*, see also through verse 23).

It is this "spirit of wisdom and revelation" that is so important in worship. In His presence, the "eyes of our hearts are flooded with light" so that we might know Him and the "...riches of the glory of His inheritance." (*AMP* and *NKJV* combined). Prophetic worship is inseparable from revelation. We can expect to receive revelation from God and His Word at any moment because He is alive, and His Word is alive in us and among us. This revelation can take us from a purely intellectual connection with the Lord to a supernatural and transformational relationship that affects our personal lives and our entire world.

THE GOAL OF PROPHETIC WORSHIP

Worship must be pleasing to God. It is all about Him. We come to minister to Him rather than have our own needs met, wait on Him rather than squeeze Him into our church program, hear His voice rather than attend a programmed religious concert, abandon ourselves before Him rather than be part of a groomed program and be changed by His glory rather than simply seek His seal of approval for our personal agendas. In the process of worship, He does meet our needs, and His presence becomes a vital part of our lives.

PROPHETIC WORSHIP AND PROPHECY

The overwhelming majority of biblical prophecy does not involve the predicting of the future. It is primarily concerned with confronting a backslidden people who have God's claim on their lives. When I use the term *prophetic*, I am using it in its fullest sense where God's voice, will, and character are made known to His people.

In the New Testament, one of the main purposes for prophecy is to edify the church. "But he who prophesies speaks edification and exhortation and comfort to men he who prophesies edifies the church" (1Cor. 14:3–4).

Prophecy and worship are closely related. Prophecy is the mind of God permeating the mind of man. Praise and worship produce the natural atmosphere for entrance into the prophetic realm, the place to receive His mind, heart, and attributes. Sorge concurs: "Praise and worship are natural complements to the functioning of the gifts of the Spirit (see 1Cor. 12:4–11), particularly prophecy. Both relate to and interact with the prophetic ministry."[4]

In First Chronicles 25:1-7, we find David's chief musicians and worship leaders—Asaph, Heman, and Jeduthun—listed as prophets and seers in Israel. They and their families prophesied with various instruments and were skillful in the prophetic song.

The primary Hebrew root word for *prophecy*, used on this and many other occasions, is *naba* (Strong's #H5012) meaning *to prophesy, to speak or sing by inspiration, to boil up, to pour out words with emotion.* A secondary meaning is *to chant, to sing sacred songs, to praise God while under divine influence.*

The work of the Holy Spirit is accomplished through the *prophetic anointing*. The primary work of the Holy Spirit in the earth is to uncover the character, nature, will, and purposes of the Father and Christ, His Son. The prophetic anointing is not the same as a prophetic word that is given to an individual or a group; it is the life and breath of the Holy Spirit in the midst of His people. The prophetic anointing keeps every aspect of our worship from being a dead form and opens our hearts to the voice and image of God.

Imagine the very life and breath of God upon every aspect of your worship service—every song, prayer, reading, vocal gift of the Spirit, the preaching, and the offerings. Through these gifts and expressions, the character of God is made known. The entire service holds a sense of the prophetic anointing. What that means in a practical sense is that we *meet* God there and will forever be changed. Sorge makes this insightful statement concerning prophecy and the prophetic anointing: "When we testify of Jesus, the prophetic Spirit rests upon us; and when we prophesy, we should testify of Jesus."[5]

The foundational purpose of all prophecy is to build up the Body of Christ. The focus of all prophetic truth is Jesus Christ and His continuing work in the earth (Luke 24:25–27). Prophecy can be delivered as an inspired utterance, song or action, or whenever we speak with divine authority and uncover the thoughts, plans, character, and nature of God. In *Nelson's New Illustrated Dictionary,* there is an excellent statement concerning the way God uses His people to express His will. "The full panorama of God's will takes many forms; it may be expressed through people, events, and objects."[6] The prophetic realm opens all our senses to behold Christ. Paul invites every believer to experience the presence of the Lord in such a way that we see Him and all His glory with the eyes of our heart or understanding (Eph. 1:18).

A Call to Prophetic Worship

Prophetic worship can be the norm for every congregation. Sometimes we take our age-old traditions too seriously. If we return to the simplicity of loving Jesus and welcoming His manifest presence among us, we can experience prophetic worship regularly.

Robert E. Webber was at the forefront of the worship renewal movement for over two decades as a speaker, author, and teacher. Beginning in 1968, he held the post of Professor of Theology at Wheaton College. Up until the time of his death in 2007, he was involved in the development of a school for pastors and other church leaders, *The Institute for Worship Studies*. He is the editor of *The Complete Library of Christian Worship*, a comprehensive seven-volume set. Webber's writings and those of numerous other authors are included in these volumes. They are insightful and beneficial for Christians from all traditions and are often quoted in this book. Webber has some helpful comments concerning changes that need to take place among us.

First, he calls for an understanding of our past—the valuable traditions of the Church—and an honest evaluation of our present worship:

> I find American evangelicalism to be secularized in its attitude toward history. There is a disdain for the past, a sense that anything from the past is worn out, meaningless, and irrelevant it is all relegated to tradition and dismissed as form. At the same time, no critical examination is directed toward present distortions, which have been elevated without thought to a sacred position. Evangelicals who want to reform their worship must therefore abandon their disdain of the historical, and return to a critical examination of the worship of the church in every period of history.[7]

It is time to examine our worship based on the true history of every Church found in the Book of Acts and the revivals throughout the ages. May we have a fresh worship revival in the entire Church that is passionate, prophetic and life-changing – infused with the presence of God from beginning to end.

THE IMPORTANCE OF WORSHIP

It is impossible to exaggerate the importance of worship. A. W. Tozer writes candidly, "The world is perishing for lack of the knowledge of God, and the church is famishing for want of His presence."[8]

Tozer emphasized the priority of worship. He believed that "the whole work of God in redemption was to undo the tragic effects of (sin)"—which wrenched us loose from the presence of God—"our right and proper dwelling place, our first estate."[9] He considered conscious communion with God—living in the presence of God as Adam and Eve did—to be the "central fact of Christianity. At the heart of the Christian message is God himself waiting for His redeemed children to push in to conscious awareness of His presence."[10]

If we desire to worship God, then let us pursue Him as He desires and allow Him to enter into the joyful communion with us. Only in this exchange will we realize what we have missed—His profound, glorious, and unfolding presence.

Prophetic worship is a journey into God.

Prophetic worship is a divine conversation between heaven and earth.

Prophetic worship gives expression to our passion and communion with God.

Prophetic worship is presence worship.

WHERE IS PROPHETIC WORSHIP IN THE BIBLE?

Revelation 19:10 – "And I fell at his feet to worship him. But he said to me, 'See that you do not do that! I am your fellow servant, and of your brethren who have the testimony of Jesus. Worship God! For the testimony of Jesus is the spirit of prophecy.'" The spirit of prophecy is the essence or atmosphere of prophecy that permeates the service and unlocks prophetic worship. John bowed down to worship an angel, but the angel told him not to do that. The angel clarified the situation by saying that Jesus was the One who was making Himself known through the spirit of prophecy in that place. It is normal for a spirit of prophecy to accompany Jesus as He makes Himself known to us. Everyone can flow in prophetic ministry in this atmosphere where Jesus is made known. The central focus of all prophecy is Jesus – His voice and His message to us.

Luke 1:46-55 – In the midst of an awesome season of God-encounters and revelation of God's grace and miraculous power, Mary started to speak/sing of the greatness of God.

Acts 16:25-29 - Paul and Silas had their own prophetic worship service in prison. As they sang and worshiped, the manifest presence of God filled the prison and there was an earthquake. The doors of the prison were opened. In this prophetic atmosphere, the Lord did not say anything – He demonstrated His power and the jailor was saved.

1Cor. 14 - The first 33 verses of this chapter describe a prophetic worship service with instrumental, singing and spoken prophetic utterances. Paul is instructing the church to be free in the prophetic atmosphere and to be in order as they do so. Everyone is encouraged to participate – the entire congregation (vs 1, 23-26) and when it is done correctly, even unbelievers will be convicted and join in the worship (vs 24-25).

2Cor. 3:18 - Although this passage doesn't mention the word, "worship," this verse perfectly describes the process of prophetic worship: we all come before the Lord with unveiled faces and interact with His glory. We are always changed in His manifest presence and become carriers of His glory wherever we go.

The Book of Revelation is filled with worship where the Lord is seen and heard.

Gen. 22:1-19 - This is the first mention of the word "worship" in the Bible (v5). This story is filled with God's voice and manifest presence. He met Abraham in the midst of a great test and revealed His name, Jehovah-Jireh. Everything changed when Abraham turned his sacrifice into worship.

Ex. 33-34 - Moses cried out for the presence of God and for His glory. God answered Moses' cry and hid Moses in Christ (the rock) while He passed by and revealed His names and character to the Patriarch. The people were afraid of the manifest presence of God, but they did worship from their own tent doors. Moses went in and out from the presence of God during this season – his face shone with God's glory. Joshua remained with God and didn't leave the tabernacle (33:11).

Joshua 6 - Joshua's army surrounded the city of Jericho with the sound of trumpets and shouts of praise. God had given specific instructions for this worship service and as Israel obeyed God, they were able to witness a spectacular display of God's might. With the sounds of the trumpet and His presence in their shouts, the massive walls of Jericho fell completely flat – the city was utterly destroyed even to this day.

1Chron. 15-16 - David brought the Ark of God's presence back to Jerusalem with great joy, dancing, music and song. Prophetic songs were birthed on that day (16:7-36) and a new order of prophetic worshipers were inaugurated in David's Tabernacle.

2Chron. 5:1-14 - As Solomon prepared to dedicate the temple, the people and all the leaders assembled to worship and offer lavish sacrifices to the Lord. As they sang and played music, the Lord filled the temple with His cloud and the priests couldn't even continue their ministry because of the weight of God's glory and presence.

2Chron 20:1-30 - Judah's defeat of the armies of Moab, Ammon and Mount Seir is one of the most remarkable descriptions of prophetic worship in the Word because no weapons were drawn except the praises of the singers. The power of praise and God's manifest presence is fully on display throughout the ages. Clearly, God's presence rested on the praises and utterly destroyed the enemy.

Many of the Psalms - The Book of Psalms is a record of many of the songs that were sung prophetically in David's Tabernacle. These songs were "birthed" in the atmosphere of God's presence.

Is. 6 - This passage is an account of an encounter that Isaiah had with the worship of heaven. Isaiah caught a glimpse of angelic worship and immediately became a part of the worshiping throng. As a result, he was touched and changed by this encounter. Isaiah saw, heard and felt the manifest presence and voice of God.

These are just a few examples. Worship encounters fill almost every book of the Bible. These are a good sampling of true prophetic worship. There are so many instances of prophetic worship in the Bible that occurred outside the "normal" services where we might expect God's presence. Any worship is prophetic when it contains the voice and message of God – where he is made known and encountered.

> *"In worship, there is no audience – only communing hearts."*

CHAPTER TWO
WHAT IS THE DIFFERENCE BETWEEN PRAISE AND WORSHIP?

*Praise is an expression of faith
that results in our declaration of what God has done,
what He is doing, and what He is going to do.
Worship is ultimately a relationship of love
in which we focus on and respond to God.*[1]
—Tom Schwanda

Defining and understanding praise and worship will release greater depths of their expression in our lives. Through understanding, doors are opened, and greater dynamics realized. Worship, in particular, involves the vast encounter we have with the Lord on a daily basis. Worship is our reverent devotion and response to His very presence and acts. While worship is more difficult to define than praise, it includes the communion and fellowship with God that fills every part of our lives.

There is one thing we do on earth that we will continue to do in heaven. That is to praise and to worship God. That is why we view life on earth as choir practice for heaven. To say that praise and worship is the most important category of music today is an understatement. "There is no more important activity of the human heart than to praise and worship God."[2]

> "Simply put, praise is the preoccupation with and declaration of God's acts; worship is our reverent devotion and response to His very presence"

Defining Praise

A biblical definition of praise is found in Hebrews 13:15. The writer to the Hebrews sums up the key elements of praise in this one verse:

> Therefore by Him let us continually offer the sacrifice of praise to God, that is, the fruit of *our* lips, giving thanks to His name. Through Him, therefore, let us constantly *and* at all times offer up to God a sacrifice of praise, which is the fruit of lips that thankfully acknowledge *and* confess *and* glorify His name (Heb. 13:15, NKJV and AMP).

Here is an outline:

- Praise is born in Him.
- Praise should exude from us at all times.
- Praise is directed to God.
- Praise is a sacrifice.
- Praise involves our lips—it is difficult to praise Him without some form of outward expression.
- Praise is like fruit—it has purpose, it grows, it nourishes, and it is capable of reproducing itself.
- Praise includes giving thanks and glory to God.
- Praise is preoccupied with His name.

> *"When we praise God, there must be faith intermingled with the praises."*

The Nature of Praise Leading into Worship

Praise requires faith. Faith is essential whenever we come before the Lord in praise. "But without faith *it is* impossible to please *Him*, for he who comes to God must believe that He is, and *that* He is a rewarder of those who diligently seek Him" (Heb. 11:6).

The Greek word for "comes" in this passage is *proserchomai* (Strong's #G4334). This word means *to come near, visit or worship*. The word "seek" is the Greek word *ekzeteo* (Strong's #G1567), which means *to search out, investigate, crave, demand, worship, require, seek after carefully and diligently*. There is an implication in this scripture concerning those who come to God to worship Him; they are rewarded with *His presence*.

Every time we lift our hearts in praise, we must accept God's:

Person:	*His character and nature*—He desires to reveal himself to us.
Presence:	*His omnipresence*—He is everywhere and always with us.
Promises:	He is faithful to meet us in the midst of our praises.
Power:	He is omnipotent, all-powerful; nothing is too difficult for God.
Perfection:	It is impossible for God to make a mistake with our lives.

Praise requires sacrifice. "Therefore by Him let us continually offer the sacrifice of praise to God" (Heb. 13:15). Since the beginning of time, God has called mankind to the principle of sacrifice. Sacrifice to the Lord is fundamental to worship and walking in obedience to Him. The first mention of the word *worship* in the Bible is found in Genesis 22:5, when Abraham told his servants that he was going to worship the Lord by offering the sacrifice of his only son, Isaac.

Biblical sacrifice has three basic underlying meanings:

- Giving – There is an expectation that we would give something of ourselves, not something we have found or stumbled upon. A true sacrifice will cost us something.

- Substitution – The sacrifice stands in the place of the one making the offering. In the case of blood sacrifices, the

- Drawing near – The Hebrew word "sacrifice" is *korban*, which comes from the root *karov* - meaning to "draw close" or to "come near" (Ez. 44:15). When we bring sacrifices of praise to God our hearts find pathways to draw near to God over and over again.

> *"Our ministry to God is less of an event; it is a lifestyle."*

One of the primary reasons for bringing a sacrifice in the Old Testament was to gain forgiveness for sin. Because Jesus made himself the final and perfect offering for sin, we no longer need to offer blood sacrifices. What is required of us are "spiritual sacrifices" (2Peter 2:5, 9), the sacrifice of praise being one of them (Jer. 17:26; 33:11; Hos. 14:2; Heb. 13:15).

Three principles of the sacrifice of praise:

a) *The sacrifice of praise involves giving. It is costly.* We must become like David, who would not offer a sacrifice to the Lord that cost him nothing. "I will surely buy *it* from you for a price; I will not offer burnt offerings to the Lord my God with that which costs me nothing" (2Sam. 24:24).

b) *The sacrifice of praise is pure.* All sacrifices were to be set apart from their ordinary usage and consecrated to God. The priests would examine the sacrifices for blemishes before they were offered (e.g. Lev. 22:21; Deut. 15:21). In the New Testament, Jesus became the perfect unblemished sacrifice that was offered to the Father on our behalf (1Pet. 1:19), that He might present it to himself a glorious church, not having spot, or wrinkle, or any such thing; but that it should be holy and without blemish (Eph. 5:27, *KJV*). In the same manner, we examine our hearts and make sure that the things we are singing and saying to the Lord when we praise Him represent the full intent and purpose of our hearts.

c) *The sacrifice of praise is vocal.* Unless we have some kind of physical disability, it is not enough to think thoughts of praise, but never give voice to ardent expressions of thanks and exaltation before the Lord. The sacrifice of praise must be spoken or sung. It must come from our lips. The writer of Hebrews refers to this sacrifice as the "fruit of our lips." In order for there to be fruit, there must be a tree or other source of life. "Praise involves the use of words audibly expressed. Silent prayer is not a Hebrew practice."[3] Our lives and relationship with the Lord should be the source of a continuous flow of praise heard from our lips.

UNDERSTANDING THE SACRIFICE OF PRAISE

When we come into the presence of God, our focus should not be upon the things we can get from the Lord, but on the offerings, we have to give to Him. "Give to the Lord the glory *due* His name; bring an offering and come into His courts" (Ps. 96:8).

"Our primary purpose in praise is to proclaim and to show the marvelous excellencies and perfections of God" (1Pet. 2:9, *AMP, NASV*). We rehearse the things He has done throughout the ages; we admire and boast about His present acts of greatness as He moves among His people; and we triumph in the certain victories and wonders of the days to come.

The *Life Application Bible* says, "The basis of praise is declaring God's character and attributes in the presence of others. When we recognize and affirm His goodness, we are holding up His perfect moral nature for all to see."[4]

Paul punctuated his epistles with thanksgiving and spontaneous outbursts of praise (2Cor. 9:15; 11:31). Many of his letters began or ended with such praises (Rom. 16:27; 1Cor. 1:4; 2Cor. 1:3; Eph. 1:3–14; Col. 1:3; 2Tim. 1:3; 1Pet. 1:3). Praise should also permeate our everyday speech and influence our thoughts day and night.

DEFINING WORSHIP

The *Oxford English Dictionary* defines worship as "to honour or revere as a supernatural being or power, or as a holy thing, to regard or approach with veneration or devotion, or that attitude expressed in particular actions."[5] Judson Cornwall captures the essence of worship succinctly: "Worship is one person responding in his or her spirit to the one true God."[6]

Sally Morgenthaler focuses on the aspect of relationship and response between the Lord and His people in the context of worship:

> Worship is two-way communication between believers and God, a dialogue of response involving both actions and speech. God reveals His presence; our need for intimacy with God is met, and we respond in thanksgiving and praise. God speaks through the Word; we are convicted and repent. God extends mercy through Jesus Christ; we respond with adoration. In other words, real worship provides opportunities for God and God's people to express their love for each other. It is not just a roomful of people thinking inspired thoughts. Nor is it human beings speaking and acting as if God were incapable of reply. In real worship, we carry on an exchange of love with the God who is present, the God who speaks to us in the now, who has done and is doing marvelous things. And it is supernatural exchange— this interaction between the God of Scripture and God's people—that is the primary difference between a public Christian event and Christian worship.[7]

Worship must infiltrate every area of our lives. It becomes the reason for our existence, the basis for every belief system we hold dear, and the center of our worldview. The Church's ultimate mission on earth is to minister praise and worship to God and to summon all people to partake of the triumph of His kingdom here and in the world to come. "True worship consciously sets God at the center of all life, celebrates His gifts in creation and providence, but reserves an unshared place for what He has done in the redemption of the world through our Lord Jesus Christ."[8]

THE ORIGIN AND USE OF THE WORD *WORSHIP*

The English word *worship* comes from the Anglo-Saxon word *worthship*. It denotes the worthiness of the one receiving special honor or devotion and means "to attribute worth" to someone or something. The word is still used in this manner in Commonwealth countries, where the Mayor is referred to as "His Worship, the Mayor." Used in this manner, *worship* refers to the respect and dignity, which is given to a person of honorable office.

We must never lose sight of the primary reason for worshiping the Lord: *He is worthy above all things in heaven and earth to receive praise and adoration.* Everything within us cries out for relationship and communion with God, but we must not use that relationship to try and "soften" God as He works to perfect us in His presence. "Because of the fallen nature of man, worship has become distorted. It has become a means of covering up the dirt on the conscience of man rather than the expression of pure adoration and reverence for the Creator."[9]

Many reduce the meaning of *worship* to a Sunday service. David Peterson, a lecturer at Moore Theological College in Sydney, Australia, indicates the difficulty we experience with language as we try to define worship. "The problem for translation and for theology is that the English word 'worship' is generally used too narrowly."[10]

There are angels whose created purpose is to stand and bow before the throne of God and cry aloud His attributes. After millions of years, the worthiness of our King will not be fully declared. Eternity will not afford these angels the time needed to adequately proclaim His excellency. All of this, and yet these heavenly beings know nothing of being redeemed. How, then, can we who are sons and daughters of God remain silent in the presence of His Majesty, the King of Kings and Lord of Lords? We cannot allow the angels to confess His magnificence with more vigor and passion than we who are His children, His Bride, and His servants. It is this relationship and intimacy with the Lord that I want us to focus on as we explore various aspects of praise and worship.

The Difference Between Praise and Worship

There is a difference between praise and worship. English author Paul Sarchet-Waller makes the reason for definition clear. "The object is to give the believer a clear concept of praise and worship from the scripture that will lead to a greater expression of both praise and worship."[11]

Likewise, Sorge believes they are different endeavors. "Praise and worship are mutually cooperative activities and are frequently very similar in the way they are outwardly expressed, but they are not one and the same. Each has its own nature and purpose."[12]

The difference between praise and worship does not rely on what style or tempo of song we are singing, what hymnal we are singing from, or what posture we are in; it is dependent on what the Lord is doing. When we praise Him, we leave our songs and words before Him as a sacrifice—like the Old Testament priests did with their burnt offerings. The Lord is in a place of receiving our praise, much as a king would receive a gift or a father would receive his children.

> "As we praise, we draw near to God. Worship results when God draws near to us."

Worship, on the other hand, cannot take place unless the Lord draws near to us and manifests himself to us. As we praise, we draw near to God. Worship results when God draws near to us. He uses our praises as a vehicle to draw near to His children:

> When God is enthroned upon our praises, He manifests, reveals, or *uncovers* himself before us. We catch a glimpse of Him, layers of His character we may never have seen before. If we spend every moment for a thousand years receiving wave after wave of the knowledge of His Father-heart, we would scarcely peel back the first layer of the revelation of God. Man will never uncover all of God. "A God comprehended is no God.[13]

Esteemed Christian author and leader Judson Cornwall

emphasizes this same point in many of his writings on praise and worship:

> Fundamentally, worship is a person responding to a person, so we can't worship until we get a glimpse of God. We can praise out of our memory circuits, but we must worship out of a present relationship; that is, we must be in God's presence to worship. True worship will not begin to flow until we get a good glimpse of Christ Jesus.[14]

Once He has inhabited our praises, we will not be able to keep ourselves from worshiping. The sight of Him—every glimpse, every whisper, and every sense of His wondrous presence will take our breath away. True worship will ruin us forever, and we will never be the same again. We will have little heart for the uninspired, inflexible, and mundane moments of traditionalism that exist throughout the modern Church.

> *"His wondrous presence will take our breath away."*

The following table is a summary of the major differences between praise and worship:

Table 1

Major Differences Between Praise And Worship

Praise	Worship
God dwells in our praises.	God reveals himself in our worship.
Praise is a sacrifice requiring faith.	Worship is a response—requiring the sight of God.
In praise, we declare His acts: What He has done, is doing, and will do.	In worship, we commune with Him in intimacy.
Praise brings us to the presence of God.	Worship responds to the presence of God.
We praise God for what He has done.	We worship God for who He is.
We praise God as we come before Him with thanksgiving.	We worship God when He comes before us by revelation.
We praise God from afar.	We worship God face to face.
Praise involves the remembrance of God.	Worship involves a present glimpse of God.
Praise is increased through faith.	Worship is increased through relationship with, and revelation of God.
Praise invites us to break in upon God.	Worship invites God to break in upon us.

Chapter Three

The Foundation of Worship

*True worship is that exercise of the human spirit
that confronts us
with the mystery and marvel of God
in whose presence the most appropriate
and salutary response is adoring love.*
 - Ralph P. Martin

Our theology of worship is supremely important. What we practice in worship comes directly from what we believe about worship. There is no need to become intimidated by a word like "theology" when speaking about worship. Theology is really the study of God and His thoughts about a matter and the beliefs that we hold as a result of finding out God's mind.

A first principle of Christian theology is that God alone can speak His own word about himself. Consequently, the first and continuing task of Christian theology is to listen to and then reflect upon what it hears. When this is faithfully done, Christian theology is the reflective and obedient response of the church to the Word that God speaks about himself in Jesus Christ.[1]

> *"God's relationship with us cannot fail to affect the way we respond to Him."*

Theology Affects Our Relationship with God

I am not sure how I came across this quote (attributed to Les Hawkins), but it is an excellent description of the importance of a sound theology of worship: "Worship without theology is a bit like dancing without music."

Webber calls theology "a reflective discipline."[2] We are bound to model or reflect our theology as we worship, since our worship expressions and experiences are shaped by our theology. We must have both good theology and good worship; they go hand in hand. You cannot have one without the other. While worship expresses the heart's love for God, theology expresses the mind's love for God.[3] Both are needed for us to respond fully to Him as worshipers.

THE RELATIONSHIP BETWEEN WORSHIP AND THEOLOGY

Consider the relationship between worship and theology:

- Worship is integrally related to both theology and ethics.[4]
- Our way of worship is inseparable from our way of believing.[5]
- If our worship has good theology and our theology has good worship, from the beginning of the service to the end it is a worship experience.[6]

It is important that we develop our understanding of worship and our theology of worship. Without this foundation, we are prone to allow our experience of worship to fit our inaccurate grasp of true biblical worship. Morgenthaler states, "Christian worship is not anything and everything we want it to be. Worship has biblical parameters with which we need to acquaint ourselves. Until we do, we will continue to offer worship substitutes."[7]

Henry Jauhiainen stresses the need for greater theological discussion on the true nature of worship.

> A serious defect of Pentecostal and Charismatic worship is the lack of intense, in-depth, biblical and theological reflection upon the nature of worship. As a result, worship tends to be a means to an end, whether that is church growth, personal fulfillment, or the defeat of God's enemies. Worship tends to become a utility or self-absorbing "experience." Worship style is adjusted

frequently to meet consumer appetites. Pragmatism wins over theology; that which attracts and holds a crowd is seen as that which God endorses.[8]

Jauhiainen's point about pragmatism winning over theology is excellent. I believe every denomination—not just the Pentecostals—is guilty of thinking that the Lord endorses their particular worship practice. Some denominations see the success of their centuries-old existence as proof the Lord is on their side of the worship style debate. Further understanding should bring us to the conclusion that the purpose of theology is not to explain or defend our statements of faith or our worship expressions, but to express clearly in the light of God's own desire what we believe and hold dear.

There are at least four benefits to studying and organizing our beliefs into a personal theology of praise and worship:

1. *Our theology enhances our worship experience.* If we understand both *what* we are doing and *why* we do it, we will gain greater meaning and purpose from our experience of worship.

2. *Our theology of worship deepens our relationship with God.* Any theology of worship should bring us into a greater knowledge of God. Worship presupposes and further examines the majesty, sovereignty, and transcendence of God.

3. *Our theology of worship affects how we worship God through the Word.* Theology brings us to God's Word for truth and accuracy. Those who rely on the Word find their worship enlivened by scripture. He responds to us through His Word and by His Spirit during our worship.

4. *Our theology of worship improves our relationship with other believers.* If every church asked the Holy Spirit to unfold the Lord's definition and expectations of praise and worship, we would be centered around His priorities in worship rather than our own traditions.

> *"With the focus upon the presence of God, rather than traditions, we all come united in worship around His throne."*

My goal in writing about prophetic worship is not that we should all come to the same experience of worship, but that every church would regularly encounter the presence of God in a dynamic and prophetic manner in their services. With the focus upon the presence of God, we all come together in worship around His throne. This is true biblical worship.

THE RELATIONSHIP OF THEOLOGY AND FORM IN WORSHIP

It is possible to worship in a manner that is not pleasing to the Lord. (See the example of Cain and Abel in Gen. 4:3–7.) Just because we call what we do in our church *praise and worship* doesn't mean that we are automatically correct in our theology, attitude, or expression of worship. Devotional writer Richard Foster says this:

> Forms and rituals do not produce worship, nor does the disuse of forms and rituals. We can use all the right techniques and methods, we can have the best possible liturgy, but we have not worshiped the Lord until Spirit touches spirit Singing, praying, praising all may lead to worship, but worship is more than any of them. Our spirit must be ignited by the divine fire.[9]

Author Kevin Conner addresses forms of worship:

> Of himself, man does not know how to worship God, yet he longs to worship. It is for this reason that man designs forms of worship or some sort of program for religious services and then asks God to bless his program. Also, because man does not know how God desires to be worshiped, he develops a variety of forms. People generally congregate to the particular form that suits their tastes, their spiritual disposition, and which does not offend their mentality.[10]

Forms, then, are not the central issue of our worship; it is the heart. The forms or expressions of worship from all our church traditions are merely the vehicles by which our hearts ascend to the Father and His voice is heard in our spirits. For this reason, we must reject any semblance of spiritual elitism that assumes "my way of worship is the only right way to worship." If true worship is a matter of the heart and not dependent upon outward forms, then we must find it in our hearts to remain open—always a student of His presence, His Word, and His work among mankind.

Each of us has drawn boundaries as to how far he thinks he should go in the expression of his love for God. Some want to sing with only the accompaniment of an organ or piano. They believe that all other instruments do not belong in church and have drawn a line in their hearts at this place of musical expression. Others don't want instruments in church at all. Still others like a variety of instruments in their worship, and some like to see the congregation dancing, clapping, or lifting their hands to the Lord. In some churches people bow or kneel before the Lord. Other congregations allow banners and streamers to be lifted in praise processions and in celebration before the King. Which line is correct theologically? How far does God allow us to go? Are we wrong for setting limits and drawing lines for God on this matter?

Our patterns for *correct worship* are the biblical examples of worship, including the worship in heaven. If we study the worship that takes place around the throne of God, we might be surprised at the things the Lord allows in His presence. Our goal should be pleasing Him, not keeping traditions and meeting certain standards. When worship flows freely from our spirits and is based on biblical principles, there is no limit to the way we can abandon ourselves in the presence of the Lord. (Not that we would be ridiculous and strange just for the sake of it, but that we would give our all to Him without regard to man-made rules, customs, and practices.)

Paul warns us not to put men's ideas and traditions above the

Lord's expectations. "Beware lest anyone cheat you through philosophy and empty deceit, according to the tradition of men, according to the basic principles of the world, and not according to Christ" (Col. 2:8).

JESUS: OUR EXAMPLE OF A WORSHIPER

Jesus is our best example of a worshiper (Jn. 13:15). He knew how the Father desired to be worshiped. From His conception, birth, and throughout His life, worship, prayer and devotion surrounded Jesus. People regularly came into His presence with worship and praise (Matt. 21:15–16; Mk. 14:3–9; Lk. 17:15–16; 18:38–43; 19:37–40; Lk.7:37).

Teachings on praise and worship found their way into many of His sermons and conversations (Matt. 5:12; Lk. 6:23; 15:5–6, 9, 22–32; Jn. 4:5–42). At His crucifixion there is mention of His heart of praise (Ps. 22); and worship was the first thing the disciples did after the Resurrection (Lk. 24:50–53). Jesus is still singing praise today in the midst of the Church (Heb.2:11–12). The Spirit of God now dwells in every believer to bring us into continuous praise and worship of the Father.[11]

WHAT IS CHRISTIAN WORSHIP?

My quest is to answer the question, "What is Christian worship?" Jauhiainen focused on this question in his article, "A Pentecostal/Charismatic Manifesto" (published in *The Complete Library of Christian Worship,* Volume Two).

> This is not a call to a bland eclecticism, nor a denial of so-called Pentecostal or Charismatic distinctives. It is a call to join other evangelicals in recovering from historical amnesia and regaining a sense of continuity with the worshiping church through the ages, thus enriching our present experience.[12]

Gerrit Gustafson has described five principles of Christian worship:

1. *The Activation of the Priesthood (1Pet. 2:5)*—the intervening presence of the Holy Spirit activates the priestly functions of worshipers.
2. *Spirit, Soul, and Body (Mk. 12:30)*—worship involves the whole person.
3. *Entering His Presence (Ps. 100:2, 4)* — worship is a progression into the manifest presence of God.
4. *Praise and Power (2Chron. 20:22)*—worship creates an atmosphere where God's power is revealed.
5. *Beyond the Song (Heb. 13:15–16)*—worship is more than singing; it is serving.[13]

Just as the theology of salvation applies to all Christians, so should our understanding of worship. Our worship is *Christian* before it is Pentecostal, Charismatic, Baptist, Lutheran, Presbyterian, or any other denomination. Certain expressions of worship tend to take place in the Pentecostal-Charismatic context, but they are in no way owned by this branch of the Body of Christ. If churches from any tradition base their worship expressions on sound biblical theology, those same worship experiences should make sense to all of us and lead us into intimate satisfying fellowship with God.

> *"Our definition and theology of worship must bring us to a preoccupation with God and His attributes."*

Gregory Wilde lists the following points as being central to worship theology:

1. The Word of God, prayer, and personal devotion.
2. Openness to the prompting and moving of the Holy Spirit both in oneself and in others.

3. Evangelism and personal holiness.
4. The power and authority of Christ and His name in intercession, whether in prayer, healing, exorcisms, evangelism, or general Christian concern.[14]

Finally, our definition and theology of worship must bring us to a preoccupation with God and His attributes. Unfortunately, some people use the worship experience to become consumed with the things He can do for them or the experiences He can give them. Worship must be about God— not us, or it will become corrupted. We must not become absorbed with the things God can do for us, or what we are supposed to be doing for God. True worship will lead us to absolute and all-consuming adoration of His loveliness. Our goal as worshipers is to adore God for His own sake.

UNDERSTANDING THE PRESENCE OF GOD

Throughout this book, we will be examining the presence of God. Three aspects of His presence need to be understood in any discussion on praise and worship.

1. *His abiding presence*—The Lord will never leave us nor forsake us (Heb. 13:5). He has promised to abide with us forever. The Holy Spirit lives in us, and there is never a moment He is not with us. We abide in Him and He in us. Without His abiding presence, we are unable to do anything. "And I will pray the Father, and He will give you another Helper, that He may abide with you forever—the Spirit of truth, whom the world cannot receive, because it neither sees Him nor knows Him; but you know Him, for He dwells with you and will be in you. I will not leave you orphans; I will come to you" (Jn. 14:16–18). See

> *"True worship will lead us to absolute and all-consuming adoration of His loveliness."*

also: Ps. 61:4, 7; 91:1; Jn. 15:4; 15:5–10; 1Jn. 2:28; 3:6, 24.

2. *His omnipresence*—He is everywhere at all times. God is the only One in heaven or upon earth who is able to be present in all places at all times. He is also the only One who is omnipotent and omniscient. The omnipresence, omnipotence, and omniscience of God are all related—He is God who is present everywhere, all-powerful, and all-knowing. (See Deut. 4:39; Prov. 15:3; Jer. 23:23–24; Amos 9:2.)

David knew that he could not escape the presence and gaze of God when he cried, "Where can I go from Your Spirit? Or where can I flee from Your presence?" (Ps. 139:7; see vv. 6–16.)

For the worshiper, God's omnipresence makes worship much simpler. We do not have to rely upon a particular location, building, liturgy or format in order to worship Him. Our hearts are His tabernacle, even when we are swimming under the ocean, climbing a high mountain, or in the midst of hundreds of people at a shopping mall. "The omnipresence of God ... guarantees that the actual nearness of God and a real communion with Him may be enjoyed everywhere, even apart from the places hallowed for such purposes by a specific gracious self-manifestation."[15]

3. *His manifest presence*—"Manifest" describes God's revelation of himself for His will and purpose. The *abiding* presence and omnipresence of God are a continuous fact, but His *manifest* presence is an act of God toward His people that takes place in a certain moment of time. "You *are* God who does wonders; You have declared Your strength among the peoples" (Ps. 77:14; see also: Ps. 90:16; Ez. 28:25; Jn. 17:6; 1Cor. 12:7; Col. 1:26).

When we worship God, we are completely dependent upon Him to manifest himself to us. It is a work of grace in response to our hunger. Prophetic worship is not possible unless His presence is made manifest. David knew he could never get away from the omnipresence of the Lord (Ps. 139:7). "Do not cast me away from Your presence, and do not take Your Holy Spirit from me" (Ps. 51:11).

Imagine a room full of people. If I were to say to them that there is a doctor in the room, everyone would look around to see who it is. Though the doctor is present in the room, no one yet knows who he is. But if the doctor begins to administer medication to sick people in the room, he would then be *manifesting* or revealing himself through his actions.

The presence of the Lord is very much like that. When we gather for worship, we know that God is present with us, because He abides with us at all times. But at certain moments in the service, the Lord may choose to speak to an individual or to the whole church through songs, prayers, gifts of the Spirit, preaching, body ministry, fellowship, etc. God always wants to manifest himself. We must give Him room to do so. "For where two or three are gathered together in My name, I am there in the midst of them" (Matt. 18:20).

Our hearts have to be filled with an attitude of surrender and receptivity, as we wait for the Lord to move within us by a sovereign revelation of His person. Our part is to give ourselves with all earnestness to seek His face and relinquish self so that our hearts become a holy sanctuary fit for the Almighty.

The manifest presence of God is revealed when His abiding presence is known. In other words, those who have made their hearts a sanctuary for His presence and live as if God is with them are the ones who are likely to experience His manifest presence.

Jesus manifested the power of God because God was with Him (Jn. 3:2; Acts 10:38). When Martha questioned Jesus concerning raising Lazarus from the dead, Jesus said to her, "Did I not say to you that if you would believe you would see the glory of God?" (Jn. 11:40). We need to expect God to manifest himself to us because

The Foundation of Worship

He is with us and we believe in Him. Cornwall explains the rabbinical understanding of the manifest presence of God:

> The rabbis chose to speak of God's manifested presence on the earth as the *shekinah*. This is not a biblical word, but it is consistently used in the Jewish Targums—rabbinical commentaries on the Old Testament—to designate "the divine presence" or "the divine manifestation." ... *Shekinah* means "to dwell." The rabbis used this word to avoid any localization of God. They consistently conceived of God as being omnipresent but they fully recognized a sense in which God revealed His presence among His people. They referred to this as the *shekinah*.[16]

And I heard a loud voice from heaven saying, "Behold, the tabernacle of God *is* with men, and He will dwell with them, and they shall be His people, and God Himself will be with them *and be* their God" (Rev. 21:3b).

Gregory Wilde gives us an excellent summary for understanding the place of worship and of God's presence within Charismatic theology.

> *"God desires to manifest Himself to everyone – He has no favorites."*

> For the charismatic, the idea that the Lord inhabits the praises of his people says much. This is because for those who truly are charismatic, all of life has become Eucharist; all of life has become a praise response to God's initiative of love. The gathered praises of God's people voiced on Sunday mornings are only symptomatic of a lifelong reality of praise, for by the power of the Holy Spirit every day has become the Lord's Day, every day a day of death and resurrection. Charismatic communities can be thought of as "epicletic communities"[17] for the lives of people have become instruments for constantly calling upon the Holy Spirit to come and transform into new creation everything that the believer is, says, does, and touches. True theology is the Church's word about God, which responds to and is controlled by the word that God himself has spoken in His self-revelation.[18]

CHAPTER FOUR

UNDERSTANDING THE ANCIENT WORDS FOR PRAISE AND WORSHIP

*Worship is . . . the acknowledgment
and celebration of God's utter perfection.
Enjoyment of God begins
with the privilege of discovering Him.*[1]
—Andrew Wilson-Dickson

The ancient Hebrew and Greek words for *praise* and *worship* are essential for understanding the biblical concepts of praise and worship. As we study these words, we can gain a clearer understanding of what the Holy Spirit intends. David Peterson describes the proper perspective from which to approach this study: "The biblical words for worship do not represent discrete concepts but are part of a whole mosaic of thought about the way to relate to God."[2]

More than 50 different words are used in the Hebrew Scriptures to denote *praise*. Not all these words have been translated *praise*, yet they all describe the action of praising God.[3] Over the past 30 years I have studied these ancient words in depth and gleaned insight from many sources. I intend to outline the most significant of them. The definitions presented here are either paraphrased from my research or taken directly from *Strong's Exhaustive Concordance, Theological Wordbook of the Old Testament,* or *An Expository Dictionary of New Testament Words.* I have included the numbers and phonetic pronunciations from *Strong's Exhaustive Concordance* as an aid to further study.

ANCIENT HEBREW WORDS FOR *PRAISE*

There are seven key biblical Hebrew words for p r a i s e . These are presented beginning with the quietest proclamation and ending with the most exuberant or extreme expressions. The spiritual state of true worship is really indescribable by words alone, though the richness of worship and devotion to God is revealed from Genesis to Revelation. Very few biblical references to praise indicate silence of any sort. Most praise is not only loud, but also in the company of others.

The important thing to notice about all these verbs for praise in the Old Testament is that they are words of SOUND. Praise in the Old Testament is always accompanied with sound. It is vocal, it is public, and it is excited.[4]

1. ***barak*** (baw-rak') (Strong's #H1288) The King James Version translates *barak* as "praise" only twice: Jdgs. 5:2; Ps. 72:12-15. In more recent translations, *barak* has been translated as "praise" up to 70 times.

   - To kneel, bless, on bended knee
   - To remember joyfully—He is the source of all our blessings.

2. ***yadah*** (yaw-daw') (Strong's #H3034) 2Chron. 20:21; Ps.9:1; 28:7; 43:4; 111:1; 138:1. "Lift up your hands in the sanctuary and bless the Lord" (Ps. 134:2).

   - To confess with outstretched hands
   - To revere or worship with raised hands

     Yada incorporates the Hebrew word *yad*—which means "hand"—implying the stretching out or holding out of the hands, and possibly pointing, throwing, casting, extending or shooting out of the hands. The name *Judah* (praise) also comes from this root word (Heb. 7:14).

   - To publicly declare God's works or attributes—an active rather than passive praise

Understanding the Ancient Words for Praise and Worship 59

3. ***towdah*** (to-daw') (Strong's #H8426) Ps. 50:23; 69:30; 107:22; Is. 51:3

   - Thanksgiving—the sacrifice of praise offered in faith for what God is going to do.

   Towdah is a noun (derived from *yadah,* meaning *the extending of one's hands*) and implies an outward display of faith expressed through praise.

4. ***zamar*** (zaw-mar') (Strong's #H2167) Found more than 40 times; Ps. 47:7; 57:7; 68:4; 144:9; 147:7; 149:3

   - Literally "to touch the strings"
   - To make melody
   - Instrumental and sung praises—making music in praise to God

   Zamar is a key word for *praise* as well as being a musical term. This word is used exclusively in poetry, most often in the Book of Psalms. Always used in reference to instrumental music, singing may or may not be involved. The Greek Bible translates this word as *psallo: to sing hymns*

5. ***shabach*** (shaw-bakh') (Strong's #H7623) Ps. 35:27; 63:3; 145:4; 147:12; Dan. 2:23; 4:34, 37. "O praise (shout or speak loudly) all ye nations; praise (triumph and address loudly) Him all ye people" (Ps. 117:1 AMP).

   - To commend or laud
   - To shout or address in a loud tone
   - To give glory or triumph in praise

   Note the call for all nations and people to *shabach* the Lord. No allowance is made for any nation, denomination or people to be excused from shouting to the Lord, It is important to note that it is the Lord who inspired and directed the writing of Scripture. This is how HE expects to be addressed.

6. halal (haw-lal') (Strong's #H1984) 1Chron. 16:4, 36; 23:5, 30; 25:3; 29:13; 2Chron. 5:13; 7:6; 8:14; 20:19, 21; 30:21; 31:2; Ezra 3:10–11; Neh. 5:13; 12:24; Ps. 22:23, 26; 34:2; 35:18; 44:8; :4; 63:5; 69:30, 34; 74:21; 84:4; 99:3; 105:3; 107:32; 109:30; 111:1; 119:30, 164, 175; 145:2; 148:1-7; 149:3; 150:1-6; Prov. 31:28, 31; Jer. 20:13; 31:7; Joel 2:26.

The grand climax of the entire Book of Psalms, number 150, uses *halal* in every verse, beginning and ending this glorious worship manifesto with a resounding hallelujah![5]

- To acknowledge God's glory, to praise
- To make a clear and brilliant tone or sound
- To celebrate God's goodness

This is the most commonly translated word for praise, used approximately 121 times in the Old Testament. According to the *Theological Wordbook of the Old Testament, halal* was considered an essential expression of public worship. It comes from the imperative: "Hallelujah!" (combining *halal* and *Jah,* an abbreviated form of *Yahweh*— the name of God), meaning: "Praise the Lord!"

7. tehillah (teh-hil-law') (Strong's #H8416) The noun *tehillah* is a derivative of *halal*. The plural, *tehillim,* is the Hebrew name for the Book of Psalms. The Bible cites more than 300 commands to sing praises to the Lord: Ex. 15:11; Deut. 10:21; 1Chron. 16:35; Neh. 9:5; 12:46; Ps. 9:14; 22:25; 34:1; 47:6–7; 48:10; 51:15; 71:6, 8, 14; 79:13; 102:21; 106:2; 109:1; 111:10; 119:171; 145:21; 149:1; Is. 42:8, 10, 12; 48:9; 60:6; 43:21; Jer. 13:11; 17:14; 33:9; 51:41.

- To sing, celebrate with song
- To laud, sing '*halals*'
- High praise

The word *tehillah* is not the word translated most frequently as "praise," nor does it indicate the loudest expression of praise, but almost every time *tehillah* is used in Scripture, something special seems to be occurring in the praise. The Lord inhabits or manifests himself in the midst of this praise. This characteristic of *tehillah* shows a link to the prophetic.

Consider each of these occasions where *tehillah* was translated as *praise*. Although the situations were very different, the reality of the presence of God was made quite noticeable through supernatural events:

2 Chron. 20:22—"When they began to sing and *to praise*, the Lord set ambushes against the people of Amon, Moab, and Mount Seir, who had come against Judah..." Other words for *praise*—*yadah* and *halal*—were used to describe the types of praise that were offered to the Lord prior to verse 22. From this, we know that this army of singers went out with their hands lifted in praise to God and their mouths filled with boisterous exaltation. However, the Hebrew word for *praise* changes to *tehillah* in verse 22. It was at this point that the Lord descended in their praises and defeated the enemy. The enemy is not afraid of noise—he is capable of making plenty of noise himself. He is, however, afraid of the sound that comes from a people who have the manifest presence of God in their songs and dances. Praise of this sort will be like a two-edged sword (as described in Ps. 149:6—another instance of *tehillah* praise*)*.

Ps. 22:3—"You are...enthroned in the *praises* of Israel." The Lord sits in the midst of our praise as a king would sit upon a throne. We experience His kingdom authority as He inhabits our praise (see also Ps. 114:2). God is the King of heaven and earth—with or without our praises, but through praise, He makes this known to us in a special way.

Ps. 33:1—"*Praise* is comely for the upright" (KJV). Another version says, "For praise from the upright is beautiful" (Ps. 33:1, NKJV). Psalm 33 describes praise as an act of beauty. When God's people praise Him rightly, it is something beautiful they do. They bring beauty to him.

...Praise is an act of beauty to God![6] The very faces of God's people are made supernaturally beautiful as we encounter Him in the *tehillah* praises. (See Ps. 147:1.)

Ps. 34:1—"His *praise* shall continually be in my mouth." Such *tehillah* praise accompanied by the presence of the Father makes continuous exaltation a delight. True worshipers are quick to praise the Lord and find communion with God only a breath away. "Rejoice in the Lord always" (Phil. 4:4). (See also Ps. 35:28.)

Ps. 40:3—"He has put a new song in my mouth—*Praise* to our God; many will see it and fear, and will trust in the Lord." The *tehillah* song of praise is able to be seen. This song is not like any other. It is more than mere music. The *tehillah* song contains the very sight and manifest presence of God. If we wait on God for the prophetic song, the rest of this promise will come to pass—"many will see it and fear (revere, worship) and will trust in the Lord." The greatest days of evangelism are ahead for the worshiping church that sings songs that are not only heard, but seen.

Ps. 65:1—"*Praise* is awaiting You, O God." "To You belongs silence (the submissive wonder of reverence which bursts forth into praise)" (Ps. 65:1, AMP) In this instance the *tehillah* praise is born out of silence. Learn to wait upon God for His appearing in your soul. In these days of great visual and audible stimuli, it is more necessary than ever to learn how to linger in the presence of the Lord, and still our hearts in His presence as His awe and wonder grip our hearts.

Ps. 100:4—"Enter His gates with thanksgiving, and His courts with *praise*." I believe that this *tehillah* praise is the doorway between praise and worship. We are ushered into His very courts through this praise.

Is. 42:10—"Sing to the Lord a new song, and His *praise* from the ends of the earth." The *Amplified Bible* says that this song of praise is a song that has never been heard before in the heathen world. No matter how creative or talented the composers, musicians, and singers, there is no way that any one of them will

Understanding the Ancient Words for Praise and Worship

be able to match the aesthetic beauty of the new song of *tehillah* praise that is arising from all the nations of the earth. One sound of heaven, touched by the glory of God, will surpass every other musical endeavor yet attempted on this earth.

Is. 60:18—"But you shall call your walls Salvation, and your gates *Praise.*" Salvation provides the protective wall around God's people; *tehillah* praise is the gate to the very habitation of the Lord.

> "One sound of heaven, touched by the glory of God, will surpass every other musical endeavor yet attempted on this earth.

Is. 61:3—"The garment of *praise* for the spirit of heaviness." Any who mourn in Zion (the place of the presence of the Lord) are offered three things: a diadem, or crown of beauty (see AMP); the oil of joy, and a garment of *tehillah* praise. We are to wear *tehillah* (God enthroned in our midst) as a garment.

Is. 61:11—"So the Lord God will cause righteousness and *praise* to spring forth before all the nations." (See also Is. 62:7; Hab. 3:3; Zeph. 3:19-20.) *Tehillah* praise brings us face to face with the Lord. It is here that all nations will see and know the power and grace of God.

ANCIENT HEBREW WORDS FOR *WORSHIP*

There appears to be one primary word in Hebrew for the worship of God: *shachah*. The spiritual state of true worship is really indescribable by words alone, though the richness of worship and devotion to God is revealed from Genesis to Revelation. (Other words are used only when referring to the worship of idols.) *Shachah* draws its meaning from the actions of our bodies as we worship the Lord. The ancient Hebrews found no better way to define worship than to describe the process of positioning our bodies to show total humility.

shachah (shaw-khaw'), (Strong's #H7812)
- To depress, i.e. to prostrate, bow down flat, do reverence, worship.
- To humbly beseech.

The verb *shachah* is used 170 times in the Hebrew Bible. The literal meaning of the root is the act of falling down and doing obeisance or even groveling on the ground before royalty (2Sam. 14:22; 1Kings 1:16) or deity (Exod. 34:8; 2Sam. 12:20; 2Kings 19:37). The basic idea conveyed is unworthiness and humility. The word pictures an inferior being in the presence of a superior being.[7]

> *"The spiritual state of true worship is really indescribable by words alone, though the richness of worship and devotion to God is revealed from Genesis to Revelation."*

Additional Hebrew words have been used in the context of worship, translated variously as:
- *darash* (daw-rash') (Strong's #H1875) To seek or inquire (Ezra. 4:2; 6:21; Ps. 24:6; 69:32; Is. 11:10)
- *abad* (aw-bad') (Strong's #H 5647) To serve (Ex. 3:12; Is. 19:21, 23)
- *sharath* (shaw-rath') (Strong's #H8334) To minister (Deut. 10:8; 18:5–7; Ps. 103:21).

A familiar concept in the Old Testament, when speaking about worship, is *the fear of God*. Closely associated with this concept are words such as *awe, respect, worship,* and *veneration*. Whenever the fear of the Lord is mentioned in the Word, it is also calling us to worship. The fear of God is not just an attitude of the heart, but a lifestyle to be diligently pursued.

The Hebrew word used in this context is *yare* (yaw-ray'), (Strong's #H3372), used over 300 times in its various forms, meaning to fear, revere, dread, frighten, to stand in awe, and worship. We can learn much about the fear of the Lord by studying the passages where the Lord instructs us to walk in His fear. As you read the following verses, consider how the fear of the Lord stands as a foundation for worship:

Ex. 14:31—"Thus Israel saw the great work which the Lord had done in Egypt; so the people feared the Lord, and believed the Lord and His servant Moses."

Deut. 31:12-13—"Gather the people together, men and women and little ones, and the stranger ... that they may learn to fear the Lord your God ... and that their children ... learn to fear the Lord your God."

Ps. 19:9—"The fear of the Lord is clean, enduring forever."

Ps. 25:14—"The secret of the Lord is with those who fear Him."

Ps. 31:19—"How great is Your goodness, which You have laid up for those who fear You."

Ps. 33:18—"Behold, the eye of the Lord is on those who fear Him."

Ps. 34:7, 9—"The angel of the Lord encamps around all those who fear Him; and delivers them. there is no want to those who fear Him."

Ps. 86:11—"Unite my heart to fear Your name."

Ps. 96:4—"For the Lord is great and greatly to be praised; He is to be feared above all gods." and "Let all the earth fear the Lord" (Ps 33:8).

Ps. 103:11, 13, 17—"For as the heavens are high above the earth, so great is His mercy toward those who fear Him the Lord pities those who fear Him ... the mercy of the Lord is ... on those who fear Him."

Ps. 111:10—"The fear of the Lord is the beginning of wisdom." (Also Prov. 1:7; 9:10; 15:33.)

Ps. 112:1—"Blessed is the man who fears the Lord."

Ps. 147:11—"The Lord takes pleasure in those who fear Him, in those who hope in His mercy."

Prov. 14:27—"The fear of the Lord is a fountain of life." (Also Prov. 19:23.)

Prov. 22:4—"By humility and the fear of the Lord are riches and honor and life."

The Lord often links the concept of loving and revering Him with obedience (Jn. 14:23)! My favorite verse on the fear of the Lord is Ecclesiastes 12:13. These are possibly some of the last words of the wisest man who ever lived. In translating this verse, the *Amplified Version* includes some helpful insights concerning the fear of the Lord. Each line of thought in this verse can be separated and meditated on independently.

> "All has been heard; the end of the matter is,
> Fear God [revere and worship Him,
> knowing that He is]
> and keep His commandments;
> for this is the whole of man
> [the full, original purpose of creation,
> the object of God's providence,
> the root of character,
> the foundation of all happiness,
> the adjustment to all inharmonious circumstances
> and conditions under the sun]
> and the whole [duty] for every man" (Eccl. 12:13, AMP)

> *"It is crucial that every Christian regains a holy fear and reverence for the Lord, a respect for His Word and an esteem for His presence, that prevails over every other priority and interest in our lives."*

Notice the three components of the fear of God outlined here.
1) Worship: "revere and worship Him."
2) The knowledge of God and understanding of His character: "knowing that He is."
3) Obedience: "keep His commandments."

Lack of reverence for God and an incorrect fear of God have weakened the modern church. Christians must regain a holy fear and reverence for the Lord, a respect for His Word, and esteem for His presence, which prevails over every other priority and interest in our lives.

I cannot remember where I found these two quotes, but they both describe how the fear of the Lord brings us into His presence, not turning from Him with dread.

- To fear God is to stand in awe of Him; to be afraid of God is to run away from Him.[8]
- Holy fear is a loving anxiety to please God.[9]

NEW TESTAMENT GREEK WORDS FOR *PRAISE* & *WORSHIP*

As in the Old Testament, New Testament writers found it is easier to describe what one *does* in praise and worship rather than the inner feelings of the heart.

PRAISE:

1. *ainos* (ah'ee-nos) (Strong's #*G136*), from #*G134*
   - Praise of God (Matt. 21:16; Lk. 2:13, 20; 18:43; 19:37; 24:53; Acts 2:47; 3:8-9)
2. *epainos* (ep'-ahee-nos) (Strong's #*G1868*), from #*G1909* and #*G134*
   - To laud and commend (Rom. 2:29; 13:3; 1Cor. 4:5; 11:2, 17, 22; 2Cor. 8:18; Eph. 1:6, 12, 14; Phil. 1:11; 4:8; 1Pet.

1:7; 2:14)

3. *humneo* (hoom-neh'-o), (Strong's #*G5214*) from #G5215
   - To sing and celebrate in song
   - A song or hymn of praise (Heb. 2:12)
4. *doxa* (dox'-ah) (Strong's #*G1391*)
   - Glory, honor or esteem
   - Reputation (Lk. 14:10; Jn. 9:24; 12:43; 1Pet. 4:11)
5. *eulogeo* (oo-log-eh'-o) (Strong's #*G2127*) from #*G2095* and #G3056
   - To speak well of
   - To bless or pronounce blessing or benediction upon
   - To thank (Lk. 1:64)
6. *eusebeo* (oo-seb-eh'-o) (Strong's #*G2151*) from #*G2152*
   - To be reverential or pious towards God
   - To respect (Acts 17:23)
7. *arete* (ar-et'-ay) (Strong's #*G703*) from #*G730*
   - Excellence
   - Praise (1 Pet. 2:9)

WORSHIP:

1. *therapeuo* (ther-ap-yoo'-o) (Strong's #*G2323*) from #2324
   - To wait upon
   - To attend to, or serve
   - To cure or heal (Acts 17:25)

   It is interesting to note the link between worship and healing. When we worship with *therapeuo*, we come face to face with the God whose name and character is "the

Lord who heals" (Ex. 15:26). When we worship Him, all of His goodness and virtue is poured back upon us and we are healed, changed, and made whole. Matthew and Mark describe occasions when some approached Jesus for help and healing by worshiping Him (Matt. 8:2; 9:18; 15:25; Mark 5:6). They did not make their requests known to the Lord until they had first drawn near to Him with worship in their hearts.

> "The best place for physical, emotional and spiritual healing is in the midst of worship—right in the presence of the Lord."

The best place for physical, emotional and spiritual healing is in the midst of worship—right in the presence of the Lord.

2. *ethelothreskeia* (eth-el-o-thrace-ki'-ah) (Strong's *G1479*) from #G2309, #G2356
   - Religious observance, sanctimony (Col. 2:18)

3. *latreuo* (lat-ryoo'-o) (Strong's #*G3000*)
   - To worship publicly
   - To minister to God
   - To serve—sometimes through the devout and upright life (Acts 7:42; 24:14; Rom. 1:9; Phil. 3:3; Heb. 10:2)

   Worship is more than singing; it is serving. Wholehearted worship will cause us to be wholehearted in our service within the community.

4. *proskuneo* (pros-koo-neh'-o) (Strong's #*G4352*) from #*4314*, from *pros* (meaning toward) and *kuneo* (meaning to kiss). This word is used over 50 times in the New Testament and is the word most commonly translated as *worship*.
   - To kiss the hand; to kiss

- To offer adoration
- To prostrate oneself in homage
- To do reverence, worship
  (Matt. 2:2, 8; 4:9-10; Lk. 4:7; Jn. 4:20-24; 12:20; Acts 7:43; 8:27; 24:11; 1Cor. 14:25; Heb. 11:21, as well as the entire book of Revelation, use this word for *worship*).

5. *sebomai* (seb'-om-ahee), Strong's #G4576
   - To venerate, to awe (Matt. 15:9; Mk. 7:7; Acts 16:14; 18:7, 13, 19:27)

   Three ideas sum up the Hebrew and Greek words used for praise and worship in Scripture:

- Adoration expressed through visible acts of reverence
- An inner attitude of humility and self-abasement
- Adoration through service and sacrifice with no thought of reward

  The New Testament is filled with a constant attitude of thanksgiving, praise, and worship—particularly surrounding the life of Jesus:

- At the conception of Jesus (Lk. 1:46–55)
- At the birth of Jesus (Matt. 2:1–12; Lk. 2:13–14, 17, 20, 38)
- At the dedication of Jesus (Lk. 2:28–32)
- During the life and teaching of Jesus (Matt. 5:11-12; 6:9–10; Matt. 21:15-16; Matt. 26:26–27; Mk. 14:22–25; Lk. 6:23; 10:17–21; 15:5-6, 9, 22–32; 17:15-16; 18:38, 43; 19:37-40; 24:50–51; Jn. 4:5-42; 6:11, 23; 11:41)
- After the resurrection of Jesus (Matt. 28:9, 17; Luke 24:50-53; Jn. 20:20, 28)
- In the present ministry of Jesus (Ps. 22:25; Heb. 2:11-12)

The first thing that the disciples did after Jesus ascended into heaven was to worship. They did not go and seek their former employment after Jesus ascended. They went to the temple and the upper room and continued waiting upon the Lord in prayer, praise, and the blessing of God (Lk. 24:52–53; Acts 1:14). On the day of Pentecost, when the believers were all filled with the Holy Spirit, they began to speak in tongues. Devout men from every nation heard the Christians praising God in their own language, and 3,000 of them were saved (Acts 2:11, 41). Likewise, when the Gentiles received the Holy Spirit, they also praised God in tongues (Acts 10:46). Believers today are called to this same life of continuous praise through the example of the Early Church and through the teachings of the Apostles.

The Book of Revelation is filled with worship. It is a glorious revelation of the exalted Christ and the atmosphere of continuous worship in heaven. The throne of God is central to this book—it is mentioned 32 times—suggesting that an understanding of authority is a key to true worship. Richard Leonard calls this book "the supreme worship book of the New Testament."[10] What a fitting way to conclude the written Word of God! Genesis begins with our awesome Creator walking with man, face to face in intimacy with Him. Revelation concludes the story of redemption, with man again restored for all eternity to the place of worship and intimacy.

Part Two

II Corinthians 3:18

The Scriptural Pattern for Prophetic Worship

> *Worship is extravagant love*
> *and extreme submission.*
> —Charlotte Baker

INTRODUCTION TO PART TWO

The truth and practice of worship is simple enough that even the youngest child can experience its wonder. Yet, much study is required to fully explore its length, breadth, depth, and height. What a vast and endless journey the Lord has us on as we seek to know Him more fully and intimately!

In an attempt to simplify and encapsulate the concepts of prophetic worship, I have outlined what I believe is the Scriptural pattern for worship, based on seven key points taken from Second Corinthians 3:18. I have been fascinated with this verse my entire Christian life as it bridges the philosophical and intellectual aspects of our faith in God with His unlimited invitation to a personal and intimate encounter.

This pivotal passage is a summary of the essential theological elements of prophetic worship:

> *"But we all, with unveiled face, beholding as in a mirror the glory of the Lord, are being transformed into the same image from glory to glory, just as by the Spirit of the Lord"* (2Cor. 3:18).

It is interesting to note that the word "glory" is mentioned three times in this one verse. Whenever a concept is uncovered in scripture with three layers such as this, it signifies that:

- This is the completion of a matter. The number three denotes divine perfection and completeness.
- There is a principle in these three things that will uncover something of God's plan to us.

Herbert Lockyer adds these insights concerning the number three: "Three...is a prominent number that indicates what is real, perfect, substantial, complete, and divine. It also suggests the resurrection."[1]

Pythagoras calls three the perfect number, expressive of beginning, middle, and end, and therefore a symbol of Deity.[2]

The seven key principles of prophetic worship are drawn from this passage, and each one has its own chapter. Within the chapters, the points are highlighted by using the relevant italicized phrase from Second Corinthians 3:18, which you will see at the beginning of every point. Here are the next seven chapters:

1. *But we all*—the **priests** of worship—worship is all-inclusive.
2. *With unveiled face*—the **preparation** for worship—worship requires transparency.
3. *Beholding as in a mirror*—the **priority** of worship—worship is prophetic.
4. *The glory of the Lord*—the **presence** in worship—worship is transcendent.
5. *Are being transformed into the same image*—the **purpose** of worship—worship is transforming.
6. *From glory to glory*—the **pathway** of worship—worship is eternal.
7. *Just as by the Spirit of the Lord*—the **power** of worship—worship is initiated by the Holy Spirit.

We will examine each of these principles in greater depth in the chapters that follow.

Chapter Five
Worship is for Everyone
"But We All..."

*God is an unutterable sigh,
planted in the depths of the soul.*
—Jean Paul Richter

"But we all"—In contrast to the time when only chosen leaders like Moses could come before the face of the Lord, we are all beckoned into the very presence of God to commune with Him as a friend. "So the Lord spoke to Moses face to face, as a man speaks to his friend. And he would return to the camp, but his servant Joshua the son of Nun, a young man, did not depart from the tabernacle" (Exod. 33:11).

As New Testament believers, all of us are now invited to such an encounter. According to Second Corinthians 3:18, there are no restrictions based on age, intelligence, or the length of time one has been a Christian. Passionate and intimate worship is available to everyone.

The Lord has made the most momentous and profound aspect of Christianity—worship—available to all of humanity. No props, degrees, callings, or special talents are needed; only hungry hearts and thirsty souls.

Consider the following truths that grant each of us access to the very throne of God:

- The death of Jesus—He has made a way for us through the veil of His flesh (His blood)—Eph. 2:13; Heb. 10:19-20
- Repentance—Heb. 10:22

- The washing of pure water (the Word of God)—Heb. 10:22

As related in Acts 17:23, Paul found some in Athens who were worshiping an "unknown God." He told them it was Jesus they were worshiping.

It is unusual to worship God without even knowing His name, since His name is so entwined in the revelation of His person. Yet, God—gracious and desirous that all men would worship Him—gave these idolaters a glimpse of himself.

Likewise, we are all welcome in the place of devotion: the saved and the sinner, the rich and the poor, the young and the old, the wise and the foolish, the humble and the arrogant, the strong and the weak. Let everyone be invited to the courts of the King!

In many parts of the world today, multitudes are coming to faith in Jesus Christ without having heard preaching or having seen the Bible. Jesus is making Himself known to them in the depths of their hearts. Out of relationship with Him and worship, they are becoming disciples and followers of Christ.

WE ALL HAVE A PART—WE ALL ARE PRIESTS

"But we all"—It would be hard to overemphasize the part that every member of the Church has to play in worship. The Bible clearly indicates that worship is the universal occupation of all creatures: "Let everything that has breath praise the Lord. Praise the Lord!" (Ps. 150:6).

The apostles Peter and John describe every believer as a priest (1Pet. 2:5, 9; Rev. 1:6). Every one of us is a priest of His presence. God's master plan is for His kingdom to permeate the entire world through a nation of holy, royal priests. Each member of every congregation is part of His personal company of worshiping priests. If the Church could worship with an understanding of this profound truth, it would not only change worship services, but every area of Church life and service.

Priests have always been those who have stood between man and God. As priests, we bring our devotion to God and then God's ministry into the earth. The Hebrew word for "priest" is *cohen* or *kohen*, meaning "the one who draws near to the divine presence" (Ex. 19:22; 30:20). Worship is our main responsibility as priests. It is our privilege to draw near to God and minister to Him. Not only do we draw near for ourselves, but we make a way for others to draw near as well.

For the past 2000 years of the Church, we have left the "priesthood" to specially trained and ordained believers. This is primarily based on the Old Testament model where Aaron, his sons, and their descendants were set aside as those who stood before the Lord on behalf of the Israelites. However, in the New Testament, there is no mention of a professional priest. Every mention of the word "priest" in the New Testament is either referring to priests in the Old Testament, our role as Believer Priests of the New Covenant.

The New Testament writers clearly show that every Christian is a priest – no matter how young in age or how long they might have known the Lord. Your entire congregation must understand their role as holy, royal priests. If they do, it will change the way they approach worship because they will come as those with priestly responsibilities in His presence rather than as spectators.

Paul instructed the Church to set aside a new type of leadership for His people: Eph. 4:11-12 *And He Himself gave some to be apostles, some prophets, some evangelists, and some pastors and teachers, for the equipping of the saints for the work of ministry, for the edifying of the body of Christ.* This five-fold group of leaders has the task of equipping the *congregation* to do the work of the ministry, and the chief ministry of every believer is worship.

A healthy church is a worshiping church. Healthy worship calls for full congregational participation. As a result, this worship will affect every area of our lives. The presence of God we encounter in worship will permeate our entire communities. When *we all* encounter God in worship, *we all* carry God through our lives into the world as true priests of His presence. Those who

> *"We are all welcome in the place of devotion: the saved and the sinner, the rich and the poor, the young and the old, the wise and the foolish, the humble and the arrogant, the strong and the weak. Let everyone be invited to the courts of the King!"*

do not come to church now have a priest who has encountered God. I believe the whole world is longing for the Church to take her place as holy, royal priests and who enter the courts of the Lord. I say this because so many are truly yearning for God whether they know it or not. They have had no priest to bring them near to Him. They have seen and heard our religion and our opinions...it is time for them to encounter Christ in us. The glory we experience in God's presence will be glory we carry into the world. The greatest revival in the history of the world will come when *we all* worship.

Michael Marshall expresses it this way: "Nothing in the human experience lies outside the scope of true Christian worship."[1]

WE ALL MUST WORSHIP IN UNITY

"But we all"—In Second Corinthians 3:18, Paul calls us all to worship, regardless of our denomination, generation, culture, or preferences. He is calling all of us to receive *His* understanding, intimate communion with Him that we call "worship."

The Lord intends us to become passionate and exuberant in our worship from time to time. The Word is full of directives such as these:

> "Oh, clap your hands, all you peoples! Shout to God with the voice of triumph!" (Ps. 47:1).
> "All the ends of the world shall remember and turn to the Lord, and all the families of the nations shall worship before You" (Ps. 22:27).
> (See also Ps. 22:29; Ps. 45:17; Ps. 66:4; Ps. 67:3,

5; Ps. 79:13; Ps. 86:9; Ps. 96:9; Ps. 98:4; Ps. 106:48; Ps. 117:1; Ps. 145:10, 21; Isa. 42:10; 66:23; Rom. 15:11; Rev. 15:4.)

Not only are all peoples and nations called to worship, we are all called to a life of untiring and consistent praise. "I will bless the Lord at *all* times; his praise shall *continually* be in my mouth" (Ps. 34:1, Emphasis mine). (See also Ps. 35:28; Ps. 44:8; Ps. 71:8.)

No exception is made in Scripture for shy people to settle back with a more reserved style of worship, or for a particular denomination or culture to be exempt from continuous, expressive, heartfelt praise and worship.

When Paul called us to transparent, life-changing worship encounters, he had no idea that the Church would ultimately be wrought with such diversity (and controversy) in matters of worship form, preference, and style. That fact does not diminish the universal summons to appear before the face of God and respond to His awesome presence with impassioned, genuine devotion.

I am not saying that those who minister to the Lord quietly are incorrect in their expression. There are definitely times for that and occasions for a great variety of styles and expressions of devotion before the Lord. The biblical injunction to praise God has more to do with the heart than it does with the outward expression. Therefore, it would be wrong to insist on a simplistic interpretation of these scriptures. It is important to note, however, that the Word stresses repeated, exuberant, and public expressions of praise that are born from passionate and sincere hearts. Webber says, "Passive worship cannot be justified on the grounds of Scripture, theology, or history."[2]

When Paul calls us all to worship, he is reinforcing the call to unity within corporate worship. The Lord is blessed by our unity as much as by our songs and words of adoration. During praise and worship, we should come to a place of unity in heart, mind, and voice. "That you may with one mind *and* one mouth glorify the God and Father of our Lord Jesus Christ" (Rom. 15:6).

WE ALL MUST CHOOSE TO WORSHIP

"But we all"—In order for us to be consistent in our devotional lives, we must bring our will into subjection. Ritual is easier than revelation. True worship costs us our time, energy and emotions. We must learn, like David, to say, "I will." David instructed himself more than 100 times to praise and worship the Lord.

> "But as for me, I will come into Your house in the multitude of Your mercy; In fear of You I will worship toward Your holy temple" (Ps. 5:7).
>
> "I will praise *You*, O LORD, with my whole heart; I will tell of all Your marvelous works. I will be glad and rejoice in You; I will sing praise to Your name, O Most High" (Ps. 9:1–2).

The Lord is a gentleman. He has given us a free will, which He honors in worship as in every other part of our lives. We are not robots, who worship because we are commanded to, but friends who embrace intimacy with Him by choice. Worship is forever a choice. You will find, time and again, that He responds to our choices with His delightful presence. As James puts it, "Draw near to God and He will draw near to you" (James 4:8).

Graham Kendrick, a worship leader and author from England, writes,

> Sometimes worship starts spontaneously because it is felt in the heart, sometimes it is an act of the will. Either way it is His worthiness that is the important thing, not our fickle, unreliable feelings. The will to worship is our part, while God's part is to supply the fire that ignites it within us. [3]

We are drawn by God, but we must choose to be part of this holy and intimate communion.

Chapter Six

Worship is the Place for Transparency
"...*With Unveiled Face*"

*Worship is the occupation of the heart, not with its needs
or even its blessings, but with God himself.*
—Judson Cornwall

"*With unveiled face*"—The Lord desires to call to the deepest parts of our hearts and reveal His glory and His secrets (Ps. 42:7; Ps. 92:5; Dan. 2:22; 1 Cor. 2:10). Only when we come with honesty, transparency, and holy expectancy will we see the desire of our hearts fulfilled in His presence. The secrets of His Person and His Word can only come to those whose faces are uncovered.

Removing the Veil to Behold His Glory

We all have a veil of some sort over our hearts. Sin and hurts cause us to hide from one another and from God. There are two ways we can become unveiled. Either we remove the veil by our own honesty and pursuit of transparency, or the Lord—the great "Render of Veils" (Matt. 27:51) will tear it for us if we ask. The Word of God, personal prayer, and worship do the best work of rending the veil, plowing

> *"Worship uncovers our faces and allows the unfathomable mysteries of God to be dropped upon our hearts."*

our hearts and making us ready for His glory. Charles Spurgeon says, "Thoughts and reasonings are like the steel wedges, which give a hold upon truth. But prayer is the lever which forces open the iron chest of sacred mystery. Then, we may get the treasure hidden within."[1]

THE FATHER SEEKS THREE KINDS OF PEOPLE

Worship uncovers our faces and allows the unfathomable mysteries of God to be dropped upon our hearts. There are three kinds of people the Lord opens His treasures to:

> *Those who fear (worship) Him*—"The secret [of the sweet, satisfying companionship] of the Lord have they who fear (revere and worship) Him, and He will show them His covenant, *and* reveal to them its [deep, inner] meaning" (Ps. 25:14, AMP).

> *The righteous*—"His confidential communion *and* secret counsel are with the [uncompromisingly] righteous (those who are upright and in right standing with Him)" (Prov. 3:32b, AMP).

> *His prophets*—"Surely the Lord GOD does nothing, unless He reveals His secret to His servants the prophets" (Amos 3:7).

THE COST OF TRUE WORSHIP

"With unveiled face"—True worship is the most exposing and costly act that we can engage in. We must be willing to be exposed and laid out before Him, never knowing what area of our lives His hand of love might touch. When we worship the Lord, there can be no place for covering our faces. When He died, Christ rent the veil that stood between us and the Father (Matt. 27:51; Mk. 15:38; Lk. 23:45). We must allow the full meaning of that to affect our worship and remain transparent before the Lord. All pretense goes as we enter the Holy of Holies. Sometimes when I am worshiping the Lord, I catch myself "wandering" somewhere else,

or thinking about other things. I have to remind myself, "Look at Jesus!" It is only with an unveiled face that we can look Him in the eye.

The unveiling of our faces includes the unveiling of our minds and the thoughts and weaknesses in our lives that He wants to address. For example, some Christians are gripped with fears, conquered by sins, or struggling with a distorted self-image. Godly men and women may be unaware of areas in their lives that cause pain to the Lord, themselves, or to their brothers and sisters. Everyone around them may see their problem areas clearly, but they remain either unaware of them or ignorant of how deeply rooted they are. Through worship, we are to set our gaze upon Him who has already won the victory over sin and death on our behalf.

Only as we cry out to the Lord for His unveiling of our faces and minds can we see the grave state of our hearts and be changed in His presence. Worship is the place for this work. Jesus commanded us to, "Love the LORD thy God with all thy heart, and with all thy soul, and with all thy mind" (Matt. 22:37; Mk. 12:30).

The following scriptures reveal Paul's emphasis on the process of transformation that needs to take place in our minds:

1. "And do not be conformed to this world but be transformed by the renewing of your mind" (Rom. 12:2).
2. "And be constantly renewed in the spirit of your mind" (Eph. 4:23, AMP). "Now it's time to be made new by every revelation that's been given to you" (TPT).
3. "Let this mind be in you which was also in Christ Jesus" (Phil. 2:5).
4. "Your hope wholly *and* unchangeably on the grace (divine favor) that is coming to you when Jesus Christ, the Messiah, is revealed" (1Pet. 1:13, AMP).

Tozer speaks of this veil of flesh that remains in our hearts and hinders intimate worship.

> A veil ... shutting out the light and hiding the face of God from us. It is the veil of our fleshly, fallen nature living on, unjudged within us, uncrucified and unrepudiated. It is the close-woven veil of the self-life which we have never truly acknowledged, of which we have been secretly ashamed, and which for these reasons we have never brought to the judgment of the cross. ... We have but to look into our own hearts and we shall see it there ... an enemy to our lives and an effective block to our spiritual progress.[2]

The truth is costly because it creates a choice; we must choose either to agree with God—embracing His likeness in exchange for our inadequacies and unworthiness—or to return to darkness. For this reason, alone, worship is most costly. We cannot cling to our former selves and remain ignorant of even the smallest issues of our character.

I remember being at odds with someone right before worship. As soon as I entered the presence of God, I knew that the Lord was not pleased with my attitude. Being right or wrong was no longer the point. My heart was unacceptable in His presence, and I had to humble myself and run to the person and ask for forgiveness. Brace yourself. Worship is an adventure of the soul. He takes us to the depths of self, so that we might become transparent before Him in the beholding of His glory.

THE WORK OF UNVEILING

"With unveiled face"—There is a degree of unveiling that we must do ourselves, but the greatest work is done by Him, the 'Render of all veils.'

When I see this phrase, I am reminded of one of the greatest moments of any wedding ceremony, when the groom lifts the veil off the face of his bride and kisses her. Our Bridegroom has come to unveil us and cause our hearts to become transparent before Him. Our worship is the kiss of devotion that we give to our true love, Jesus Christ.

The Song of Solomon begins with the Shulamite woman asking her beloved for a kiss. "Let him kiss me with the kisses of his mouth—for your love *is* better than wine" (Song of Sol. 1:2). As we kiss the Lord, we need to be reminded of these points. [3]

1. We can only kiss one person at a time. Worshipers only have eyes for Him.
2. When we kiss, we have to stop talking. There are times in worship when we need to stop talking and commune with Him from the inner sanctuary of our hearts.
3. A kiss is a face-to-face encounter. Worship is all the more delightful because it, too, involves a face-to-face encounter.

> "Our worship is the kiss of devotion that we give to our true love – Jesus Christ"

Hosea 2:14–23 speaks prophetically of the Lord alluring His love, the Church, into the wilderness. Here is where He desires to meet with us, betrothing us to Him forever. In the wilderness, He...

- Turns our desert into a vineyard—v. 15
- Turns our valleys into doors of hope and opportunity—v. 15
- Turns our sorrows into songs—v. 15
- Turns our hearts which worship false gods (Baals) into hearts which cry "My Husband"—vv. 16–17
- Turns our broken promises into a fresh covenant—vv. 19–20

How the Lord delights in his people! He draws us, cleanses us, and restores us to right standing with Him.

1. "Who *is* this coming out of the wilderness like pillars of smoke, perfumed with myrrh and frankincense, with all the merchant's fragrant powders?" (Song of Sol. 3:6)
2. "Who *is* this coming up from the wilderness, leaning

upon her beloved?" (Song of Sol. 8:5).

Worship is the place of our encounters with God, time and again. When He ravishes our hearts in the wilderness, we become like a pillar of smoke which represents a city conquered; we smell like Him—the fragrances of His victories—as we lean upon Him with utter dependence, every devotion centered in Him.

JESUS RENT THE VEIL ON CALVARY

"With unveiled face"—As Christians, we are able to approach the Lord with every man-made veil and hindrance between us removed because of Calvary. These passages reveal the confidence that adorns the Church as we are invited to come to His very throne with boldness. "Let us therefore come boldly to the throne of grace" (Heb. 4:16). "Therefore, brethren, having boldness to enter the Holiest by the blood of Jesus, by a new and living way which He consecrated for us, through the veil, that is, His flesh...let us draw near" (Heb. 10:19-20, 22). (See also Eph. 2:13.)

As He was being "wounded for our transgressions and bruised for our iniquities" (Is. 53:5), the veil in the temple was rent from top to bottom, a sign that Christ had given us access to God. How He longs to reveal himself to every believer!

In Exodus 33:18, Moses uttered the most dangerous and most wonderful prayer in the Bible: "Please, show me Your glory." This is a cry for deep and intimate fellowship with God. The Lord told Moses that no man could see His face and stay alive, so Moses was only permitted to see God's back as He passed by. God's glory must be found in His face.

To this day, flesh is consumed in His presence. When we see Him, flesh melts away, and we will be like Him (1 Jn. 3:2). We still need to be hidden to see His glory. For now, God "hides" himself from His people so that only smaller, bearable glimpses of His glory are seen. The blood of Jesus acts as a veil to hide us and allows us to stand in the presence of His *shekinah* glory.

Consider each of these five hiding places of God. They are secret entrances into His holy place and into intimacy with Him.

- The secret place of darkness (Job 20:26; Ps. 18:11; Is. 45:3)
- The secret place of His tabernacle (Ps. 27:5)
- The secret place of His presence (Ps. 31:20)
- The secret place of thunder (Ps. 81:7)
- The secret place of the stairs (cliff, mountain), (Song of Sol. 2:14)

"With unveiled face"—Worship and intercession are closely related. God's transparent people must be an interceding people. The Father only seeks three kinds of people: the lost (Lk. 15:11-32), the worshipers (Jn. 4:23), and the intercessors (Is. 59:16). These three remain inextricably linked forever in the place of worship.

WE SEEK HIS FACE

"With unveiled face"—As we remove the veil from our faces, we are more able to receive the blessing that comes from the face of God (see also Ps. 119:135; Ps. 67:1). "The LORD make His face shine upon you, and be gracious to you" (Num. 6:25). It is His face, or presence, that we seek. The Hebrew word for "face" is the same as the word for "presence."

> *"Press into God with all your heart. Seek His face and allow the glory of the Lord, His beauty, and His character to shine like a light from your face for everyone to see.*

- *paniym*. To see His face is to be in His presence and confronted by His glory.

"You have said, Seek My face [inquire for and require My presence as your vital need]. My heart says to You, Your face (Your presence), Lord, will I seek, inquire for *and* require [of necessity and on the authority of Your Word]" (Ps. 27:8, AMP).

Press into God with all your heart. Seek His face and allow the glory of the Lord, His beauty, and His character to shine like a light from your face for everyone to see.

CHAPTER SEVEN

WORSHIP IS PROPHETIC

"...BEHOLDING AS IN A MIRROR"

> *To behold Him is to love Him,
> and to love Him is to worship Him.*
> —Judson Cornwall

"*Beholding as in a mirror*"—The key word here is 'beholding.' We have made worship about the music, but it is really about gazing on the beauty of God. When we unveil our faces we see the glory of God. He makes worship alive, full of meaning and completely delightful rather than dry and ritualistic. The greatest hope of every believer is to see God, and the greatest worship comes from the things we have seen and experienced of Him. That is what makes worship prophetic.

In 1997, worship leader and composer, Paul Baloche, wrote "Open the Eyes of My Heart," aptly expressing the thoughts in 2Cor. 3:18:

> *Open the eyes of my heart, Lord Open the eyes of my heart*
> *I want to see You, I want to see You (x2)*
> *To see You high and lifted up*
> *Shining in the light of Your glory*
> *Pour out Your power and love*
> *As we sing holy, holy, holy.*
> *Holy, holy, holy Holy, holy, holy Holy, holy, holy*
> *I want to see you.*

GAZING UPON GOD

The yearning heart of the worshiper is described by the

psalmist, "Unto You I lift up my eyes, O You who dwell in the heavens. Behold, as the eyes of servants *look* to the hand of their masters, as the eyes of a maid to the hand of her mistress, so our eyes *look* to the LORD our God, until He has mercy on us" (Ps. 123:1–2).

The true worshiper has every opportunity to gaze upon God, not during a few select moments of life, but whenever our hearts desire to meet with Him. The inward eye of the spirit needs only to focus upon His presence. Cornwall emphasizes this point:

> Thanksgiving and praise are often responses to Christ's deeds, but worship is always based on His person. Fundamentally, worship is a person responding to a person, so we can't worship until we get a glimpse of God we must be in God's presence to worship. True worship will not begin to flow until we get a good glimpse of Christ Jesus.[1]

Because David clothed himself in the righteousness of Christ, he was able to look upon the face of the Lord, just as Moses did. We must also be clothed in righteousness as we draw near to the Lord. Entirely a work of His grace, there is nothing we can do to earn His approval. When we behold the Lord, we will cry out with David, "As for me, I will see Your face in righteousness; I shall be satisfied when I awake in Your likeness" (Ps. 17:15).

There is an important spiritual principle revealed in our text (2Cor. 3:18): *we become like the God we look upon and worship.* This makes worship far more than a duty to be performed. It is a holy exchange of life and devotion between the Lord and His people. David made his desire to see God an urgent request, one that was even commanded by God in His Word.

> One thing have I asked of the Lord, that will I seek, inquire for, *and* [insistently] require: that I may dwell in the house of the Lord [in His presence] all the days of my life, to behold *and* gaze upon the beauty [the sweet attractiveness and the delightful loveliness] of the Lord and to meditate, consider, *and* inquire in His temple You have said, Seek My face [inquire for and require My presence as your vital need]. My heart says to You, Your face (Your presence),

Lord, will I seek, inquire for, *and* require [of necessity and on the authority of Your Word]" (Ps. 27:4, 8, AMP).

> *"It is because of the beholding that worship is prophetic."*

We have the opportunity to become worshipers who behold the face of God. Because of His great grace, Christ, the Rock (Rom. 9:33; 1Cor. 10:4), has made a way for us to be hidden in Him. "For you died, and your life is hidden with Christ in God" (Col. 3:3). Anyone who desires to see Him must first be hidden in the Rock.

- Moses was hidden in a rock (Ex. 33:21–22)
- David was hidden in a rock (Ps. 27:5)
- Jesus was hidden in a rock (Matt. 27:60–28:2)

What a magnificent plan! He died and rose again so that He might live in us! "Christ within *and* among you, the Hope of [realizing the] glory" (Col. 1:27b, AMP).

Many Christians accept Christ as their Savior, but do not avail themselves of the second part of this great mystery, that we must also die (to self) and live as ones who are hidden in Him.

I will never forget attending Shekinah Church in Tennessee some years ago. The Lord was visiting this body in an extraordinary way. They would hold prayer meetings every day in the morning and again at night. In every service, the Lord moved supernaturally upon hearts. Such was the overwhelming presence of the Lord, that I attempted to "hide" under my chair–all the while knowing that this was futile. There was no hiding from His face, nowhere to take cover from His presence. If I could have ripped up the carpet and climbed underneath it, I would have tried that, but I was trapped by the gaze of God. All I could do was to cry out with Isaiah "Woe is me, for I am undone!" (Is. 6:5). I was sure that He could see every sin I had ever committed and that each of those present could see each fault in graphic detail. The purpose for such an encounter is not to leave us clothed in layers of shame, but broken over sin, renewed by His grace, and made holy through a face-to-face encounter.

"Beholding as in a mirror"—In Lockyer's comments on Hebrews 9:24–28, we see three aspects of the Lord's appearing: past, present, and future. For easier reference, I have organized his thoughts into a table, along with Vine's Greek definitions (Table 2). It is obvious that the Lord is not passive on the issue of appearing before His people. [2]

"Beholding as in a mirror"—Worship always includes some aspect of beholding God. When we are focused on Him, our eyes turn away from ourselves and see the only One who is worthy of worship. Worship is only possible when we see Him and surrender our hearts to Him in humility, abandon, and adoration. We waste so much time in His presence while we are thinking only about ourselves, our needs or our surroundings.

We have made worship about the music, but true worship focuses on *seeing* Him.

All heavenly beings look for Him when they worship, and they become consumed with the sight of Him in all His light and splendor. The Book of Revelation is filled with John's descriptions as they gather around the throne of God in adoration. Worship in heaven centers on the sight of God.

THE MIRROR

"Beholding as in a mirror"—When we look into a mirror, we see our own reflection. But when we look into *this* mirror, we behold the face of God, and we are changed into His likeness. The only way this supernatural beholding can work is through the abiding presence of God in us—"Christ in you the hope of glory" (Col. 1:27). This is the essence of prophetic worship.

The very nature of a mirror conveys an exact image of the one looking. Only to the degree that we allow ourselves to be unveiled by Christ will we see accurately in the mirror.

Mirrors in antiquity consisted of a metal surface, made usually of copper, silver, gold, electrum, or, especially in Palestine during the postexilic period, of bronze.[3]

TABLE 2

THREE ASPECTS OF THE LORD'S APPEARING

Heb. 9:26 The past appearing	Heb. 9:24 The present appearing	Heb. 9:28 The prospective appearing
He has appeared to put away sin	... now to appear in the presence of God for us.	... He will appear a second time.
phaneroo[2]—Gk. for *appear:* to be manifested or revealed in one's true character as opposed to one who might appear in a false guise or without disclosure of what he truly is.	***emphanizo***—Gk. for *appear:* "to shine in," used literally of physical manifestation (Matt. 27:53; Jn.14:22) or metaphorically of the spiritual experience of Christ by believers who abide in His love (Jn. 14:21).	***optomai***—Gk. for *appear:* "to see." The English word *optical* comes from this word.
This appearing is past and permanent.	This appearing is present and progressive.	This appearing is prospective and perfect.
We have salvation from the penalty of sin.	We have salvation from the power of sin.	We have salvation from the entire presence of sin.
Looking back, we see Jesus dying for us.	Looking up, we see Jesus pleading for us.	Looking forward, we see Jesus returning for us.

Because the ancient mirror was made of metal, it was liable to rust or tarnish and needed regular attention to be kept bright. Likewise, we must read the Word of God and minister before Him in worship on a regular basis, so that our vision of Him will remain clear.

I believe the mirror in Second Corinthians 3:18 represents the Word and presence of God. When we stand in the light of these, that same light is strangely reflected in and through our lives. Bible commentator, Adam Clark, expresses it this way:

> Now as mirrors among the Jews, Greeks, and Romans were made of highly polished metal, it would often happen, especially in strong light, that the face would be greatly illuminated by this strongly reflected light; and to this circumstance the apostle seems here to allude. So by earnestly contemplating the Gospel of Jesus, and believing on Him who is its Author, the soul becomes illuminated with His divine splendor, for this sacred mirror reflects back on the believing soul the image of Him whose perfections it exhibits; and thus we see the glorious form after which our minds are to be fashioned; and by believing and receiving the influence of His Spirit ... our form is changed ... into the same image, which we behold there; and this image of God, lost by our fall, and now recovered and restored by Jesus Christ: for the shining of the face of God upon us, i.e. approbation, through Christ, is the cause of our transformation into the divine image.[4]

When we look into the Word of God with open hearts and unveiled faces, there is the potential to behold aspects of Christ we have never seen.

> Anytime and anywhere people have discovered the truth of the Scriptures, it has resulted in a great awakening of their hearts to worship the Lord Jesus. ... Something dynamic happens when the Bible is opened. Lives are changed. Christ is exalted. And worship flows from the hearts of God's people. The miracle that transpires in the hearts of people is inexplicable.[5]

We usually look into a mirror as we clothe, beautify, and perfect ourselves. As we look into the mirror of Christ, let us adorn ourselves with His glorious attire, the beauty of His character, and the perfection of His holiness.

LOOKING FOR HIS COUNTENANCE

"Beholding as in a mirror"— Paul contrasts the plight of the Hebrews, who were not able to look upon the light that shone from Moses' face, with this invitation to us all to look into the glorious face of God. Paul proposes, "But if the ministry of death, written *and* engraved on stones, was glorious, so that the children of Israel could not look steadily at the face of Moses because of the light of his countenance, which *glory* was passing away, how will the ministry of the Spirit not be more glorious? For if the ministry of condemnation *had* glory, the ministry of righteousness exceeds much more in glory" (2Cor. 3:7–9).

Moses needed to veil his face after he had been with God, but Jesus was more glorious than that. Yet the multitudes were never blinded or repelled by His light. Sinners were never put off by the grace and truth that shone from His face. The touch of His hand, the gaze of His eye and the sound of His voice only served to heal broken and desperate seekers. We must continue to run to His light.

"Beholding as in a mirror"—We are to worship as *a prophetic people*, not merely as a people who believe in prophecy. Prophetic people look for the Lord at every opportunity. David Blomgren speaks of a corporate "prophetic unction which brings a dimension of divine quickening into our worship. ... The prophetic spirit coming and permeating the worship atmosphere is a witness of the presence of Jesus being manifest in the service."[6]

"Beholding as in a mirror"— The Holy Spirit uses a great variety of means to make Christ visible to us in praise and worship. Each of these causes us to see Him more clearly. (You can see a list of the ways and places to hear God's voice in Chapter twenty-four.)

> *"Whenever we look into the Word of God with open hearts and unveiled faces, there is the potential for us to behold aspects of Christ that we have never seen before."*

All art forms can become wonderful tools for prophetic worship. It is through the arts that we are able to catch a glimpse of eternity and hear the voice of the Lord. The arts open our spiritual and natural senses to God. When music is ministered as part of the prophetic "uncovering" of the Lord, it is almost as if there is a "sound within the sound." This is not a sound that is heard with the ear, but an anointing that is only perceived in the heart. It is a layer of the sound of God in what we do, sing, and play in His presence.

> *"Prophetic worship is dependent upon music that contains a 'sound within a sound.'"*

Chapter Eight

Worship is Transcendent

"...THE GLORY OF THE LORD"

Worship is eternally and inseparably linked to the glory of God.

"*The glory of the Lord*"—What a sight! According to 2 Cor. 3:18, we are privileged to behold the very glory of God whenever we worship. In fact, the chief goal of worship is to bring mankind into contact with the glory of the Lord. The Lord is known in Scripture as *The Lord (or God) of Glory* (Ps. 24:8, 10; 29:3; Acts 7:2; 1 Cor. 2:8; Eph. 1:17; Jas. 2:1). Cornwall points out that He cannot be God without His glory.[1]

The *International Standard Bible Encyclopedia* states, "*Glory of God*—In the ultimate sense, no subject is more important than this."[2] I would venture to say that the main subject of the whole Bible is the glory of the Lord. The entire book is about our God who, in His infinite wisdom, created a universe that is being formed into the likeness of His glory.

The plan of God is simple, profound, and powerful. He has created a people who would worship Him of their own free will. In the context of worship, the people behold His glory, become changed into His likeness and serve as ministers of His glory in the earth.

> As clearly as we can see our own natural face in a mirror, [we can also see] the glorious promises and privileges of the Gospel of Christ; and while we contemplate, we anticipate them by desire and hope, and apprehend them by faith, and

are changed from the glory there represented to the enjoyment of the thing which is represented, even the glorious image—righteousness and true holiness—of the glory of the God of glory.[3]

"The glory of the Lord"—In the Hebrew, the primary word for 'glory' is *kabod* (kaw-bode', Strong's #H3519), meaning *weight, splendor, glorious, copious, heavy.* It is like a sublime heaviness that rests upon the soul. His weight is not a burden or imposition of any kind. Every thought of Him and every layer of the knowledge of His character are the joy, nourishment, delight and full satisfaction of every person. "For the biblical worshiper, God is not an idea; he is a compelling reality encountered at the deepest level of being."[4] We must allow the weight of His glory to rest upon every area of our lives until His virtue permeates our thoughts, breath, and every desire of our hearts. Through these encounters with God, we become the "hiding place of his glory" – His secrets are our quest and finding him out is our goal and honor:

> God conceals the revelation of his word in the hiding place of his glory.
> But the honor of kings is revealed by how they thoroughly search out the deeper meaning of all God says.
> (Prov. 25:2 TPT)

Some years ago, I attended an intercessor's meeting at my home church. A friend gave me a ride home, and we both had the distinct impression that the Lord had not finished with us, that we needed to spend more time in His presence. As soon as she arrived at my house, she turned off the car and immediately the *kabod* of God filled the car. The only way I can describe it is that it seemed like a hand was pushing me down in the seat. It was not an uncomfortable experience. I was unable to speak and could hardly breathe, yet I was not afraid at all. I felt a little silly and wondered if my friend was expecting me to get out of the car. (I later found out that she was experiencing the same thing.) Several hours passed by as if they were minutes, and still He pressed his glory into me. We finally were able to conclude this time, but that same presence remained with us for several weeks. Even to this day, I encounter Him in this manner, the delightful pain of the weight of His presence.

> *"The chief goal of worship is to bring mankind into contact with the glory of the Lord."*

Whenever we have an encounter with God, it is not for the experience alone, but to form something of God within our hearts. I believe He was tuning my heart and "calibrating" me for the glory. I have never gotten over this, and I pray I never will.

THE GLORY OF GOD FILLS OUR SENSES

"The glory of the Lord"—The glory of the Lord is more than a supernatural manifestation that will be seen in the earth during the last days (Hab. 2:14). It is also His nature and character revealed to us through our spiritual and natural senses—sight, sound, touch, taste and smell. Through these, God has made a way for us to know Him more deeply. He desires to draw nearer to us and uses every means available to do so. By filling the universe with His presence, He demonstrates His intentions.

> He is delightful to every sense, to the eye most fair, to the ear most gracious, to the spiritual nostril most sweet. The excellencies of Jesus are all most precious, comparable to the rarest spices. . . all sweetness meet in Jesus, and are poured forth wherever he is present.[5]

In Exodus 33:18–23 and 34:5–7, Moses prayed that most dangerous, yet delightful of all prayers, he asked God if he could see His glory. God's response was very interesting. It shows us two important ways we can experience the glory of God:

1. *Seeing*—God told Moses that no one could see His face and stay alive. (That is why Moses' prayer was so dangerous.) We must assume that the sight of God's glory somehow involves the sight of His face. (Other scriptures that refer to seeing the glory of God: Ex. 16:7; Ps. 63:2; 97:6; Is. 35:2; 40:5; 62:2; Matt. 24:30; Mark 13:26; Luke

21:27.)

The sight of His glory may include supernatural manifestations, such as healings, miracles, a visible cloud of glory in the room, or other unusual effects. On one occasion, during worship at Shady Grove Church, some ceiling lights fell out of their sockets, and the lights all surged on and off as if they were unable to contain the power and the glory of God! That day, great miracles of deliverance took place in the presence of God.

2. *Hearing*—The Lord allowed Moses to be hidden in the cleft of a rock while He walked back and forth before him declaring His name. Moses was only permitted to see the back of God and hear His voice. Moses also heard God's voice out of the burning bush, and he was changed forever. ("I Am"— Ex. 3:4–14.) There are layers of glory that He desires to reveal to us through sound.

> *"There are layers of glory that He desires to reveal to us through the sound of His name and every time He speaks to us."*

3. *Tasting*—The Lord invites us to taste and see that He is good (Ps. 34:8). His words are sweeter than honey (Ps. 119:103), and his fruit delights the taste of the bride (Song of Sol. 2:3). It is interesting that the Lord doesn't say, "See, and then you will taste." Somehow, by taking His Word into our hearts and "tasting" Him, our eyes are opened to His glory. In the Garden of Eden, Adam and Eve tasted the fruit of the knowledge of good and evil and their eyes were opened (Gen. 3:5). That one taste closed their hearts to greater and greater depths of God's glory and sent all the earth into a tailspin of destruction. Now, it is through tasting that our seeing is restored, and fellowship with Him is renewed.

4. *Smelling*—The Lord's wedding garments smell of myrrh,

aloes, and cassia (Ps. 45:8). The Shulamite sang of our Lord, whose name is like fragrant ointments (Song of Sol. 1:3). He is described as a "bundle of myrrh" and is the merchant who has fragrant powders (Song of Sol. 3:6). The cry, "Abba Father," (Mk. 14:36; Rom. 8:15; Gal. 4:6) means "Daddy, I love your smell."[6]

5. *Touching*—Many knew that if they could only touch Jesus—even the hem of His garment—they would be healed (Matt. 9:21; 14:36; Mk 3:10; 5:28; 6:56; 8:22; 10:13; Lk. 6:19). I have experienced the touch and weight of the glory of God in prayer and worship on numerous occasions, where His hand has pressed me into a chair or onto the floor, where I could not move for hours. At other times, His love causes delightful pangs within my heart, and He takes my breath away. In no way are these frightening experiences. He overtakes us with love. Every touch of His hand and every contact with His glory only mean that another portion of my heart has been conquered and laid bare for the imprint of His nature.

The sight, sound, taste, smell and touch of God are freely available for all believers.

LAYERS OF GLORY

"The glory of the Lord"—There are more than 450 references in Scripture concerning the glory of the Lord. I was surprised to find that around half of these are found in the New Testament. We can learn the following facts about the glory of God:

The location—The glory of God is able to come into and leave the sanctuary (Ez. 10:4, 18; 44:4). The glory of God sanctifies the tabernacle (Ex. 29:43). It sometimes fills the whole sanctuary (2Chron. 5:14; 7:1–3; Ps. 63:2; Ez. 43:5; 44:4; Rev. 15:8). The glory of God will fill the whole earth (Num. 14:21; Hab. 2:14; Ps. 57:5, 11; 72:19; 108:5).

The glory of God is to be declared in all the nations (1Chron. 16:24; Is. 42:12; 66:18). It is to be declared by all people everywhere (1Chron. 16:28–29; Ps. 29:1–2; 96:3, 7–8). The heavens declare the glory of God (Ps. 19:1; 97:6), and it is declared continuously before the throne of God (Is. 6:3; Rev. 4:8). The glory of God accompanies His presence (1Chron. 16:27).

The effect—The glory of God has, at times, caused people to be unable to stand (1Ki. 8:11; 2Chron. 5:14; 7:2; Ez. 44:4; Acts 22:6). The glory of God is a fearful thing (Ps. 102:15; Is. 2:10, 19, 21; 59:19; Lk. 2:9).

The crown--God is clothed and crowned with glory (Job 40:10; Heb. 2:9). God's people form a crown of glory for the Lord (Is. 62:3). God will become an eternal crown of glory to His people (Is. 28:5; 1Pet. 5:4). Our God is the King of glory (Ps. 24:10).

In the last days and through eternity—The Lord is going to appear in glory (Ps. 102:16). Everyone on earth will see the Lord coming in glory (Matt. 24:30). It will endure forever (Ps. 104:31; Matt. 6:13; 1Pet. 5:11; Rev. 4:9, 11; 5:12–13; 7:12; 19:1). The glory will provide light for all eternity (Is. 60:19; 21:23).

Possession—The glory of God is the inheritance of the wise (Prov. 3:35). This glory cannot be shared with anyone; it is God's alone (Is. 42:8; 48:11). Sin has caused mankind to fall short of the glory (Rom. 3:23). Our greatest hope is the glory of God (Rom. 5:2; Col. 1:27). God gives us all a spirit of wisdom and revelation in order that we might receive greater understanding of Him and the work of His glory in our lives (Eph. 1:17–19).

The revelation—The glory of God will be seen upon His people

(Is. 60:1–2; 62:2; Hag. 2:7). God is intent upon revealing His glory in and through His people (Is. 43:7; 60:7; Jn. 17:10, 22; Rom. 8:18, 30; 1Cor. 2:7; 10:31; 2Cor. 10:17;

Gal. 6:14; Eph. 3:21; 5:27; 1Pet. 5:1)—accompanied with great rejoicing (1Pet. 4:13; 5:1), surrounds those who serve Him (Is. 58:8), and is manifested in and through Jesus (Jn. 1:14; 2:11; 12:23; 13:31–32; 14:13; 17:1, 4–5). Only God is worthy to receive all glory (Rev. 4:11; 5:12).

GLORY TRANSCENDENT AND NUMINOUS

"The glory of the Lord"—True worship invariably contains an element of transcendence, vertical worship where we tend to sing and minister *to* God rather than singing *about* Him. Transcendent worship draws us away from focusing on our needs and lifts us into an encounter of the awesome and glorious God, our King and Father. In this day, where we have lost so much respect for authority, it is easy to become self- absorbed and familiar with God. We have forgotten that our every breath is in His hand (Job 12:10; 34:14–15); that His face shines with the same brilliance as the sun (Rev. 1:16); that He is clothed in greatness, power and majesty (1Chron. 29:11; Ps. 93:1; 104:1); that He alone is full of wisdom, perfect in beauty, beyond compare, and completely past finding out (Job 9:10; 11:7).

LaMar Boschman refers to transcendent worship in his writings. He insists that Christians focus more upon the majesty of the Lord in worship, rather than spending long periods of time singing to the Lord about our needs and His power to meet those needs.

> When we touch transcendent worship the temporal is transformed and abased...When we experience this level of worship there is an awareness of the awesome presence of God. ... Our worship should transcend our feelings, needs and circumstances.[7]

Richard Leonard describes transcendent worship: "In genuine biblical worship, the focus is on the *One who is worshiped*. The biblical worshiper comes before the Creator with an overpowering sense of reverence, awe, even dread before the divine mystery. This aspect of worship is known as the *numinous.*"[8]

An encounter with the numinous aspect of God's presence may range from the sweet impressions He makes upon our hearts of His nature and will, to a visible encounter, which is known as a *theophany*. It is here where encounters with God transcend selfish and intellectual thought and our whole being is consumed with the sight of Him. Foster refers to this experience as "being invaded by the Shekinah of God."[9]

THEOPHANIES

Many theophanies have been recorded in the Bible. Several of those are outlined in Table 4, "Encounters With God." The purpose in making a study of theophanies is to recognize the preparation needed to encounter God and the diverse manifestations and effects of His glory on humankind.

Our goal should not be just to experience supernatural manifestations, but to attain a deep knowledge of Him. We would do well to pursue God with the same intensity and devotion of some of these biblical characters.

In the chart, I have attempted to show the place of their encounter; how long they spent seeing God; what they did to prepare their lives for such a privileged sight; what they actually saw, or the supernatural manifestation that was revealed to them; the revelation they received; the resulting effect on their personal lives, and what lasting changes came as a result of the visitation of God.

THE GLORY OF THE LORD

The glory of the Lord is the most powerful force in the universe. Worship creates an atmosphere where God's power and glory are revealed. Our lives are to be a statement of that power, life, and glory, "Therefore, whether you eat or drink, or whatever you do, do all to the glory of God" (1Cor. 10:31).

To the believer, the light of God is not a blinding force, but the illuminating knowledge of the true nature of God; it is divine revelation. We will never know God or understand this life by our own wisdom. Our understanding of God and our worldview must stem from the light of His presence and Word. Then will we understand from God's perspective. "In Your light we see light" (Ps. 36:9).

> *"The glory of the Lord is surely the most powerful force in the universe."*

"The Holy Ghost lights up the dark recesses of our heart's ungodliness. . . one ray from the throne of God is better than the noonday splendour of created wisdom."[10]

TABLE 3
ENCOUNTERS WITH GOD

NAME	PLACE	LENGTH / TIME	PREPARATION	MANIFESTATION	REVELATION RECEIVED	RESULT	AREA OF LIFE CHANGED
ADAM/EVE Gen. 2-3	Eden Gen. 2-3	?	God formed and initiated relationship with them	God walked openly before them Gen. 3:8	Whatever God showed them of Himself	1. Oneness with God 2. Sinlessness	We can only presume they grew from glory to glory
ENOCH Gen 5:22-24	?	Three hundred years	He walked with God in habitual fellowship	?	?	God took him	He was given a glorified body
ABRAM Gen. 12:7	Shechem	?	Obedience to the commands of God	The appearance of God	An unconditional promise to Abram and his	He built an altar	He grew as a man of faith
ABRAM Gen. 17:1-22	?	?	Obedience to the commands of God	The appearance of God	Abramic Covenant and the promise of a son	He fell on his face and laughed	His name was changed
ABRAM/ SARAH Gen. 18:1	By the oaks (terebinth trees) of Mamre	?	Obedience to the commands of God	Three men (God) stood by him	Is anything too hard for the Lord? Confirmation of previous promises destruction of Sodom & Gomorrah	He ran to greet and to minister to God bowed down	?

Worship is Transcendent

NAME	PLACE	LENGTH / TIME	PREPARATION	MANIFESTATION	REVELATION RECEIVED	RESULT	AREA OF LIFE CHANGED
SARAH Gen. 21:1	Gerar	?	Faith in the promises of God Heb. 11:1	?	?	Her body was renewed she was able to conceive	Sarah had a child
JACOB Gen 28:10-22	Probably Mt. Moriah	One night	Separation from family & inheritance	V12 Open heaven/ladder between heaven & earth/angels ascending and descending / the Lord stood beside him	Renewal of Abramic covenant / v16 "The Lord is in this place"	V17 Awe and fear of God	Beginning of a heart change/ Jacob started to give to God v22
JACOB Gen. 32:22-32	Peniel (The face of God), over the brook – Jabbok	One night	V9 Prayer / v22-23 He passed over Jabbok (emptying) and left everything that he trusted behind	Jacob fought all night with the Lord – he saw God face to face v30	Jacob had a revelation of Himself as he faced God. The Lord changed his name	1. v2 repentance 2. v26 He fought God for His blessing	1. v28 His name and character were changed (he became a prince with God) 2. v25:31 His walk – he limped

109

NAME	PLACE	LENGTH / TIME	PREPARATION	MANIFESTATION	REVELATION RECEIVED	RESULT	AREA OF LIFE CHANGED
MOSES Ex. 3:4-7	Mt. Horeb (desert) possibly a part of Sinai	3 days	40 years in Egypt, 40 years in the desert. Moses was prince of Egypt who had become humble	1. The bush burned but was not consumed 2. Appearance of an angel 3. God's voice 4. The rod changed from serpent to rod again 5. Hand became leprous then healed	V14 This is the first time that God gave Himself a name – I AM. "I have manifest, I do manifest, I will manifest."	1. Moses hid his face in fear 2. Removed his shoes	The call of God – from shepherd to deliverer
MOSES Ex. 19-24:8	My. Sinai Thorns)	3 days	1. v10 the people were sanctified 2. v11 the waited for 3 days	1. 19:9 Gods presence in a thick cloud 2. 19:16; 2018 Earthquakes, thunders, lightnings 3. v18 Mt. Sinai smoking, fire 4. 20:21 Thick darkness 5. 19:19 God's voice	Exodus 20:1-17 The Ten Commandments	1. Fear and trembling 2. Moses stood afar off 3. Death if any came too close	Ex. 19:6 Moses was called to be a priest as well as a deliverer. Ex. 20:21 Moses drew near to God

Worship is Transcendent

NAME	PLACE	LENGTH / TIME	PREPARATION	MANIFESTATION	REVELATION RECEIVED	RESULT	AREA OF LIFE CHANGED
MOSES Ex. 24:9-32	Mt Saini	40 days and nights	Ex. 24:4-5 Moses built an altar of worship – the young men offered sacrifices Ex. 24:16 Six days waiting in God's presence	1. 24:9-11 They saw God & His glory 2. 24:16-17 A cloud of glory and fire	1. 24:12 The Law and Commandments 2. 25-31 Instructions concerning Tabernacle of Moses	1. 24:11 They ate and drank in God's presence 2. 24:18 Moses drew near to God	Ex. 32:7-28 Moses was called by God to be a judge
MOSES Ex. 33:34	Base of Saini/Horeb then up the Mt.	40 days and nights	Ex. 33:7 Separation from the camp of sin	1. 33:10 Cloudy pillar 2. 33:11 God speaking face to face 3. 33:23 View of the back of God	1. Ex. 34:6-7 The goodness and severity of God found in His name 2. Ex. 34:28 The Ten Commandments	Ex. 34:8 Moses immediately bowed down to worship	Ex. 34:29-35 Moses' countenance shone like Gods face and had to be veiled
JOSHUA Josh. 5:13-6:5	Gilgal (rolling away) near Jericho.	?	1. Josh. 5:2-9 Obedience 2. Keeping Passover	A man with a sword drawn in his hand – The Captain of the Lords Host (Jesus)	Josh. 6:2-5 The battle plan for victory at Jericho	He fell on his face and worshiped He removed his shoes	He call of God – Joshua was now a warrior as well as a deliverer

111

NAME	PLACE	LENGTH/TIME	PREPARATION	MANIFESTATION	REVELATION RECEIVED	RESULT	AREA OF LIFE CHANGED
ELISHA 2Kings 2:1-14	Jordan	A moment	1. Elisha was a servant to Elijah 2. Persistence from Gilgal	1. Chariot of fire 2. Horses of fire 3. Elijah taken up	2Kings 2:9-10 Double portion anointing	1. V12 He cried out 2. Rent his clothes 3. V14 Smote the water with Elijah's mantle	The call of God – Elisha was now a prophet as well as a servant
ISAIAH Is. 6:1-13	Probably in Jerusalem	?	Death of Uzziah – Isaiah's father figure	1. The Lord high and lifted up 2. V 1-4 Seraphim 3. V4 he saw the doors of heaven shake 4. V8 He saw the Trinity in discussion	5 Sin nature of man 8-10 The heart of God for His people	1. v5 Repentance 2. V6-7 Cleansing 3. V8-9 Call	1. His cry – went from, "Woe unto them" in chapter 5 to "Woe is me" 2. His cleansing v6-7 3. His call – "send me"
EZEKIEL Ez. 1:1-13	Probably by the river Chebar	?	Captivity	The entire book is filled with visions, Cherubim, fire, whirlwind, cloud, throne of God, four creatures, the glory of the Lord, open heavens. The Spirit of God entered Ezekiel as He spoke to him; he was lifted by his hair between earth and heaven	1. God's glory and His prophetic plan for His people . He saw and heard God as He spoke	1. 1:28; 3:23 He fell on his face 2. 3:15 He remained silent and astonished for 7 days	3:8 God gave Ezekiel a firm, inflexible will and character to endure great hardships in order to bring his prophetic message to God's people

NAME	PLACE	LENGTH / TIME	PREPARATION	MANIFESTATION	REVELATION RECEIVED	RESULT	AREA OF LIFE CHANGED
SHARACH MESHACH ABEDNEGO Dan. 3	Babylon	?	Godliness in captivity	1. V25 The Sn of Man in the fire with them 2. The fire had no ability to burn	The power of God	3:29 A decree was issued – the nation would serve the Lord	V30 Promotion in the court of Nebuchadnezzar
DANIEL Dan. 7:9-28	Babylon in the first year of Belshazzar	?	Godliness in captivity	1. V9 The Ancient of Days 2. V9 God's Throne 3. V10 Angelic Ministers of God	1. V9 God's Name "Ancient of Days" – The only name given to God the Father in Scripture 2. V 14 The Kingdom of God 3. God's eternal plan	7:15, 28 Grieved, troubled, alarmed	V28 Daniel was troubled by his thoughts. His countenance changed but he kept his visitation a secret

NAME	PLACE	LENGTH/ TIME	PREPARATION	MANIFESTATION	REVELATION RECEIVED	RESULT	AREA OF LIFE CHANGED
DANIEL Dan. 10	Beside Hiddekel/Tigris river	?	1. Prayer 2. 10:2-3 3 weeks mourning 3. 10:12 Daniel's heart of understanding; his humility and words before God caused God to respond with His presence	V5-6 An extraordinary man (Christ)	1. Future events Daniel caught a glimpse of the battle between good and evil supernatural powers	1. V7 Great trembling, fear, hiding 2. Strength was sapped 3. V8 His face went pale 4. V9 deep sleep 5. V9 he fell on his face to the ground 6. Unable to speak	V18-19 Renewed strength
MARY Luke 1:26-38	Nazareth – a place of no reputation – bordered by heathen	?	V28 Meekness. Mary's relationship with God resulted in her being greatly favored and blessed	1. V26-38 The angel Gabriel spoke with her 2. V35 The overshadowing of the Holy Spirit	V32-33 That she would conceive and bring forth the Messiah whose kingdom had no end	1. V29 Troubled 2. V38 Humble submission	She became fruitful and bore our Messiah

Worship is Transcendent

NAME	PLACE	LENGTH / TIME	PREPARATION	MANIFESTATION	REVELATION RECEIVED	RESULT	AREA OF LIFE CHANGED
PETER, JAMES, JOHN Matt. 17:1-13	A high mountain	?	Closeness with Jesus	1. V2 Transfiguration of Jesus 2. V3 Moses and Elijah 3. V5 A bright cloud 4. The voice of God	V13 Some revelation of the teachings of Jesus	V6 The fell on their faces and were afraid	Nothing perceptible
(The disciples had other encounters with the glorified Christ during His life on earth and as he ascended into heaven)							
STEPHEN Acts 6:15; 7:55-60	Jerusalem	Possibly only hours	6:3-5, 8, 10; 7:55 He grew in the wisdom, honesty, faith, power and fullness of the Spirit	1. 6:15 His face had the appearance of an angel 2. He saw the glory of God and Jesus standing at the right hand of God 3. 7:55-56 He saw the heavens opened	Stephen had a revelation of the glory of God. (His sermon starts and finishes with the glory of God)	7:54-47 – the hearers: 1. Were cut to the heart 2. Gnashed at him with their teeth 3. Cried with a loud voice 4. Stopped their ears 5. Ran upon him	6:15 His face shone

NAME	PLACE	LENGTH / TIME	PREPARATION	MANIFESTATION	REVELATION RECEIVED	RESULT	AREA OF LIFE CHANGED
PAUL Acts 9:3-8	On the Road near Damascus (Some of us meet God on the road alone)	?	Martyrdom of Stephen and the persecution of the Church	1. V3 (Acts 26:13) A light shone round about him which was brighter than the sun 2. A voice from God	1. Jesus – the Light of the world 2. Self – the sinner	1. V4 Fell to the earth 2. V6 Astonishment, trembling 3. V8 Blindness for 3 days	1. His name was changed from Sul to Paul 2. His heart was changed from anger towards the Church to becoming a great Apostle 3. Paul's life was surrendered to the Lord
JOHN Book of Rev.	Rev. 1:9 Island of Patmos	?	1. 1:9 Tribulation 2. 1:10 Walking in the Spirit	13:16 One like the Son of man, with a vice like a trumpet	1. The Lamb of God 2. The Alpha and Omega 3. The Throne of God 4. The Church 5. The end times 6. Heaven 7. Eternity	V17 He fell at His feet as if he were dead	Blessed

Chapter Nine

Worship is Transforming

"... ARE BEING TRANSFORMED INTO THE SAME IMAGE"

The gods we worship write their names on our faces, be sure of that. That which dominates will determine man's life and character. Therefore, it behooves us to be careful what we worship, for what we worship we are becoming.
—Ralph Waldo-Emerson

"Are being transformed into the same image"—We are created in the image and likeness of the Lord, but sin has separated us from Him. As we worship, we draw near to the Lord and become more and more like Him. John Dryden wrote of creation,

> Man only of a softer mold was made
> Not for his fellows' ruin but their aid:
> Created kind, beneficent and free,
> The noble image of the Deity.[1]

There is a cyclic effect that occurs as we behold Him. The more we unveil our faces and see Him, the more we are transformed. The work of our transformation will then create new desire to see Him again and be further changed into His image. This is one of the great biblical principles of worship.

Morgenthaler says that in worship, self is abandoned in His presence, and layer after layer of His heart and likeness are embraced by the worshiper. "Essentially, Christian worship is the spirit and truth interaction between God and God's people. It is an exchange."[2]

"Are being transformed into the same image"—It is impossible to worship without being eternally transformed. Such is the power of encountering God. If we say we have worshiped yet we have no evidence of change in our lives, we are deceived. It simply means that we did not see Him and did not unveil our faces in worship. Perhaps we sang and whispered prayers, but the songs and words have no ability to change us. It is the presence of God and an encounter with His grace that changes our hearts.

God offers us change to the very core and fiber of our being—change in the way we think, feel, believe, act, speak, and live. We are changed in order to bring our lives into accordance with His divine will and purpose. "All the doors that lead inward, to the sacred place of the Most High, are doors outward—out of self, out of smallness, out of wrong."[3]

John Stevenson adds, "You will either leave transformed by the power of God or you will leave convicted by the power of God."[4] Worship offers an eternal exchange. At the altar of worship, we leave something of self behind and gain the likeness of Christ.

"Are being transformed into the same image"—The tense used in this phrase is known as the present continuous tense. The transforming power of God is at work in us now and will continue as we behold Him again and again. Transformation continues as long as we gaze on His glory. There is no limitation to this process.

> "We are changed in order to bring our lives in accordance with His Divine will and purpose."

WORSHIP GIVES US A DIFFERENT PERSPECTIVE

Praise and worship provide a different perspective on everything. Part of laying self aside means that we lay down thinking that is born out of the seat of brokenness and sin in our heart.

As I speak of God encounters and the change that is woven into our lives, some may be tempted to think in terms of smoke, fire, wind, heavenly voices, and so forth. While such events indeed transpired throughout the Bible and occur even today, we must not expect them to be the norm for *every* encounter with God.

We often say we have "heard His voice," "met God," "sensed His presence," "seen His glory," or any other such phrase that indicates some form of encounter with Him. This communion should be normal for believers. It is His manifest presence. He desires continual fellowship with us, and His arms always invite our response to His loving pursuit of our lives.

When God confronts us, it may be in the form of a whisper, an impression in our hearts or minds. He might put His finger on something, and we notice it for the first time. His hand might make an almost imperceptible adjustment in our thinking or at the seat of our desires. He can speak to us through His Word, music, friends, leaders or through His creation. We may know things that we did not learn, be sensitive when our hearts were hard, feel longings that have been breathed into us by God himself, or have grace for others when it has been sadly lacking on previous occasions. We may witness for Christ with words and passion that have been foreign to us, see new light at the end of our personal struggles, or experience victories in battles that appeared hopeless—the possibilities of our meeting with Him are as endless as God himself.

No matter how He shows himself, there will be transformation. Sometimes it seems He reveals himself to us in layers—and layers of self are changed. The transformation of the early Apostles was noticed even by unbelievers: "Now when they saw the boldness *and* unfettered eloquence of Peter and John, and perceived that they were unlearned and untrained in the schools [common men with no advantages], they marveled; and they recognized that they had been with Jesus" (Acts 4:13, AMP).

There must have been something about the way they spoke and the look in their eyes that caused amazement. These were "unlearned and untrained ... common men with no advantages," all the more reason for amazement. The abilities and character now displayed in the lives of Peter and John could not have come from themselves. Within a few days, the sight and communion of the glorious Christ had transformed them.

My prayer is for that same reaction to take place when people observe the worshiping Church. When we go to restaurants, grocery stores, our homes, and places of employment, people should be able to take one look at us and know that we are different—that we bear upon our lives the likeness of Christ.

David offered the perfect prayer for worshipers who desire life-changing encounters with God:

> At each and every sunrise you will hear my voice
> as I prepare my sacrifice of prayer to you.
> Every morning I lay out the pieces of my life on the altar
> and wait for your fire to fall upon my heart.
> (Ps. 5:3 TPT)

GOD'S PLAN FOR THE EARTH CONCERNS HIS GLORY

God's plan for the spread of His glory throughout the earth is simple: Worship causes us to become partakers of the divine nature (2Pet. 1:4). Then we go into the world as ministers of that same glory. God "through us spreads *and* makes evident the fragrance of the knowledge of God everywhere, for we are the sweet fragrance of Christ" (2Cor. 2:14b–15a, AMP). When we see Him through worship, prayer, or communion, His likeness penetrates the very core of our being—we will never be the same again. They "looked to Him and were radiant" (Ps. 34:5).

"Are being transformed into the same image"—Our goal is not to be transformed into the likeness of any man or his gifting. We are not to imitate the most popular TV preacher or the last prophet to visit our church. Our goal is the likeness and imitation of Christ:

> [For my determined purpose is] that I may know Him [that I may progressively become more deeply and intimately acquainted with Him, perceiving and recognizing and understanding the wonders of His Person more strongly

and more clearly], and that I may in that same way come to know the power outflowing from His resurrection [which it exerts over believers], and that I may so share His sufferings as to be continually transformed [in spirit into His likeness even] to His death (Phil. 3:10, AMP).

> *"When we see Him through worship ... His likeness penetrates through our countenance to the very core of our being and we will never be the same again."*

WE BECOME LIKE THE ONE WE WORSHIP

Every time we worship, we are being changed into the likeness of the one we worship. This principle applies whether we worship false gods or the Lord himself. Consider these scriptures:

> Their [the Gentile's] idols are silver and gold, the work of men's hands. They have mouths, but they do not speak; eyes they have, but they do not see; they have ears, but they do not hear; noses they have, but they do not smell; they have hands but they do not handle; feet they have, but they do not walk; nor do they mutter through their throat. *Those who make them are like them; so is everyone who trusts in them* (Ps. 115:4-8, emph. mine). (See also Ps. 135:15-18.)

Paul was not advocating a meager transformation of thought processes or an easy path to spiritual enlightenment. His example and challenge beg us all to come to complete death of self. As Richard Foster puts it, "Worship ... is not for the timid or comfortable. It involves an opening of ourselves to the adventurous life of the Spirit."[5]

The Psalmist is describing a spiritual reality—those who make or worship any god other than the Lord will come to look like, sound like, act like, think like, and live like that god. For example, some people worship the gods of power and self. These influences are easily recognized in the words and actions of their lives.

We also see this principle at work in the peoples and nations who do not know the Lord as their God. I have visited countries where some worship snakes. As these snake worshipers leave their temples, it is common for them to fall to the ground and writhe like snakes. What barrenness and despair!

Compare this with David's prayer, "As for me. I will see Your face in righteousness; I shall be satisfied when I awake in Your likeness" (Ps. 17:15). Or in another version, "As for me, I will continue beholding Your face in righteousness (rightness, justice and right standing with You); I shall be fully satisfied, when I awake [to find myself] beholding Your form [and having sweet communion with You]" (Ps. 17:15, AMP).

David was able to look upon the face of God in the same manner as Paul does in our text, Second Corinthians 3:18. His satisfaction is complete when he awakens in the morning with the likeness and communion of God marking his life. The apostle John wrote, "But we know that when He comes *and* is manifested, we shall [as God's children] resemble *and* be like Him, for we shall see Him just as He [really] is" (1 Jn. 3:2b, AMP).

We do not have to wait until the final end-time manifestation of God's glory to become like Him. Even now, God is manifesting His glory in the earth. Even now, when we see Him, we are changed into His likeness. "The Mighty One, God, the LORD, speaks and summons the earth from the rising of the sun to the place where it sets. From Zion, perfect in beauty, God shines forth" (Ps. 50:1–2, NIV).

"We do not have to wait until the final end-time manifestation of God's glory to become like Him.

THE CALL TO WORSHIP IS FOR EVERY NATION

The Lord calls all people to come before Him and behold His glory. His worshiping people, the people who love His presence, are named Zion. These are perfect in beauty. The Lord shines out of them for they have seen Him!

"Are being transformed into the same image"—this transforming process is a mystery. Certainly, there are decisions

to be wrestled with in order to fully perfect the transformation process; however, the majority of the work has been done for us on Calvary. Our part is to agree with and yield to the miracle of the Lord's work in our lives. That work is nothing short of miraculous. Paul wrote to the Church in Rome of the magnitude of the change that is wrought within us by Christ: "Do not be conformed to this world (this age), [fashioned after and adapted to its external, superficial customs], but be transformed (changed) by the [entire] renewal of your mind [by its new ideals and its new attitude]" (Rom. 12:2a, AMP).

The radical meaning of *transformation* is scarcely perceived by most Christians. Consider the full meaning of this word. *Transformed* is translated from *metamorphoo* (met-am-or-fo'-o)—(Strong's #G3339, from #G3326 and #G3445). The same Greek word is often translated as *transfigure,* meaning to *change into another form.* Vine's dictionary says,

> ... the obligation being to undergo a complete change which, under the power of God, will find expression in character and conduct. 2Cor. 3:18 describes believers as being "transformed into the same image" (i.e., of Christ in all His moral excellencies), the change being affected by the Holy Spirit.[6]

Our English word *metamorphosis* is closest in meaning to the Greek word, *metamorphoo. Metamorphosis* means,

> [1.] A change in form from one stage to the next in the life of an organism, as from pupa to butterfly. 2. A change of form, structure, or substance as by magic. 3. A remarkable change, as in appearance." [7] and [2.] "Change in the way a person or thing looks or acts.[8]

The changes that need to take place in us are as extreme as the metamorphosis from caterpillar to pupa or pupa to butterfly. The following are only a few examples of the extraordinary changes the Lord works into our lives:

- *He is able to take any darkness within us and infuse it*

with His light—"For You *are* my lamp, O LORD; The LORD shall enlighten my darkness" (2Sam. 22:29). Also: "For God Who said, Let light shine out of darkness, has shone in our hearts so as [to beam forth] the light for the illumination of the knowledge of the majesty *and* glory of God [as it manifests in the Person and is revealed] in the face of *Jesus* Christ, the Messiah" (2Cor. 4:6, AMP). (See also: Job 12:22; Ps. 112:4; Is. 9:2; Dan. 2:22; Micah 7:8; John 12:46; Rom. 2:19; 1Pet. 2:9.)

- *He brings life out of death and calls into existence things that do not yet exist*—"God, who gives life to the dead and calls those things which do not exist as though they did" (Rom. 4:17).

> "There is no book large enough to describe the transformation that the Lord skillfully weaves into every willing life."

- *He turns our troubles into doorways of hope* (Hos. 2:15).
- *He turns dry and thirsty places within our hearts into streams and pools of water* and teaches us how to rejoice and blossom there (Is. 35:1, 7; 43:19; 44:3, etc.).
- *He deliberately chose the foolish, insignificant, weak and despised things within us to rise up and triumph* over man's wisdom, self-promotion, strength and arrogance (1Cor. 1:27).
- *He who knew no sin, not only took our sin from us, but He became that sin so that He could pay the full penalty for us. We, who are born in sin and are rotten to the core, were received and have become the righteousness of God* (2Cor. 5:21).

"To stand before the Holy One of eternity is to change... In worship an increased power steals its way into the heart sanctuary, an increased compassion grows in the soul. To worship is to change."[9]

WORSHIP FORMS US IN THE IMAGE OF CHRIST

We are being formed into the image of Christ—not the other way around.

> The pursuit of God will embrace the labor of bringing our total personality into conformity to His. I speak of a voluntary exalting of God to His proper station over us and a willing surrender of our whole being to the place of worshipful submission, which the Creator-creature circumstance makes proper.[10]

"Are being transformed into the same image"—The transformation that Christ works in us is a process. Neither worship nor transformation was intended to be a one-time event. Neither is our transformation an option. If we worship, we will be transformed. "We are united to him, gazing here by faith upon him and his meaning, able to advance to greater perfection."[11]

Paul's words to the Philippians reveal his understanding of the transformational process. (I really like the *Amplified Version* here.)

> Yes, furthermore, I count everything as loss compared to the possession of the priceless privilege (the overwhelming preciousness, the surpassing worth, and supreme advantage) of knowing Christ Jesus my Lord, *and* of progressively becoming more deeply *and* intimately acquainted with Him, [of perceiving *and* recognizing and understanding Him more fully *and* clearly]. For His sake I have lost everything and consider it all to be mere rubbish (refuse, dregs), in order that I may win (gain) Christ, (the Anointed One), And that I may [actually] be found *and* known as in Him, not having any [self-achieved] righteousness that can be called my own (Phil. 3:8–9a, AMP).

ALL CREATION IS SUBJECT TO HIS TRANSFORMING GLORY

"Are being transformed into the same image"—anything that has ever been created is likely to be transformed at the sight of God. For example,

- Fire sometimes doesn't burn when the All-Consuming Fire reveals himself through it: Ex. 3:2–4; Dan. 3:21–26
- In the presence of Jesus, the Water of Life, water may:
  –become a highway—Ex. 14:21–22
  –burst out of rocks—Ex. 17:6
  –become a roadway for men to walk upon—Matt. 14:25–29
  –be turned into wine—Jn. 2:6–10
- He is the Rock, and in His presence, rocks or mountains will sometimes:
  –tremble or quake—Ex. 19:18; Ps. 68:8; 114:7; Is. 64:1; Matt. 27:51; Acts 16:26
  –smoke—Ex. 19:18; 20:18; Ps. 104:32
  –bow down before the Lord like the stone god, Dagon—1Sam. 5:3–4
  –skip or leap—Ps. 114:4, 6
  –melt like wax—Ps. 46:6; 97:5
  –be threshed like wheat and made into chaff—Is. 41:15–16
  –sing—Is. 44:23; 49:13; 55:12
  –be turned to bread—Lk. 4:3
  –grow lips and sing praises—Lk. 19:40
  –grow legs and run into the sea—Matt. 17:20; 21:21–23; Mk. 11:23
  –roll away and reveal an empty tomb—Lu. 24:2
- The Lord is the Alpha and Omega, the Beginning and the End. In His presence the sun, which is the keeper of time, might:
  –stand still in the sky—Josh. 10:12–13
  –go backwards—Is. 38:8

If these elements are capable of such dramatic and supernatural changes, how much more should we change in the presence of the Lord who became flesh for us that we might become more and more like Him?

The *Amplified Version* of our text reads, "are constantly being transfigured into His *very own* image in ever increasing splendor" (2Cor. 3:18, AMP). The progress of our change must be constant; the magnitude of our change is only limited by our degree of transfiguration.

"Are being transformed into the same image"—In light of these glorious truths, we might well ask why Christians seem so often weak and powerless in their daily walk. I believe that the sad state of the Church today can largely be traced to a lack of worship and of the *manifested* presence of God in our lives. If we regularly met face to face with the Lord—who is "All Powerful," "Full of Wisdom," a "Wonderful Counselor," our "Healer" (the One who makes us whole), our "Redeemer" and "King"—then we would reflect these same characteristics in our lives and act as representatives of His virtue here on earth.

If worship brings transformation into the likeness of God, then we must examine ourselves. Are we becoming more holy; more loving; more whole in body, soul and spirit; more zealous for the lost to be saved? If not, are we truly worshiping? Richard Foster challenges the Church to engage in true worship and to live obediently, "If worship does not propel us into greater obedience, it has not been worship . . . Holy obedience saves worship from becoming an opiate, an escape from the pressing needs of modern life."[12]

Tozer writes of this aspect of our spiritual growth through worship and the presence of God:

> The instant cure of most of our religious ills would be to enter the Presence in spiritual experience, to become suddenly aware that we are in God and God is in us. This would lift us out of our pitiful narrowness and cause our hearts to be enlarged. This would burn away the impurities from our lives as the bugs and fungi were burned away by the fire that dwelt in the bush.[13]

WORSHIP SHAPES OUR INNER BELIEF AND OUTWARD RESPONSE

"Are being transformed into the same image"—Worship not only changes our inner lives; it also affects the expression of our faith and service to God in the world around us. Satan tried to tempt Jesus in the wilderness by offering all the kingdoms of the world if Jesus would bow down and worship him. Jesus' response was powerful: "Away with you, Satan! For it is written, 'You shall worship the Lord your God, and Him only you shall serve'" (Matt. 4:10).

This illustrates a great principle of worship. Whatever we worship we ultimately will end up serving. The more we worship something or someone, the more our commitment increases, and the more we become like the thing we worship.[14]

If we aspire to a more excellent heart for service and Christian witness, then we must surrender to His presence and His ongoing claims upon our lives. Our love and worship of God will cause us to serve Him with greater devotion and desire.

Chapter Ten
Worship is Eternal
"...From Glory to Glory"

God is a sea of infinite substance.
—St. John of Damascus[1]

"From glory to glory" ("*from one degree of glory to another*" AMP)—God's glory can be measured in endless degrees of incomparable beauty and perfection; the depths of which can never be exhausted. Therefore, our progress in His glory must never cease; it should expand throughout eternity one degree at a time, beginning at our salvation. The change that is worked within our lives through worship and beholding His glory will remain and mature forever. This thought could not be expressed more excellently than through these words of Bernard of Clairvaux: "God in himself is incomprehensible, the beginning and the end. He is the beginning without conclusion, and the end without any more excellent end."[2]

When we are born again, we receive Christ and His glory into our hearts. Our salvation is not the end of the story (2Cor. 3:18). We need to continually behold Him and be transformed. There is no such thing as "arriving" as a Christian. We continue to allow the Lord to work His likeness into our hearts. The favor we are granted in worship is His glory and likeness. It will never fade and cannot be sold. Our lives are changed forever when confronted with His glory. The sight of God will bankrupt every mediocre place in our hearts. "The knowledge of God is God himself dwelling in the soul. The most we can do is to prepare for his entry, to get out of His way, to remove the barriers, for until God acts in us there is nothing positive that we can do in this direction."[3]

> *"The favor we are granted in worship is the ultimate – His glory and likeness!"*

WORSHIP AND ETERNITY

"From glory to glory"—There is something eternal in this statement. "The Bible declares that He is the same yesterday, today and forever" (Heb. 13:8). With regard to worship, we need to understand what this means. He was worshiped, He is worshiped, He will be worshiped for all eternity. When we worship the Lord, we participate in the eternal. We proclaim and enact His Kingdom. We declare His sovereignty in the earth and we pronounce His attributes for all to hear. When we worship, we join the heavenly beings and shout through the hallways of all time, echoing the song of worship which is never interrupted day and night and never ceases. "Holy, holy, holy, Lord God Almighty, who was and is and is to come!" (Rev. 4:8).

"From glory to glory"—The same glory that shone out of darkness to create the earth is the glory that shines in our hearts to reveal Christ to us:

> For God Who said, Let light shine out of darkness, has shone in our hearts so as [to beam forth] the Light for the illumination of the knowledge of the majesty *and* glory of God [as it is manifest in the Person and is revealed] in the face of *Jesus* Christ (the Messiah) (2Cor. 4:6, AMP).

If complete and utter darkness can be penetrated with God's light, and life is able to be born from there, then that same light of glory is able to give birth to the knowledge and character of God within us.

Again, it is a mystery that the glory of God should find its home in our hearts. God's secrets and mysteries are there for everyone to discover. They are not an exclusive or hidden plan for just a few to experience. When God indicates in the Word that something is a mystery, it means that it cannot be understood by man unless God reveals it to us. The Father desires to give to every believer the spirit of wisdom and revelation in order that we might know Him more completely and partake of the riches of His glory (Eph. 1:17–19).

OUR SANCTIFICATION AND HIS GLORY

The mystery of our sanctification and completion in Him is wrapped up in these scriptures on the glory of God. Sin caused mankind to lose his ability to embody the life, image and glory of God. Yet, He has made a way for us to be restored to full fellowship. When we worship and behold God's glory, we will be changed, cleansed, renewed, and sanctified by the experience and encounter with God. The wholeness of every Christian depends upon the principle of beholding the glory and yielding to His work in our hearts.

> *"It is a mystery that the glory of God should find its home in our hearts."*

> This mystery has been kept in the dark for a long time, but now it's out in the open. God wanted everyone, not just Jews, to know this rich and glorious secret inside and out, regardless of their background, regardless of their religious standing. The mystery in a nutshell is just this: Christ is in you, therefore you can look forward to sharing in God's glory (Col. 1:26-27).[4]

The Father, Son and Holy Spirit are involved in our lives to bring about this work. Ralph Martin has laid out the *trinitarian structure* of this mystery, as shown in Table 5.[5]

OUR REWARD—A CROWN OF GLORY

"From glory to glory"—Our eternal reward as faithful sons of God is the incorruptible crown of glory (1Pet. 5:4). God is holy. Nothing is able to stand before Him that does not reflect His holiness and perfection. Everything that surrounds Him partakes of His glory: Angels (Lk. 2:9; 9:26; Rev. 18:1); the cherubim (Heb. 9:5); the heavenly city (Rev. 21:11); and mankind, who are the only ones who are permitted to grow in the light of His glory for

eternity. There is no essential glory in man—only those who are transformed from glory to glory will spend eternity gazing upon Him. He must make us fit for His presence.

TABLE 4
GOD IN YOU

You in God (Col. 3:3; Jn. 17:21)	God in you (Jn. 14:23; 1Cor. 6:19–20; Phil. 2:13)
You in Christ (Jn. 15:4f; Rom. 8:1; 2Cor. 5:17)	Christ in you (Jn. 14:18–20; Gal. 2:20; Col. 1:27)
You in Spirit (Jn. 4:23f.; Rom. 8:9; Gal. 5:16, 25)	Spirit in you (Jn. 14:16f; Rom. 8:9; 1Cor. 3:16)

Jesus' great prayer in the Gospel of John, chapter 17, is a plea for the believers to become one in Him and with each other by dwelling with Him and beholding His glory. "And the glory which You gave Me I have given them, that they may be one just as We are one [that they] may be with Me where I am, that they may behold My glory which You have given Me" (Jn. 17:22, 24).

> *"Beholding His glory and being changed into the likeness of His glory is a key for every Christian."*

Obviously, the Lord longs for us to participate with Him in ministering His glory in the earth. Beholding His glory and being changed into the likeness of His glory is a key for every Christian. He became flesh so that we could commune with Him and become like Him—holy and blameless, able to stand in His presence forever.

THE BEAUTY OF HOLINESS

"From glory to glory"—As the glory of the Lord is layered upon our lives, we become more and more beautiful in body, soul, and spirit.

Think of all those believers you know who are faithful in prayer, who delight in spending time with the Lord. So often they look younger than their natural years. Consider the likes of Elisabeth Elliot, Corrie Ten Boom, Billy Graham, and Mother Teresa. These are only a few who were radiant in their faces and striking in character.

In the Old Testament, the glory of God is spoken of as a visible thing. Many of the saints saw His glory, but it was only on rare occasions that anyone could be described as having His glory manifested upon their lives. Moses was one man who beheld the glory of God and received the same light of glory in his own face (Ex. 34:29–35).

In the New Testament we live with the glory of God dwelling in us. We don't just see the glory; we live with the glory upon our lives. It is shared with us on the basis of our relationship with Him. "And so we are transfigured much like the Messiah, our lives gradually becoming brighter and more beautiful as God enters our lives and we become like Him" (2Cor. 3:18, MSG).[6]

One of the greatest gifts that accompanies our lives is the beauty that comes from holiness. God is holy and can only be worshiped by a holy people. Holiness is the inner architectural structure of the believer. Without it our faith will weaken and fall. A holy life is a life of great beauty.

The seraphim declare this attribute of His character continuously before His throne (Is. 6:1–3; Rev. 4:8–9); the priests of the Old Covenant cleansed themselves, their utensils and their garments before they approached the Lord (Ex. 19:22; Ex. 28:36–43; 29:1-9, 21, 29, 35–37, 44; 40:12–13, etc.), and David cried out: "Who may ascend into the hill of the Lord? Or who may stand in His holy place? He who has clean hands and a pure heart" (Ps. 24:3–4).

Romans 3:23 declares that every man has sinned and fallen

short of the glory of God. Just as sin has taken us from God's glory, holiness will lead us to His glory. Paul's heartache in this matter is that we have fallen short, not of becoming evangelists, ministers, singers, or prayer warriors, but of the likeness of God. Worship and holiness lead us to God's glory, so that we can come out of His presence as ministers of His glory.

The writer of Hebrews encourages the worshiper to seek after holiness. Without holy lives we will not be able to see the Lord, and seeing Him is an essential component of prophetic worship. As Cornwall states, the Lord expects us to pursue holiness.

> While God condescends in grace to redeem us, He expects us to ascend in holiness to worship Him. I do not mean to imply that one must become absolutely holy in order to have a worship experience with God I am saying that holiness is an absolute prerequisite in order to become a consistent worshiper.[7]

Changing from glory to glory means that we adorn ourselves with His holiness and beautify ourselves with His grace. The character, power and graces of the Lord are our glory and beauty. The more we worship and become like Him, the more beautiful we become inside and out.

DISPLAYING HIS GLORY—THE ULTIMATE EVANGELISM TOOL

"From glory to glory"—We are not changed from glory to glory just to fulfill our own eternal purposes. We are molded into the likeness of His glory in order that the whole earth might see Him and likewise be changed.

Recall how God displayed His glory in the midst of a powerful worship service in a prison, where Paul and Silas prayed and sang praises (Acts 16:25–34). At least one purpose for that display of God's glory was the salvation of others. The prison guard and all of his household were saved. (I would not be surprised if a few of the prisoners were saved, too. We do know that they were listening and not mocking when Paul and Silas were praying and singing.)

The eternal destiny of everyone on earth depends upon the obedience of believers to the call to worship God and be changed into His likeness. Through our compliance, we gain the heart and will of God for mankind and the wisdom, grace, and strength to execute His purposes in the earth. When we are changed into the likeness of His glory, we are able ministers of His glory to those around us. "The glory of the Lord shall be revealed, and all flesh shall see *it* together; for the mouth of the Lord has spoken" (Is. 40:5).

> To Him *be* glory in the church and in Christ Jesus throughout all generations forever and ever. Amen (Eph. 3:21, AMP).

Chapter Eleven
Worship is Initiated by the Holy Spirit
"...Even as by the Spirit of the Lord"

> *Worship... is God's Spirit in man responding to God's Spirit in God. It is the Holy Spirit worshiping through us.*
> —Judson Cornwall

"Even as by the Spirit of the Lord"—"*God is Spirit, and those who worship Him must worship in spirit and in truth*" (Jn. 4:24).

The Holy Spirit is a person, and He dwells in the heart of every believer. The Holy Spirit leads us to the Father and teaches us how to worship in spirit and in truth. Whenever spirit and truth are joined in worship, there is blessing. He is the One who actively brings us into the likeness of Christ— layer by layer, from glory to glory.

The Holy Spirit is the source and inspiration for our communion with God and is the primary initiator of the intimacy between God and man. When we worship, we are responding and interacting with the Holy Spirit to bring our love, adoration, and service to the Father, through the mediation of Jesus, the Son.

In every other religion, man attempts to reach up to God. Our God initiates our relationship and reaches down to us. By the work of the Holy Spirit, every Christian is led to worship and to the likeness of Christ. Cornwall says: "While praise can be the product of the human spirit, worship is impossible without the aid of the Holy Spirit of God."[1]

It is the Lord who begins our worship journey, and the Lord who completes us through the work of the Holy Spirit. He does not override our will, but the Holy Spirit responds to our desire for His work in our hearts. As Tozer puts it: "He waits to be wanted."[2]

Foster comments on the wooing of the Holy Spirit in worship. He calls worship "our response to the overtures of love from the heart of the Father."[3] His love is made known to us through the work of the Holy Spirit. Adam Clarke teaches that it is "by the energy of that Spirit of Christ which gives life and being to all the promises of the Gospel; and thus we are made partakers of the divine nature and escape all the corruptions that are in the world."[4]

> "It is the Holy Spirit that leads us to the Father and teaches us how to worship in spirit and in truth."

We must be wholly and humbly dependent upon the Holy Spirit to draw us in worship. He is the source of every aspect of our relationship with God. We are born again by the Spirit; we must continue in the Spirit.

The Holy Spirit—Our Companion in Worship

"Even as by the Spirit of the Lord"—The Holy Spirit is our Guide and our Friend as He leads us into the knowledge and love of the Father and the Son. There are times in worship that are absolutely delightful as the Holy Spirit brings us to meet with the Lord in different ways as described below.

- *The face of God* where He speaks to us of himself (Ex. 32:30; 33:11; Ps. 17:15; 27:8; 41:12); He turns our hearts in repentance (2Chron. 7:14); and kisses us in love (Song of Sol. 1:1).
- *The hand of God* where we take our place alongside Him

as His royal bride (Ps. 45:9; Is. 62:3); we find His blessings and protection (Ps. 16:1; 18:35; 63:8; 138:7; 145:16; Is. 41:10); He molds us into vessels of honor (Is. 64:8); and He hides us (Is. 49:2).

- *The feet of God* where we fall down in worship (Matt. 15:30; 28:9; Lk. 7:37–38; Jn. 12:3; Rev. 5:14; 7:11).
- *His banqueting hall* where we sit down and feed from Him (Song of Sol. 2:4); and He prepares a table for us in the presence of our enemies (Ps. 23:5).
- *His throne room* where we come boldly and bow humbly before our King (Es. 5:1; Heb. 4:16; Rev. 19:4–5).
- *His inner chamber* where we engage in intimate and secret communion with Him (Song of Sol. 1:4); and He spreads His wings over us (Ru. 3:9; Ps. 17:8; 36:7; 57:1; 61:4; 63:7; 91:4; Eze. 16:8).
- *His seat of justice and judgment* where we obtain forgiveness and justice (Ps. 35:22–24; 68:5; 82:1; 89:14).
- *His secret places* where we grow nearer to Him and receive His treasures (Ps. 27:5–6; 31:20; 81:7; 91:1; Prov. 3:32; Song of Sol. 2:14; Is. 45:3).
- *The outer court of His presence* where we celebrate and rejoice because of His greatness (Ps. 100:4).
- *The gates of His holy place* where we become attendants of His majesty and servants of His court (Ps. 24:3; Prov. 8:34).
- *The place of prayer and intercession*—the private closet and right hand of God (Mt. 6:6; Rom. 8:26-27, 34; 1Tim. 2:1).

The Holy Spirit draws and leads us into every encounter with the Father. All we have to do is respond with all our hearts and run after Him. Prophetic worship opens the way for us to enter His presence again and again.

An Extraordinary Communion with God

"Even as by the Spirit of the Lord"—Anything the Holy Spirit initiates is pure (Ps. 24:3–4) and perfect (Deut. 32:4; Ps. 18:30; 19:7). His love, judgment, mercy, presence, and joy—as described in the Bible—might all be characterized as being consummately extreme when compared to our standards of expression, yet He requires that we commune with Him in a way that is pleasing to *Him*—not to us. We need to learn *His* definition of "normal" when it comes to worship. We have nothing to fear and nothing to lose except ourselves. We must trust the Holy Spirit to bring both liberty and order to our worship.

"Even as by the Spirit of the Lord"—Worship flows from our lives when we are filled with the Holy Spirit. "Be filled with the Spirit, speaking to one another in psalms and hymns and spiritual songs, singing and making melody in your heart to the Lord" (Eph. 5:18b–19). Our worship is based upon our relationship with God, and our relationship is dependent upon the indwelling of the Holy Spirit in our lives.

"Even as by the Spirit of the Lord"—The Holy Spirit reveals a definite purpose and intent in this verse. We are confronted with His desire in the matter of our relationship with the Lord. In the previous six points of Second Corinthians 3:18, our focus has been on the things we need to be doing: unveiling our faces, looking into His glory, yielding to His transforming work in our lives, and so forth. Now we see the emphasis has shifted to the desire and determination of the Holy Spirit in this matter.

Seven Desires of the Lord

The word "desire" in Greek is a word of passion and longing. The Lord has a fiery desire towards us. He longs for us more than we can ever know. The Lord expresses seven desires in the entire Bible (*King James Version*). They are summed up in His longing to have fellowship with us. He desires…

- *The beauty of His Bride, the Church.* "So the King will

greatly desire your beauty" (Ps. 45:11). This is the only time in the Word that there is mention of the Lord greatly desiring anything. He greatly desires to see and partake of our beauty as we are transformed into His likeness.

- *Zion to be His dwelling place forever.* "For the Lord has chosen Zion; He has desired *it* for His dwelling place: 'This *is* my resting place forever; here I will dwell, for I have desired it.'" (Ps. 132:13-14) (See also Ps. 68:15-16.) Zion is a poetic and prophetic name for the worshiping Church. The Lord desires to dwell in the midst of His worshiping people forever.

- *Truth in our inner being.* "Behold, You desire truth in the inward parts" (Ps. 51:6). The beauty of God's people begins on the inside. David is asking the Lord to cleanse him completely after being caught in sin. It is David's astounding repentance—from the core of his being—that restores his relationship with the Lord and causes him to be known forever as a man of integrity and uprightness (1Ki. 9:4); with a perfect heart (1Ki. 11:4; 15:3), and a man after God's heart (Acts 13:22). Our ongoing relationship with the Lord is only possible, if we walk in transparency and holiness to the core of our being.

- *Mercy above sacrifice, and for us to know Him.* "For I desire mercy and not sacrifice" (Hos. 6:6). God desires our righteousness and inner virtue over the external sacrifices that He instituted. The Hebrew word for *mercy* in this passage is *checed* (Strong's #H2617)—meaning *kindness, piety, beauty, favor, lovingkindness, mercy.* These qualities are more desirable in us than any form of outward religion. "For I desire ... the knowledge of God more than burnt offerings" (Hos. 6:6).

- *Intimacy with His Church—He wants all of our heart.* "I am my beloved's, and his desire *is* toward me." (Song of Sol. 7:10). The Shulamite recognized that her lover was totally devoted to her. She was the center of all His desires. This is the same way that the Lord feels about us.

His greatest love and most profound desire is for intimacy and relationship with His bride.

- *To Eat the Passover.* "Then He said to them, 'With fervent desire I have desired to eat this Passover with you before I suffer;" ...and said, "You've no idea how much I have looked forward to eating this Passover meal with you before I enter my time of suffering" (Lk. 22:15, MSG). The Lord makes himself known to us in the breaking of the bread. Communion is not simply a casual ritual of the Church, but the essential meal for believers.

- *For us to see His glory.* "Father, I desire that they also whom You gave Me may be with Me where I am, that they may behold My glory which You have given Me" (Jn. 17:24). The final desire the Lord expresses in the Word is that we would see Him as He truly is. Not only does He require that we be unveiled, but He desires to unveil himself before us in worship and show us His glory.

Churches and individual worshipers must undergo change for prophetic worship to become the norm. I want to conclude with several versions of our key text: 2Cor. 3:18. Just savor the nuances of each translation and the call to deeper intimacy with the Lord:

> *"If we are to know God, then we must become students and stewards of His divine mysteries."*

"And we all, who with unveiled faces contemplate the Lord's glory, are being transformed into his image with ever- increasing glory, which comes from the Lord, who is the Spirit." (NIV)

"So, all of us who have had that veil removed can see and reflect the glory of the Lord. And the Lord—who is the Spirit—makes us more and more like him as we are changed into his glorious image." (NLT)

"Now all of us, with our faces unveiled, reflect the glory of the Lord as if we are mirrors; and so we are being transformed, *metamorphosed*, into His same image from one radiance of glory to another, just as the Spirit of the Lord accomplishes it." (Voice)[5]

"All of us! Nothing between us and God, our faces shining with the brightness of his face. And so we are transfigured much like the Messiah, our lives gradually becoming brighter and more beautiful as God enters our lives and we become like Him." (MSG)[6]

"And all of us, as with unveiled face, [because we] continued to behold [in the Word of God] as in a mirror the glory of the Lord, are constantly being transfigured into His *very own* image in ever increasing splendor *and* from one degree of glory to another; [for this comes] from the Lord [Who is] the Spirit." (AMP)[7]

Let us yield to the work of the Holy Spirit as He forms Christ in us.

PART THREE

PROPHETIC WORSHIP: A NEW EXEMPLAR

Chapter Twelve
An Introduction to Breaking Worship Traditions

Worship is a journey into God

I was raised in a traditional Presbyterian Church and am forever indebted for the Christian foundation I received there over my early years. I deeply respect the history and rich heritage of shared, biblically-based truth that is found in all the mainstream churches. It is time, however, to challenge the rigidly held traditions and beliefs on worship that are found in all of Christendom, from the oldest denominations to the newer independent and charismatic churches. Jack Hayford says this of tradition:

> We would die for it, but we can't live with it. Its role in worship is pervasive; no part of human experience is more shaped by tradition than the way we worship. Even in the Body of Christ, frequently the force of tradition overrides the truth of God's Word.[1]

It is the truth about worship in the Word of God that I am interested in. I maintain that prophetic worship is the model that best describes biblical worship in both the Old and New Testaments. It is clearly the pattern that God gave to David, and the model of worship that continued under every godly king. The

> "Prophetic worship is the model which best describes Biblical worship in both the Old and New Testaments."

New Testament doesn't have a lot to say about music, the arts, and worship, but what is laid out from Jesus (John 4:21-24) to Revelation is dynamic, prophetic, God-filled worship.

The Lord has been developing, renewing and changing the worship formats of His people since the beginning of time, but the one thing that remains constant is that He expects us to make way for His voice and presence in all worship. So, change has been constant, but the priority of His presence has been the unifying factor of all worship through the ages.

The sacrificial system of worship that Cain and Abel participated in became an elaborate tabernacle worship spectacle under Moses. A couple of hundred years later, the Lord instructed David to offer "spiritual sacrifices" rather than animal sacrifices. Later, David's son, Solomon, built the temple, which combined worship forms taken from the tabernacles of both Moses and David.

In the New Testament, Jesus told an inquiring woman that the hour was coming when worship would no longer take place in a particular geographic location, but in the hearts of mankind (Jn. 4:19-24). The pace of change has accelerated into the Church Age. As we are all aware, the architecture of churches, styles of music, and types of instruments used in worship have changed vastly over the centuries. All we can be sure of with the Lord is that changes are bound to take place, and this book calls for a worship renewal in the Church.

> True worship renewal does not come about through superficial measures, but through recognizing that worship studies are an essential discipline of Christian theology. Renewal grows out of attention to the biblical and historical sources of Christian worship and the provision of the Holy Spirit.[2]

THE USE OF THE WORD *EXEMPLAR*

I have used the word *exemplar* in the title for the third section of this book because its meaning best captures the nuances of the message I am trying to convey. Many use the term *paradigm* or *paradigm shift* as they search for new models for worship. The term *exemplar* goes a step further and calls for *a patterning after, a way to be followed or imitated*. Thus, I use the term because I truly believe that the model for prophetic worship presented here should become the norm for *all* worship in *each* congregation in *every* nation.

Prophetic worship is not the exclusive worship model for some new type of charismatic church. It is not restricted to those congregations who have a charismatic or other particular theology of worship. Rather, it can be understood and attained by any church, irrespective of their culture, background, denomination, or size; no matter what the proficiency of their musicians and singers.

Also, prophetic worship is *not* some new *style* or preference of worship. Prophetic worship is a necessity for all churches. No matter what style of worship you already have, I am simply calling for all churches to learn how to find the voice and presence of God within the worship you already have.

Please understand I am not on a quest for all churches to worship in the same manner, to the exclusion of the distinct character of individual congregations. I believe in a unity that includes diversity. Yet, our distinctiveness should not merely be a reflection of our denomination or our culture, but a consequence of the individual journey of every congregation, the character of the people, and the unique work of God within them.

In the past, many have clamored for more consideration to be given to the individual rights and personalities of the people in worship. I am more concerned that we give full consideration to the voice, will, and character of God. The chapters that follow outline a prototype for achieving this goal in worship.

CONTRASTING TRADITIONAL WITH PROPHETIC WORSHIP

When we contrast traditional worship with prophetic worship, it is important to note that traditional worship—as it applies to any particular form or denomination—is not really the issue that is at fault. The traditional practices, themselves, may be valuable and even advantageous in the pursuit of true worship. We must bear in mind; true worship is a matter of the heart and of genuine devotion to God.

These thoughts offer some helpful insights into the role tradition often plays in our worship theology:

> It is even possible to be traditional about our non-traditionalism. Tradition has to do with the repetition of a pattern, not with the essential character of the pattern . . . The worship of Jesus Christ must never become so familiar that we simply go through the motions.[3]
> "Tradition is the living faith of the dead; traditionalism is the dead faith of the living. And, I suppose I should add, it is traditionalism that gives tradition such a bad name."[4]
> "Do not seek to follow in the footsteps of the men of old; seek what they sought."[5]

I think we sometimes deceive ourselves concerning our rituals and traditions. We assume that because they are important to us, that they must be important to God as well. So often, true prophetic worship has been stifled by our insistence upon ancient rituals that may have no heart and no devotion in them. Consider Ambrose Bierce's definition of *ritualism:* "A Dutch garden of God where He may walk in rectilinear freedom, keeping off the grass."[6]

Andrew Hill has also given an excellent definition of *ritualism*:

> Ritualism occurs when the worshiper is no longer able to participate knowingly, actively, and fruitfully. In other words, the worshiper no longer recognizes and appropriates the form or liturgy of worship as his or her personal expression of faith. Thus, participation in the outward form of worship is devoid of inward reality.[7]

As you read the following chapters, keep these questions in mind with regards to the issue of ritualism within your own worship traditions:

- Are we fashioning our worship to fit our own preferences to such a degree that we actually mar the reflection of the nature of God?

- Are we pursuing our traditions in worship over and against biblical injunctions and examples for true praise and worship? Remember, there is not a separate Bible for each denomination. We are *all* called to worship God in the way that *He* desires and how He has outlined throughout the Bible. We can't pick and choose how to worship based on our personal preferences. The entire Bible is a worship handbook for *all* denominations and peoples.
- Are we truly seeking to minister to God in our worship, or are there other, more selfish motives that drive our weekly attendance at church (such as what *we* expect to get out of it)?
- Do we find such security in our age-old liturgies and forms of worship that we do not even look for God to manifest His glory before us? In other words, does our trust and comfort come from our traditions rather than from God himself?
- Do the rituals of our weekly worship meetings even allow *a time* for God to manifest himself? Or is the Order of Service completely filled with our own expressions and activities?
- Is there any portion of our worship meetings that *requires* the manifest presence of God? In other words, if He failed to show up one Sunday, would we even realize that He was missing?

I seek to challenge rather than criticize as we compare the traditional ways of worship with the prophetic way of worship outlined in scripture. I have endeavored to treat every Christian denomination and worship tradition with respect. For it is my desire to open up to all, the tremendous possibilities of prophetic worship and the impact that it can have on any church.

It is not my intention that we use these points of contrast as items of negative criticism towards one another, but rather, that we all make an honest evaluation of our own hearts and expressions of worship. As Tippet has said, the actual style of our traditionalism is not the shortcoming; it is the lack of integrity and devotion at the core of our corporate experience. This will make any worship lukewarm, at best, and totally dead, at its most tragic.

> *"It is the weakness of our human nature that begs us to cling to the traditions and practices of the past and flee from every notion of change."*

Neither is it my intention that we study worship dynamics in order to compare ourselves with others. Please do not use these chapters as a means to evaluate your worship in the light of other churches. Let them challenge your own heart to a deeper and more honest relationship with the Lord. Allow the Holy Spirit to inspire change where it is necessary and to have His way in every aspect of your devotional life.

Also, I am not interested in churches obsessing on worship in ways that will only cause them to make insincere and superficial changes to their worship services. This does nothing but foster "liturgical hedonism," as Paul Waitman Hoon puts it.[8]

Table 6, *Traditional Worship vs. Prophetic Worship*, contains a synopsis of the major issues that distinguish prophetic worship from traditional worship. It could almost be considered a summary of this whole book. Keep in mind that these are generalizations. Again, it is not my intention to be critical, but rather, to offer suggestions for a new exemplar.

This chart shows the 12 areas of traditional church worship that need to be changed in order to make way for God's voice and presence. Every church has ties to some form of tradition that needs to be infused with God's prophetic presence. Renewal is required in each of these if prophetic worship is to become the norm.

It is the weakness of our human nature that begs us to cling to the traditions and practices of the past and flee from every notion of change. While I am encouraging every church to make courageous changes and break with dead traditions, I am not trying to eliminate the distinctive and meaningful contributions that each denomination has made within the Body of Christ. If we can learn how to hold on to the traditions that are meritorious while embracing the truth of prophetic worship, I think change will become more palatable.

The change I am talking about must come about within church leadership, worship teams, and entire congregations. Change in any one or two out of these three groups will not be enough. The way we do things and our understanding of worship ministry need refining.

An in-depth explanation of each point from this chart is contained in the chapters of Part III.

TABLE 6
TRADITIONAL WORSHIP VS. PROPHETIC WORSHIP

TRADITIONAL WORSHIP	PROPHETIC WORSHIP	CHAPTER
1. Worship is defined by what **we** are doing: our various expressions and forms of worship, etc.	Worship is defined by what the **Lord** is doing. Praise includes all our expressions of what He has done, is doing, and is going to do. Worship is our response to His manifest presence.	13
2. The worship leader is in control.	The worship leader leads but is also a doorkeeper and facilitator. The Holy Spirit is primarily the worship leader— the one directing and in control of the service	14
3. A small number function as ministers in the service. Those on the platform (pastors, singers, musicians, etc.). The congregation is treated as an audience.	The whole congregation is a holy, royal, priesthood. Each one is responsible for participating in the service and ministering to the Lord. There is no audience in prophetic worship—only communing hearts.	15
4. There are definite time limits on the worship service.	No time limits. Worship takes as long as the Holy Spirit directs.	16
5. The songs/hymns are regarded as being less important in the overall service than the preaching.	The songs/hymns, the whole worship time and the preaching are regarded as having equal importance.	17
6. Our denomination determines the way we worship and has definite ideas about worship forms.	The Word of God is our foundation and guide for worship structure and forms.	18

An Introductions to Breaking Worship Traditions

7. Our worship may be determined and greatly influenced by our culture.	Our national origin or native culture is not our focus. We belong to a new nation—the Kingdom of God—where the standard for appropriate worship is determined by the King, himself. Though flavored by our culture, our worship must be made suitable for the King.	19
8. There is an emphasis on the music. Music and other art forms are used for performance, entertainment, and accompaniment. There is art for art's sake—art forms used in worship are often an end to themselves. Success is measured by excellence in the art form.	There is an emphasis on the manifest presence of God. Music and all other art forms are used for ministry to God and His people. All art forms must be ministered in a prophetic sense. They are a means to an end. The goal is the glory of God. Success is measured by the presence of God and His fruit in our lives	20
9. There is little or no change of musical styles and repertoire over the years.	The music and songs we sing are seen as an ongoing reinforcement of the things that the Lord is showing us; therefore they are continually changing.	21
10. In order for the congregation to participate in worship they do not need to mature. Nothing more is required of the worship leader and team than to be artists.	Prophetic worship is only possible with a congregation that continues to mature and grow in the likeness of Christ. The worship leader and team are required to be students of the presence of God and to carry a prophetic anointing on their lives.	22
11. Worship is an individual experience.	Worship does not stop at being an individual experience; it must include the corporate journey.	23
12. There is little, or no expectation of hearing God's voice speak today in the worship service. The majority of the direction of our spiritual communication is from us to God.	Hearing God's voice speak today is one of the primary objectives of prophetic worship. There is openness for "two- way" or reciprocal communication with God, i.e. us to God and God to us.	24

CHAPTER THIRTEEN
REDEFINING PRAISE AND WORSHIP

*Worship, in essence,
is simply communing with God.*
—Bob Sorge

The foremost subject of the Bible and central goal of lives must be the glory of God. Every definition of worship and understanding of its workings, power and purpose stems from this comprehension. Tippit agrees, "True worship will always be wholehearted worship built upon the single foundation of the glory of Christ."[1]

Worship is rooted in God's worthiness; therefore, our primary reason for coming into the presence of the Lord is to bless Him and minister to Him. When Jesus defined worship in John 4:20-23, He emphasized the *object* of our worship (The Father) over the *place* of worship. Jesus made this statement as He was talking to a Samaritan woman. In those days, it was important which mountain one worshiped at, as it told folks what god you served. She wanted to know what true religion, or worship entailed. Jesus' statement to her was outrageous for the time. He said the *place* was not important. The Lord looks into our *heart of worship*. "But the hour is coming, and now is, when the true worshipers will worship the Father in spirit and truth; for the Father is seeking such to worship Him. God *is* Spirit, and those who worship Him must worship in spirit and truth" (John 4:23-24).

Numerous writers have given explanations of the words,

> *"The foremost subject of the Bible and central goal of lives must surely be the glory of God."*

"spirit and truth." Most seem to conclude that Jesus was referring to the mind and manner,[2] or the motive and form of worship. (It is interesting to note that Jesus referred to *himself* as a worshiper in verse 22: "You worship what you do not know; *we* know what *we* worship, for salvation is of the Jews.") The issue for true worship is the temple of the heart rather than the temple of stones; commitment to the Word of God rather than ceremonies and rituals. How we define *praise* and *worship* is supremely important since our theology and understanding of biblical worship is based on this. Matthew Henry and Adam Clarke offer these commentaries on John 4:23:

> If we do not worship God, who is a *spirit, in the spirit,* we miss *the end* of worship.[3] *In spirit* ... we must worship him with fixedness of thought and a flame of affection, with *all that is within us. In truth,* that is in *sincerity.* We must mind the power more than the form. ... The gate of spiritual worship is straight. Such worship is necessary, and what the God of heaven insists upon.[4]
>
> God is a *spirit.* This is one of the first, the greatest, the most sublime, and necessary truths in the compass of nature! There is a God, the cause of all things—the Fountain of all perfection—without parts or dimensions, for He is eternal—filling the heavens and the earth—pervading, governing, and upholding all things, for He is an infinite Spirit! A man worships God *in spirit* when, under the influence of the Holy Ghost, he brings all his affections, appetites, and desires to the throne of God; and he worships Him *in truth* when every purpose and passion of his heart, and when every act of his religious worship, is guided and regulated by the Word of God.[5]

Various methods of categorizing praise and worship music have been used over the centuries. In Charismatic and Pentecostal circles, we have long defined praise and worship by the style of our songs. One rather simplistic (and grossly inaccurate) form of this is to say, "Praise is the fast songs and worship is the slow songs."

This simple example illustrates how rarely we consider the Lord's role and place in worship. It is as if we have thought of Him as a heavenly spectator for our music and songs. Some have even referred to Him as "the audience of One." While it sounds nice, and I understand that those who believe this are trying to emphasize the active role that all worshipers must play, we need to see Him as the leader and full participant in this great communion called "worship."

THE MANIFESTATION OF THE PRESENCE OF GOD

While we are ministering to Him, He inhabits our praises and communes with us. As a result of His presence we are changed forever. Worshipers are changed as they minister to God, almost as a beneficial "side effect." As already stated, we become like the one we worship. God is omnipresent—in all places at all times—yet He *manifests*—reveals, uncovers or shows—himself in the midst of our praises and speaks of himself there. Tozer addresses these concepts:

> The omnipresence of the Lord is one thing, and is a solemn fact necessary to His perfection. The manifest Presence is another thing altogether, and from that Presence we have fled, like Adam to hide among the trees of the garden, or like Peter, to shrink away crying, "Depart from me, for I am a sinful man, O Lord" (Luke 5:8).[6]

Yet the question remains: How do we recognize His manifestation and what form does it take? We have studied in previous chapters the great variety of ways that God can speak to us. He is speaking to all of us at once on many different wavelengths. As each person expresses what God has placed within his or her heart, a coherent picture begins to take shape. Then we realize that He is revealing an aspect of himself in our midst.

For example, the Lord might choose to manifest himself in our worship as a God who is rejoicing or dancing over us with singing (as in Zeph. 3:17). At that time, the sound of our music will probably include the sound of rejoicing. During this part of the service, the worship music may very well become fast and loud as the instrumentalists become inspired by and respond to this revelation. Likewise, if He comes amongst us as a gentle Shepherd, then we will play and sing with gentleness.

Our gauge for determining worship is rooted in God's

presence, not our music. We know that worship is taking place because God is present, and the people are responding to Him. The character of His presence will determine the nature and sound of our worship: fast or slow, majestic or somber, joyous or gentle.

I will never forget the day He came amongst us as a Deliverer during a service at Shady Grove Church. The pastor had invited all who felt they needed deliverance from some spiritual oppression to come forward for prayer. The front of the church was filled, but before anyone could begin to pray for them, some dancers came onto the platform and began to dance in a warlike manner, beating out a rhythm on the wooden platform with their hands and feet. After a time, the musicians joined in with a victorious sound, and the whole congregation entered into intercession on behalf of those at the altar. The Lord healed and delivered many that day.

> "We know that worship is taking place because God is present, and the people are responding to Him."

How awesome He was in the midst of the praises of His people! It is not that the dance and music were so powerful in themselves, but they became *a prophetic expression* of the Lord's strong right arm and His delivering strength. We worshiped that day because we allowed the Lord to show himself in the midst of His people. Our worship was not based on the kinds of songs we had chosen to sing that day, but on the manifestation of His presence among us and His work in our lives.

Foster expects miracles in the midst of worship. "If Jesus is our leader, miracles should be expected to occur in worship. Healings, both inward and outward, will be the rule, not the exception. The Book of Acts will not just be something we read about, but something we are experiencing."[7]

Quite simply, praise is not "the fast songs." Rather, it is our faith-filled expression of thanks and honor because of what the Lord has done, is doing, and will do. It is the pouring out of our hearts in sacrifice before Him as priests.

We need the Holy Spirit to draw us into and teach us the language of praise. When He is allowed to lead, there will be times when praise becomes prophetic. We will be declaring the greatness of the Lord *before* we even see what He is going to do, or we will delight in His works *before* we fully understand the magnitude of His acts.

> *"The character of the Lord determines the nature of our worship."*

OUR RESPONSE TO THE PRESENCE OF GOD

Worship is our response to the manifest presence of God. The manifest presence of God is His revealed presence. We must have an expectation for His voice and His manifest presence. Worship is only possible once the Lord has "shown" himself, and we have had a revelation of Him. Then, it is impossible not to worship!

It is easy to "super-spiritualize" the word *revelation*. Having a revelation of God is not just for the few "special" saints, once or twice a year, but should be the norm for all of God's children. Revelation from the Lord is an integral part of our personal and corporate relationship with Him. It keeps our relationship alive. Several others have commented on the revelation of God in the midst of worship:

"Worship is revelation and response. ... If we fail to respond, worship has probably not occurred.[8]

> Fundamentally, worship is a person responding to a person, so we cannot worship until we get a glimpse of God. We can praise out of our memory circuits, but we must worship out of a present relationship; that is, we must be in God's presence to worship. True worship will not begin to flow until we get a good glimpse of Christ Jesus. [9]

I can remember countless occasions when the Lord revealed himself to an entire congregation. One time during a worship conference in Puerto Rico, the Lord came among us as a Shepherd evidenced by a prophetic word, followed by a lilting melody played on a recorder (wooden flute), and various scriptures that were read. Many were healed as the Lord walked among His people and anointed their heads with the oil of His Spirit. Some dancers depicted this action of the Lord through dance and mime.

I do not think anyone present that evening missed out on this incredible revelation of the Lord as the Good Shepherd. I had read Psalm 23 numerous times and was intellectually aware of the Lord's role as the Shepherd. Yet, that evening, something of His Shepherd's heart touched my heart, and I will never be the same.

REVELATION AS IT RELATES TO WORSHIP

There are so many examples in scripture where worship is preceded by a revelation of God and His manifest presence. Abraham experienced God: Genesis 18–22. This is the first time worship is mentioned in scripture. Abraham had a visitation from the Lord concerning God's promise of a son. This visitation from the Lord caused Abraham to be able to worship God by offering his son, Isaac, in chapter 22. The Lord revealed himself again on Mount Moriah as He provided a ram for the sacrifice. Abraham worshiped God after this great provision and revelation, offering the ram as a sacrifice to God. See also: Ex. 15, 34:1-9, 2Chron. 7:1-6, Is. 6:1–8, Lk. 1:39–80, Lk. 4:40-41; 5:25; 7:16; 13:13, 17; 17:15–16; 18:43.

TWO CRUCIAL ISSUES CONCERNING WORSHIP

1) By definition, all worship is prophetic because it includes the concept of God's self-revelation. Every ministry in the presence of God—whether music, dance or any other artistic expression—is an extension of the true act of worship, which is the communion between God and His people. Worship will take place whenever God fills our praises with His presence (Ps. 22:3).

2) Profound, creative, revelatory, and intimate worship should be the norm for every congregation of all denominations. Our relationship with God bids us to

expect face-to-face encounters with God on a regular basis. It is our responsibility as worship leaders to make a way for God to manifest himself before His people. He is patiently waiting to respond to our longings.

Once we have worshiped in spirit and in truth, we will be ruined for anything else, forever. We will have no patience for dead traditions of any sort. It will be easy to recognize any man's hand upon the worship service, as some would try to manipulate and control spiritual things.

"It is impossible to really worship God unless we have had a revelation of God. Once we have had a revelation of Him, it is impossible not to worship Him."

Chapter Fourteen

The Control of the Service

*What I believe about God
is the most important thing about me.*
—A.W. Tozer

Who controls the worship service in your church? Is it the pastor? Is it the worship leader? Who decides when it is time to sing? When it is time to stop singing, sit down, or take an offering?

This is one of the more difficult issues to be resolved for churches (and church leaders) that desire to pursue prophetic worship because it requires a new understanding of leadership and of spiritual authority. In prophetic worship, everyone must submit to the leading of the Holy Spirit.

The Holy Spirit as Worship Leader

In prophetic worship, the "leader" functions more as a worship doorkeeper or facilitator since the Holy Spirit is the true leader. His or her role is to craft the sight and sound of God in our midst with the excellence of a master conductor before a symphony orchestra.

If He wants the sound of His voice to be expressed through the sweetness of a flute or the innocent prayer of a child, then the worship leader must be sensitive enough to respond immediately and make space for these expressions to be heard.

As this illustrates, we need to completely "rethink" the traditional role of a choir director or worship leader. An understanding of spiritual release and delegation of responsibility to the whole congregation in worship must be learned.

The Lord has a lot to say about the direction of our worship services if we will only take the time to listen. He has a masterful plan and purpose for *every* service. His direction is already set. It is up to worship leaders to "tap into" the Lord's leading and release a wide participation in the service by all members of the congregation. It is up to the leaders to follow the life and breath of the Holy Spirit. Griffing calls it a "point of life." You can perceive what the Lord's voice and purposes are in a particular song, instrument, dance, etc., because of the *life* there.

> *"In prophetic worship, everyone must submit to the leading of the Holy Spirit."*

We might describe this as a fluid form of leadership because different people participate in and lead at various moments in the service. By 'lead,' I mean they may be inspired by the Holy Spirit to step out and call upon the congregation for a particular response. I have seen a man come forward and challenge the men of the congregation to pray; a woman gather children to dance; and a trumpet player stand and play, then direct other musicians to follow his example. During these moments, those who have stepped forward are leading the service.

On one occasion, I heard a drummer prophesy on his drums. During the service, we had all been singing songs concerning the King and were expecting Him to reveal himself in an extraordinary way. As the congregation exalted and praised the King, He heard our cry and at that moment, the trumpets played in spontaneous fanfare and announced His presence. A holy hush descended upon the people, and they appropriately fell on their faces before Him.

After a time of silence, the Lord began to speak. His voice was like thunder. The most suitable instrument to speak at that moment was the drums. For several minutes, the drummer played on the toms—not with a set rhythm, but with the cadence of one who is speaking. The walls shook with the sound, and our hearts were melted in the presence of the Lord. Sometime after the drums finished, the pastor came to the microphone explained what the Lord was saying and asked the people to remain in silence until He had finished His work in our hearts.

No one told the drummer to play, and no worship leader had directed during the 30 minutes or so that this went on. The Holy Spirit was clearly in charge, and the Lord received all the glory. I am sure that every believer in that service remembers God's thunderous voice to this day. It was an awesome sound, rather than a frightening sound, that shook our hearts to the core. We walked away softly that night with a greater hunger for God and a much fuller understanding of His impressive majesty.

There is no need for any pastor or elder to feel their authority is being compromised in this type of service. Neither is there any room for personal "kingdom building" or the usurping of authority of any sort by anyone present, when a congregation of mature, spiritual people gather to worship the Lord.

Ultimately, the Lord is the primary worship Leader of the church. Foster concurs:

> Christ is the Leader of worship in the sense that he alone decides what human means will be used, if any. Individuals preach or prophesy or sing or pray as they are called forth by their Leader. In this way there is no room for the elevation of private reputations. Jesus alone is honored.[1]

THE FEAR OF GOD

Prophetic worship leads to a greater release on the part of worshipers, but also to a greater increase of the fear or awe of God. I say *release*, because it is not up to any one individual to make anything happen. It is not necessary to fabricate the sense of God's indisputable presence.

God is completely responsible for every supernatural meeting with the congregation and for touching our lives with His grace. The worship service—for which we plan and prepare—is merely the tool, or steppingstone for God to use as He "breathes" upon the songs, words, instruments, and so forth.

We will never fully know what God is going to do in our midst.

Even so, let God have full control of the whole service. Morgenthaler addresses one of the major problems churches encounter when trying to release control of the service to the Holy Spirit—pride and self-promotion. "If we are really going to give people opportunities to encounter and interact with God in our sanctuaries ... we have to set aside some of our control issues and get out of the way."[2]

> *"Worship is rooted in the honor and fear of God."*

Set your eyes and ears upon the true worship Leader. Watch Him, wait upon Him, and work with Him as he ushers us into the courts of His awesome majesty, and deftly weaves His life and likeness into every heart.

Chapter Fifteen
The Priesthood of all Believers

True worship has no room for a spectating heart.
—Sammy Tippit

Every Christian church believes theoretically in the priesthood of all believers, but very few seem to practice this in meaningful ways. Most believers shy away from thinking of themselves as priests. We have a traditional view of the priesthood as a vocational calling alone, but God's idea on this subject differs drastically. A priest is really a bridge-builder— one who stands between God and unredeemed man. That is the priestly call upon the Church.

The term "priest" in the New Testament never refers to a professional minister or leader. It is either referring to an Old Testament type of priest, the role of Jesus as our Priest, or it is referring to every believer (2Pet. 2:5, 9; Rev. 1:6; 5:10).

The meaning of First Peter 2:1–10—where the Church is challenged to participate in Christian life and worship as a holy, royal priesthood—has yet to be fully explored and experienced by the modern church. Each believer is called to be a priest of the "spiritual house" mentioned in First Peter 2:5. This is more a corporate expression of priesthood than an individual one. Peter's intent was not to dismiss spiritual authority in the believer's life and send each person off to lead their own church. As he goes on to explain, the primary reason for the corporate priesthood is:

"to offer up spiritual sacrifices" (1Pet. 2:5) (See also Heb. 13:15–16), and

"that you may proclaim the praises of Him who has called you" (1Pet. 2:9).

We will not go wrong if we see our priestly role as ones who minister before the Lord in praise and worship and are servants of all people on earth—both the saved and the unsaved. As priests and servants to the lost, we have a great responsibility to proclaim His saving grace to all (2Cor. 5:16– 19).

Jesus and Paul clearly taught that we are the dwelling place or temple of God, priests responsible for ministering before the Lord (Jn. 14:23; 1Cor. 6:19–20; 2Cor. 6:16; Eph. 4:6). Our personal ministry before the Lord is necessary preparation for our priestly ministry within the church body, and to the world. This priestly ministry was outlined by the Lord in Deuteronomy 10:8, where we see God's three areas of ministry for all priests – for all time:

1. *"Bear the ark of the covenant"* – carry God's presence.
2. *"Stand before the Lord to minister to Him"* – worship God.
3. *"Bless in His name"* – go out and minister to one another and to all the world.

Please note that it is impossible to do the second job of the priesthood until we have accomplished the first. Carrying the presence of God is paramount. It is also impossible to accomplish the third responsibility unless we have learned how to minister to Him and before Him. Once we have carried His presence and learned how to be true priests of his presence by ministering to Him, then we are qualified to go out and bless others in his name. True worship will radically affect our understanding and effectiveness in missions and evangelism. The world is longing for priests who carry the presence of God.

> *"The world is longing for priests who carry the presence of God."*

GOD'S ORIGINAL PLAN

It has always been in the heart of God to flood the world with His glory through a holy and royal priesthood. He called the entire nation of Israel to be priests in the midst of all the nations. This was one of the most definitive occasions of Israel's history as the Lord revealed His wider purpose for their existence as a nation:

> "Now therefore, if you will indeed obey My voice and keep My covenant, then you shall be a special treasure to Me above all people; for all the earth *is* Mine. And you shall be to Me a kingdom of priests and a holy nation." These are the words which you shall speak to the children of Israel Then all the people answered together and said, "All that the LORD has spoken we will do" (Ex. 19:5-6, 8).

The people agreed with God's plan—*"All that the LORD has spoken we will do"*—so the Lord took them at their word and told them to prepare because He was going to manifest himself among them. Once the people saw and heard the Lord, they decided they did not want to pay the price to experience the presence of the Lord as His priests and they appointed Moses as the one who would hear God on their behalf:

> Now all the people witnessed the thunderings, the lightning flashes, the sound of the trumpet, and the mountain smoking; and when the people saw it, they trembled and stood afar off. Then they said to Moses, "You speak with us, and we will hear; but let not God speak with us, lest we die" (Ex. 20:18- 19).

These are some of the saddest words in Scripture, and unfortunately, the Church is still asking for pastors and leaders to find God on their behalf. The cost of having God's manifest presence in our meetings is too much for many congregations.

Many of the Psalms show us that the people of Israel understood the mandate upon their lives to bring blessing to the other nations. Psalm 67 asks God to bless them so that "Your way may be known on earth, Your salvation among all nations" (v. 2). The psalmist goes on to call all the nations to their destiny: to praise the Lord.

So, it has always been on the heart of God to touch the whole world through His priestly nation. Understanding this truth is pivotal to releasing God's presence in our churches. We are to be priests before His presence, priests in ministry to one another, and priests to our communities and in all the nations.

Priestly Participation

God never intended for the Church to have an élite caste of ministers. The vast and persistent gap that separates church leaders and platform ministers from the congregation clearly militates against prophetic worship. Several well-known authors have addressed this issue.

> "Worship is a verb. It is not something done to us or for us, but by us."[1]
>
> "Liturgy is supposed to be the work of the people."[2]
>
> The people of God are deserving of a richer share in the service than simply being hymn-singers and offering-givers, while for the rest of the service they remain a body of inert auditors and passive spectators. ... Give them an understanding that each facet of the public worship of God has meaning in which they are invited to contribute a significant activity—in praising, praying, giving, as in remembering, listening, confessing, believing, and acting out. These are all verbs of involvement and choice.[3]

Active participation in worship is the biblical norm for the whole congregation. When we gather, we have not come for a performance by the pastor, music minister, or worship team, but we have come to participate in the greatest "work" of our week. It is our highest calling to participate in ministering to God by offering him "spiritual sacrifices." (See Chapter Two for further discussion on these sacrifices.)

> *"Active participation in worship is the biblical norm for the whole congregation.*

We are *royal* priests (1Pet. 2:9). We assume our position as ministers within a royal court before a great King. Every worshiper can learn to be a gatekeeper of His court (Ps. 84:10; Prov. 8:34); a minister of incense before His throne (1Pet. 2:5); a royal bride who knows intimate communion with Him (Ps. 45:9–15; Song of Solomon); royal children of God who rule and reign with Him on earth and in His Kingdom forever (1Jn. 3:1–2).

When the pastor, priest, or music team is expected to lead every aspect of the whole service, the congregation functions as nothing more than spectators or an audience for a well- scripted, religious show.

For good or for ill, we live in a society capable of producing spectacular shows and productions on a regular basis. Multi-billion-dollar sports, media, advertising, and entertainment industries rule our finances and constantly saturate our senses.

What a pity that our children and congregations have not been shown the experience of the presence of God in worship! It is much more profound, moving, and magnificent than anything Hollywood could ever imagine or produce.

For worship to be this exciting, *it must involve the whole congregation.* Tippit and Cornwall add these thoughts:

> Music that produces worship will be participatory in nature. True worship has no room for a spectating heart; the home of worship is in the participating heart. Worship cannot sit in the grandstands of the church watching the performance of the more talented. True worship does not perform for others. It only participates in the grace and love of God.[4]
>
> Worship is one thing that cannot be done for the people; it must be done by them, for worship by identification is impossible. The Old Testament priesthood assisted the worshiper in his approach to God, but they did not perform the ritual as a surrogate for the worshiper. ... The choir's anthem cannot substitute for congregational singing, nor can the preacher's sermon replace congregational praise and worship. Worship demands involvement on the part of the worshiper.[5]

WHOLEHEARTED WORSHIP

Not only must every member of the congregation participate in worship as priests, but individuals are challenged to yield every area of their bodies, souls, and spirits to worship ministry. This is God's first and greatest commandment:

> And you shall love the Lord your God out of *and* with your whole heart, and out of *and* with all your soul (your life) and out of *and* with all your mind (your faculty of thought and your moral understanding) and out of *and* with all your strength. *This is the first and principle commandment* (Mk.12:30, AMP). (See: Deut.6:4–5; Matt. 22:37; Lk. 10:27.)

Wholehearted worship is not necessarily loud and exuberant. The Lord looks at the intent and purpose of our hearts. I know stroke patients who are barely able to speak or move yet seem to fulfill this obligation of enthusiastic and sincere worship. They strain with every fiber of their being to participate in songs and lift or clap their hands in response to the Lord. Barely a sound can be heard from their lips, and their clapping may be awkward and off-beat, but no one can dispute the earnest nature of their offering to the Lord.

Expectations of Unbelievers and Believers in Worship

First Corinthians 14 is a primary passage where Paul gives instruction to the church on how to conduct public worship services. Paul is particularly concerned that the gifts of the Spirit be ministered in an orderly manner and that the congregation understands their role in the service. Paul indicates the most likely response of any unbeliever if they encounter the presence of God in the midst of the church:

> But if all prophesy, and an unbeliever or an uninformed person comes in, he is convinced by all, he is judged by all. And thus the secrets of his heart are revealed; and so, falling down on *his* face, he will worship God and report that God is truly among you. How is it then, brethren? Whenever you come together, each of you has a psalm, has a teaching, has a tongue, has a revelation, has an interpretation. Let all things be done for edification (1Cor. 14:24–26).

In the midst of this prophetic meeting—where the whole church was flowing in the gifts of the Spirit—an unbeliever had the secrets of his heart uncovered and fell down, worshiping the Lord.

Even this unbeliever was able to recognize the presence of the Lord and be changed in the midst of true worship. How much more should we, who know the Lord, be able to hear His voice as He flows through the ministry of the whole congregation?

Other kinds of Body ministry take place during worship services such as prayers for healing or comfort for those who are suffering. Sometimes the Father turns the worship service towards Body ministry because He is our Pastor and Chief Shepherd and is acutely aware of every need and every troubled heart.

The other point of this passage is that Paul seems to expect a prophetic flow through every member of the church, each time we gather together: "Whenever you come together, *each* of you. . ." (1Cor. 14:26). Young people and those without Bible school degrees are not excluded. The whole Body is expected to function in a way that brings edification to all— even the unsaved. This kind of ministry within the church service can only be accomplished when the people are taught that they are a part of a holy, royal priesthood whose greatest work on earth is to be ministers unto the Lord in worship.

The true function of a vocational minister is to equip the Body to function in maturity in all areas of their Christian lives— including worship ministry:

> And He Himself gave some *to be* apostles, some prophets, some evangelists, and some pastors and teachers, for the equipping (perfecting—KJV) of the saints for the work of ministry, for the edifying of the body of Christ, till we all come to the unity of the faith and of the knowledge of the Son of God, to a perfect man, to the measure of the stature of the fullness of Christ" (Eph. 4:11–13).

After a service, I often encounter those who believe that the Holy Spirit was prompting them to share a particular scripture, prophecy, or song during worship, but they were too shy to come forward and share what was on their hearts. While the place of hearing and obeying the Holy Spirit is a learning process for every Christian, I cannot help but feel grieved. Their opportunities to minister have been missed, and the chance for others to respond to the voice of God has been lost because of disobedience, pride, or shyness.

I remember when a pastor and a worship team thought the worship part of the service had concluded. Everyone started to leave the platform and instruments were placed back in the cases. One singer remained with her eyes closed.

She slowly and tentatively began to sing of the power of God to heal and restore. After a short time, she gained confidence and sang with greater strength. A few of the musicians joined her in what became a powerful song of healing. The pastor called for the sick and broken to come forward, and the musicians and singers surrounded them with God's songs of deliverance. The obedience of that one singer opened up a magnificent moment for that church. Many were healed and set free from bondages. An extended time of personal ministry ensued. I hate to think what they all would have missed if that singer had sat down with everyone else.

> *"Our greatest work on earth is to minister to the Lord in worship."*

Every believer must be responsible and alert to the voice of God in worship. The Lord has chosen His priests to proclaim His voice. Corporate prophecy is not the sole prerogative of older or more mature Christians, but the responsibility of the entire church body, men and women.

Tenney made this statement about the purpose of church: "The original purpose of church was a meeting place between God and man. Church was not created for you to get anything, church was created for you to give something of yourself to Him. ... If we want a restoration of the original power of the church, we have to return to the original recipe."[6]

The original recipe that Tenney was referring to is found in Second Chronicles 7:14: "If my people who are called by My name will humble themselves, and pray and seek My face, and turn from their wicked ways, then I will hear from heaven, and will forgive their sin and heal their land."

Desperate, wholehearted seeking of God by the entire priesthood needs to be heard in the Church today if we desire the glory of God to invade our land.

Chapter Sixteen

Time Limits in the Worship Service

Time is an available instrument for reaching the eternal.
—John W. Lynch

Every moment of every day belongs to God, for the earth and everything in it is His (Ps. 24:1; 1Cor. 10:26, 28). He is the Author and Finisher of our faith, all the days we live on this earth (Heb. 12:2). Our best moments and most complete regard should always be given to the Lord as an act of worship. My late pastor and mentor, Charlotte Baker, spoke of "wasting ourselves, our time, and all we have upon Him" in the same way that Mary wasted the contents of the alabaster box upon the head and feet of Jesus.

Unfortunately, we are confined by multitudes of time restraints. It is reasonable to surmise that living under such restraints has some influence on our attitudes toward corporate worship.

Perhaps this is why some tend to treat worship as just one "segment" of a highly produced and well-packaged Sunday celebration service. Such services are designed to subject church members to as short a time as possible in fulfilling their commitment, since leaders are afraid to impose too much on the busy schedules of the average Christian. Many are the occasions I have seen anxious pastors looking at their watches and glaring at the worship leader because the "worship segment" of the service seemed to be running late. That would, of course, throw off the entire schedule for that morning's production.

Often, out of fear for his job or just because she feels it is time to move on, the worship leader will interrupt the moving of the Holy Spirit to yank everyone to their feet for a rousing finale. This can be quite frustrating for those in the congregation who are truly communing. It interrupts the intimacy they are experiencing with Christ.

An Audience With the King

The Lord is enthroned in the midst of us as we worship Him (Ps. 22:3). We have the opportunity to sit, stand, or kneel in the presence of the King and commune with Him—face to face. Worship summons us into the presence of His Majesty, the King of kings. Who on earth would want to pass up that opportunity just to keep a man-made schedule?

> *"Worship summons us into the presence of His Majesty, the King of Kings."*

If we were in the presence of an earthly king, queen, president or prime minister, I doubt that we would constantly look at our watch and anxiously gaze toward the exit anticipating the end of the meeting. More likely, we would measure our words and count every second as an honor.

If the queen asked us to spend one day with her, how quickly we would cancel all other engagements, how insignificant all other pursuits would seem. We would count the days till our appointment, tell all our friends, lay out our finest clothes, prepare ourselves for any possible questions from *Her Majesty*, pray for favor, practice our protocol, and enter with wonder, awe, and anticipation.

May I suggest that every moment of boredom in the presence of Jesus is a moment when that individual has lost sight of the One we worship? As spectacular as it would be to have an audience with *Her Majesty, the Queen*, nothing will ever come close to the encounter we are invited to every time we gather as a church. This reminds me of a nursery rhyme I learned as a child:

> *Pussy cat, pussy cat, where have you been?*
> *I've been to London to see the Queen.*
> *Pussy cat, pussy cat what did you there?*
> *I spied a little mouse under the chair!*

The cat came all the way to London to see the queen. We know that he was in the presence of the queen, because he refers to the "chair" which is the throne. Unfortunately, the cat tells us absolutely nothing about the queen. The only thing we hear about is the lowly mouse!

What would be the reply if we were to ask the members of our congregations the same questions?

> *Christian, Christian where have you been?*
> *I've been to church to see the king.*
> *Christian, Christian what did you there?*
> *I spied the pastor's wife with funny hair.*

It may not be the pastor's wife that we are looking at, but one thing is certain: anything or anyone distracting our focus from the awesome majesty of the King of kings can never stand worthy of such misdirected attention. How often we waste time in the presence of Jesus by emphasizing the trivial and concentrating on earthly matters. "Some people go to church to see who didn't."[1]

> *"Every moment of boredom for every man, woman or child in the presence of Jesus is a moment when that individual has lost sight of the One we worship."*

HONOR THE SABBATH

The time we spend with God should not be an accident, nor should it be determined by some theoretical theological calculation. The Lord is aware of how much time we need to commune with Him. Everything He has done has been in its right time—He is never early or late.

The Lord has commanded us to set aside a whole day as holy unto Him (Ex. 20:8). Vine tells us that the root meaning for the Hebrew word *Sabbath* (Heb: *Shâbath*) means: *to cease, desist*. Vine goes on to explain that the singular word has a doubled "*b*," which indicates "an intensive force, implying complete cessation or a making to cease, probably the former. The idea is not that of relaxation or refreshment, but cessation from activity."[2]

The fast pace of modern society may be responsible for our erroneous attitudes toward the day of rest and worship.

Worship services are often peppered with the sound of mobile devices. Numerous activities have been crammed into our Sabbaths, leaving little room for waiting upon God or lingering in His presence.

As I have said, the Merriam-Webster dictionary defines 'linger': "to remain or stay in a place longer than is usual or expected; to continue to exist as time passes; to be slow in parting or quitting something; to be slow to act; to pass a period of time slowly; to remain alive though gradually dying."

In most of our churches, there are set times for the worship. Worship leaders tend to fill the entire time with songs and give no time to waiting in the presence of the Lord and listening for His voice. We rarely experience time passing while we remain still— 'being slow to act or speak.'

David tells us: "Rest in the Lord, and wait patiently for Him; Do not fret because of him who prospers in his way, Because of the man who brings wicked schemes to pass" (Ps. 37:7). The NLT translates this verse: "Be still in the presence of the Lord and wait patiently for Him to act. ... think about being still in His presence. Quiet your mind and make your heart still."

SILENCE IN WORSHIP

Prophetic worship requires time to wait for God's voice and respond to Him appropriately. Spontaneous and unprepared moments are quite common in services where the Holy Spirit is the leader. Special moments of quiet or silent worship can include waiting, meditating, quiet prayer, or song, instrumental music, mime, etc. When we pray, we talk to God; when we meditate, we listen to God; when we worship, we respond to God.

The Psalmist wrote, "Be still, and know that I *am* God" (Ps. 46:10). Something of the knowledge of God is found in stillness. Holy silence and stillness are often life-changing moments in our worship. Wheaton professor, Andrew Hill, observes: "The silence of worship is equally as important as the noise of worship. Silence takes the worshiper out of time and into God's eternity. Silence is valuable in Christian worship because it is disturbing, arresting. We feel uncomfortable, helpless; we are no longer in control."[3]

When God draws us into His silence, our schedules and time constraints become irrelevant.

> With our loss of the sense of majesty has come the further loss of religious awe and consciousness of the divine Presence. We have lost our spirit of worship and our ability to withdraw inwardly to meet God in adoring silence. ... It is impossible to keep our moral practices sound and our inward attitudes right while our idea of God is erroneous or inadequate. If we would bring back spiritual power to our lives, we might begin to think of God more nearly as He is.[4]

We must combine silence with reverence and worship. Silence is a result of the awe and wonder we experience in God's presence. There are times in worship when words are inadequate and a holy hush falls upon all. Pastors and worship leaders must surrender to the time frame of the Holy Spirit as He works secretly and lovingly within our hearts.

Several years ago, Pastor David Fischer of Living Waters Fellowship in Pasadena called worshipers from all over Southern California to a day of worship. He called it a "Sabbath of Worship." There were no plans for sermons or announcements—the day was entirely devoted to worship.

Throughout the day, the Lord moved among the people in various ways. At one point, He drew us into about 45 minutes of silence, during which two mimes ministered silently and prophetically from the Song of Solomon. No words were spoken, and no sound was made as the mimes called the congregation to a greater understanding of our bridal relationship with the Lord. Instruments broke the silence as they began to play the song of the bride and the song of the bridegroom. We immediately fell back into the holy hush.

As this illustrates, there can be many different kinds of silent response to the Lord in worship. Here are two other statements on the value of silence well worth considering: "Everything true and great grows in silence. Without silence we fall short of reality and cannot plumb the depths of being."[5] "Four things go together: silence, listening, prayer, truth."[6]

> *"Waiting, lingering, resting in worship are crucial if we want to hear the voice of the Lord.*

Solomon wrote, "To everything *there is* a season, a time for every purpose under heaven" (Eccl. 3:1). We would be wise to reconsider our use of time in worship—the most important purpose under heaven. There are few who would say their church spends *too much time* worshiping. For most congregations, quite the opposite is true.

Waiting, lingering, resting in worship are crucial if we want to hear the voice of the Lord. The word "rest" in Hebrew is: *damam*. It means 'to be silent, to be quiet, to wait, to grow dumb (no speaking), to be still, to die.' Interestingly, the Hebrew for "waiting patiently" is the word *chuwl* which means 'to twist, whirl, dance, writhe, tremble, fear, travail, to be born, to wait.' So, it seems that sometimes our waiting can lead to a dance, and a "birthing" of the things God has purposed for us. Wait on Him—linger for a while and listen to His voice—turn your prayers into a dance if that is a way you can communicate with Him.

THE ALPHA AND OMEGA

Because worship is an encounter with the Alpha and Omega— God, who is the Beginning and Ending of all time— we should become accustomed to Him invading and overruling our human concepts of time and order whenever He pleases. When we enter eternity, time ceases. True worship touches eternity and transcends time. It will know no time restraints or limitations, nor will it be bound by man's expectations. "God invades our time with eternity. We are not born for time but for eternity. We are victims and prisoners of time, but creatures of eternity."[7]

In prophetic worship, the Lord frequently has us operate according to *His* time frame, eternity. Every moment of His presence is a moment that knows no earthly time frame. This does not mean that every worship service must go on for hours and hours to be seen as "successful," However, each service should provide as much time as the Lord needs to accomplish His work in us.

If He completes all that He has for us in 15 minutes, then we should stop and go on to the next phase of the service. But if He would have us sing one song for half an hour, remain in silence for 20 minutes, or bow before Him for a full hour, then what on earth should keep us from these things?

What I am suggesting is that we make an effort to give priority to the time frame of God's communion with us, which is frequently interrupted by those who insert *their own* schedules and agendas. Invariably, some just want to beat the Baptists to the restaurant!

> *"The worship service should take as long as the Lord needs to accomplish His work in us."*

Chapter Seventeen

The Emphasis and Priority of Worship

Worship renews the spirit as sleep renews the body.
—Richard Clark Cabot

Following the Age of the Apostles all churches were liturgical. Services were in Latin and the priests did everything—singing, reading, speaking, etc. The people could see the Gospel story through the stained-glass windows, the statues, icons, and other arts. The "main event" in the service was the drama and mystery of the communion table. As the services were in Latin, the "sermons" were not long or even understood. Music was not a priority and again, they were in Latin.

Beginning in the Thirteenth Century, a "popular sermon" in the vernacular of the people was added to the mass. This popular sermon was delivered by Franciscan or Dominican friars on Sundays, Feast Days, Lent, and sometimes during Advent. The format continued for 300 years.

On October 31, 1537, Martin Luther nailed his Ninety-Five Theses to the door of the Castle Church in Wittenberg, Germany. Luther explained, "The Word of God is the greatest, most necessary, most important thing in Christendom." He challenged the status quo and called for a reformation of the church. The Reformation attempted to restore the preaching emphasis of Jesus and the Apostles. The language of the people was instituted in preaching, and the invention of the printing press made Bibles more available to the common man. Hymns were also written in the everyday language and became a major tool for teaching theology to a Church that had been starved of this necessary food for centuries.

To illustrate the priority of preaching, the pulpit was raised and decorated with ornate carvings. Pastors climbed several steps to get to the preaching platform high above the people. Pulpits were often placed in the center of the church. It remains like this today in many traditional reformed churches, particularly throughout Europe.

Although the intention was to restore the Word to the Church through reading, teaching, and singing the glorious theology of the faith, the unfortunate consequence was to place all the emphasis on preaching. Music and singing only served to reinforce the preaching. This emphasis continues today. While preaching is an important part of our service, it is not more important that all other aspects of worship and ministry in God's presence.

As the Church entered the Twentieth Century, a new age dawned. The Holy Spirit was poured out afresh in Wales, India, and Azusa Street, California. Music played an important part in these early revivals, but the format of worship services was not greatly affected. We still see worship as a "support" of the preaching. Statements like that of E. W. Howe show the prevailing attitude of the day. "If you go to church, and like the singing better than the preaching, that's not orthodox."[1]

Again, Webber highlights this faulty thinking: "I graduated from three theological seminaries without taking a course in worship My seminary education left me with the impression that the only important matter in morning worship was the sermon. All else was preliminary. ... I say, 'Shame!'"[2]

The subject of worship should become a primary study in all seminaries. I believe the best preachers are those who are worshipers and who have an intimate relationship with God as their teacher and example.

We need a reformation of worship in the Church worldwide, reformation that draws us to the presence of God and makes way for Him to be the "main event" and primary purpose for our meeting. We certainly can find Him in the preaching, but surely Christ-centered worship, prophetic worship, is the easiest and greatest way to connect the congregation with the presence of God.

There may be times in the life of a church when the pastor feels more time is needed for his message. During other seasons, worship may be given greater emphasis. But on the whole, *worship and preaching should be given equal prominence in church life.* In churches where prophetic worship is practiced, there will be a healthy balance between worship and the preaching of the Word.

> *"Anointed preaching will inspire great worship in a congregation, and anointed worship will inspire great preaching."*

Teacher and author Sam Sasser expressed this thought clearly.

> We must re-focus to see that while the ministry of the Word of God is imperative, the ministry we give to a holy God, from the deep inner recesses of our hearts in sustained worship, is even more imperative. This is not to say that I seek to elevate "worship" without "word," but rather to return the reader to the distinction of worship with the word, to clarify that our focus must be on the throne before the pulpit.[3]

The power of our traditions is hard to break. Since most pastors and congregants today seem to regard the sermon as the most important part of the whole service, people come to church late believing they are not missing anything important since the preaching has not begun.

Here are some other worship leaders' thoughts on this subject:

> It is no longer adequate to defend our worship services by saying, "Well, we've always done it this way." It is equally insufficient to conceive of our worship services as "the preliminaries," something to "condition" the congregation in preparation for the truly important part of the service: the sermon. It is time to seriously consider from a broader perspective the vital role that worship plays in the life of the congregation.[4]
>
> There are Godly men and women in the church who have an inadequate and sub-biblical view of music. They think of music as a filler, as a warm-up, as passing time. They think of music as the preliminary and the sermon as the main event. By this attitude the people become listeners and note takers—well informed, highly motivated, godly people, to be sure—but with no common outlet for corporate praise of the God they love. This short-circuits the cycle of praise in their life.[5]

When prophetic worship is restored to its rightful priority, there is never a conflict between worship and preaching, since the Holy Spirit has no conflict with himself. I have witnessed many worship services where the theme of the worship has tied in directly with the preaching, even though the worship leader had no idea what the pastor was planning to preach. In a worshiping church, on occasion, the pastor may feel free to preach for a shorter period of time—or not at all, if he senses that the Holy Spirit has accomplished all that was needed during the worship time.

We should not see worship as being a hindrance to the preaching or in competition with it in any way. Rather, worship should prepare the hearts of the people for the Word and make them better able to receive all that God has to say to them through the speaker. Anointed preaching will inspire great worship, and anointed worship will inspire great preaching. Mutual respect between the pastor and worship leader will enhance both ministries.

Chapter Eighteen
Transcending Denominational Barriers In Worship

*It is always dangerous to go to church,
for there is always a chance
that God's presence will break through
the protective shell of our denomination.*
—Eugene Carson Blake

Is it possible to believe all the right things about God and embrace a correct theology of worship yet still have little passion for His presence or true devotion to God? Worship is a matter of the heart and must transcend all things—including denominationalism. Dynamic, heartfelt worship filled with expectations of God's presence should be the primary goal of all churches. Tozer provokes Christians from all denominations to a greater understanding and experience of the presence of God:

> *"Dynamic, heartfelt worship filled with expectations of God's presence should be the primary goal of all churches."*

> That type of Christianity which happens to be the vogue knows this Presence only in theory. It fails to stress the Christian's privilege of present realization. According to its teachings we are in the presence of God positionally, and nothing is said about the need to experience that Presence actually. ... Ignoble contentment takes the place of burning zeal.[1]

Each of us must recognize the impact that our own

denomination has had on our worship experiences. I must say again that there is not a separate Bible for each denomination. There is only one Bible, and in it the Lord clearly lays out how *He* prefers to be worshiped. We don't have to worship in the same manner, but there are principles of worship that apply to every denomination and all people

Some might seek to defend the status quo and accept the fact that Christians prefer to gather in groups of like theology, personality, and background. Those drawn to highly emotional forms of worship should form their own denomination and let those who prefer a more subdued atmosphere continue to have their traditional meetings (most likely, as far away as possible, on the other side of town).

My contention is that all of us, whether quiet or emotional worshipers, need to make some necessary changes to bring us closer to the biblical *pattern* of worship. It is possible to describe the music and worship of any church based on the name of the denomination. Each have traditions concerning the style of music, length of singing, use of instruments, volume of the overall sound, congregational involvement, use of hymn books, or projector for the words of songs, and other such important issues in worship. Morgenthaler points out that our Christian identities have largely been shaped by what occurs in the worship services of our particular denomination: "Too often we worship our methodologies while feigning devotion to God. And when we do this, our pride and self- reliance belie a humanism more secular and infinitely more grotesque than anything we abhor in the world."[2]

Cornwall expresses this thought excellently: "True worshipers ... will not allow themselves to be limited by the traditions of men, or bound by the worship ritual of their religious heritage. ... They will choose to be Bible-directed in all of their responses."[3] "Too often religion stifles, rather than kindles, worship responses."[4]

PROPHETIC WORSHIP AND DENOMINATIONAL STYLES

The history of our worship experiences tends to become

embodied in our favorite music and rituals, making it difficult to consider our need for growth and change in worship expressions. But we *do* need to grow, and the manner in which we propose change in our services is as important as the changes themselves.

> There are times when we are guilty of trading ritualism for ritualism. Some who consider themselves "non-liturgical" and would defend their freedom at any price have bound themselves to a liturgy even more restrictive than the avowed liturgist.[5]

Presbyterians, Baptists, Pentecostals, Charismatics—all have their prescribed ways of doing things. Some sing only hymns, while others use predominately contemporary choruses from publishers such as Hosanna! Music, Maranatha! or Vineyard Music Group. Some churches use only a piano or an organ, while others use many instruments, even large bands or orchestras. Some churches allow the free use of the gifts of the Holy Spirit in worship while others completely forbid the ministry of these gifts.

> *"Biblical worship must transcend denomination, generation and culture."*

> It is one thing to have a preference in these issues, but it is another matter entirely to legislate or restrict worship based on any denominational decree. Ordinances and sacraments are certainly scriptural, but many times God cannot be accommodated by our program or liturgy! In a lot of churches there is no room for the Lord.[6]

One of the funniest things about this scenario is that each church continues to believe they are the ones who worship "decently and in order," according to First Corinthians 14:40. They tend to consider every other denomination that is different from them, at fault in some way.

I suggest that we read the whole of chapter 14 to understand what Paul means by "all things." Our concept of what constitutes "decently and in order" should reflect what the Lord considers decent and in order, *not* what our denominational culture is comfortable with. Webber writes,

> *Protestant*-evangelical worship has followed the curvature of culture, rather than being faithful to the biblical, historical tradition of the church. *The true character* of worship is not determined by people, but by God.[7] Our task is not to be judgmental in a manner of spiritual superiority, but to dig beneath the traditions to recover the spiritual impulse that originally brought them forth.[8]

WORSHIP INVOLVES OUR WHOLE HEART

The essential point is our need to worship God with all our heart, soul, mind, and strength—this is our first commandment (Deut. 6:5; Mark 12:30, 33; Lk. 10:27). Our entire body enters into the act of worship as we become a living sacrifice (Rom. 12:1). Whatever it takes for such praise and worship to be sincerely expressed must be allowed. "God calls for worship that involves our whole being. The body, mind, spirit, and emotions should all be laid on the altar of worship. ... We are to present our bodies to God in a posture consistent with the inner spirit in worship."[9]

I learned one of the greatest lessons on whole-hearted worship several years ago in Bogotá, Colombia. I was given responsibility for the large orchestra, gleaned from among several thousand delegates. The orchestra consisted of about 60 guitars, 70 tambourines, one clarinet, a piano, bass, drums, and one little lady—stuck behind the piano, scarcely able to see or be seen—who played a pair of finger cymbals.

I will never forget the face of this lady as she stood at her post and waited with patience for me to ask her to play. Despite the fact that she was never heard by anyone except God, she stayed poised for action–eyes ablaze with expectancy–from the first note of the first song, right through to the last note of the conference. She gave her all and played her part with great diligence and devotion.

Many musicians would have clamored for the best seat and the loudest microphone before they would have consented to play during worship. This woman, however, was only interested in pleasing the Lord through her worship. She ministered to God with all her heart, mind, and strength. My life was changed as I worshiped with her. "Biblical worshipers are generous worshipers because they are wholehearted worshipers."[10]

FORMS OF WORSHIP

Did you know that kneeling in prayer or worship is not uniquely Catholic or Episcopalian? It is a biblical expression as old as our faith, and all Christians should feel free to kneel in prayer or worship (Ps. 95:6). Likewise, did you know that the clapping and lifting of hands is not essentially a Charismatic or Pentecostal form of worship? It also is a biblical expression from old (Ps. 47:1; Ps. 134:2; 1 Tim. 2:8).

These outward expressions of worship follow the inward attitudes they symbolize. When our hearts bow in reverence before the Lord, it is appropriate for us to kneel or prostrate ourselves before Him. When we are lifting up praises to Him, or reaching for His love, it is befitting to lift our hands in worship.

> "We should worship in a particular manner because the Bible teaches us that it is acceptable, not because our denomination has traditionally allowed it in our worship service."

All denominations can appropriate and encourage these expressions. Because they are clearly mandated in the Bible, consideration of personal preferences and temperament becomes irrelevant. Rather than being threatened by our differences, we learn from one another.

One day, every knee will bow before the Lord (Phil. 2:10–11). There will be no question as to the individual's culture, denomination, or preference in the matter. Surely, if it is appropriate to kneel when we see Him in heaven, it is appropriate now when we worship Him on earth. Biblical models of worship provide exuberant and artistic expressions accepted by the Lord:

- The angels and heavenly beings—over one hundred million of them—*cry with loud voices* (Rev. 5:11–12).
- David and all of Israel *danced and played instruments* with all of their might during a joyous procession into Jerusalem (2Sam. 6:14–15).
- *Colorful banners, declaring the names of God, were displayed* in David's worship (Ps. 20:5—A Psalm of David).
- Solomon *offered a lavish number of sacrifices* on the occasion of the dedication of the temple. At times, his offerings were so extravagant that they could not be counted (2Chron. 5:6; 7:4–5).
- Jehoshaphat *put anointed singers in front of his army* and saw victory in a consequential and celebrated battle. The victors returned to Jerusalem *with exuberant praises* (2Chron. 20:28).
- The praises that were offered at the rebuilding of the temple in Ezra's time were accompanied by *shouting and weeping mingled together*.

Not one of these examples was followed by a heavenly expression of shock or displeasure. Not once did God declare that He was offended with these acts of worship due to the fact that He was Presbyterian, Baptist, or Pentecostal. Since there was no cry of dismay over such passionate displays, no indication that any such fervor was inappropriate before Him, it must be assumed that He approved. The Lord has ordained His people to worship Him with enthusiastic abandon. Nowhere are there scriptures that seek to curtail genuine devotion or expressive worship before God.

In fact, when King David's wife, Michal, saw him dancing publicly in worship before the Lord and despised him in her heart, God's punishment was quite severe: Michal was made barren for the rest of her life (2Sam. 6:14–23). This contains a lesson for us.

WOULD GOD "FIT IN" TO YOUR WORSHIP SERVICE?

My suspicion is that God, himself, might not fit in to many of our worship services because of His unorthodox voice and presence. God's own voice sounds, at times, like a gentle whisper (1Ki. 19:12 NIV), many waters (Rev. 1:15), or gigantic thunder (Job 37:4–5; 40:9; Ps. 29:4–9). He shouts like a warrior in battle (Is. 42:13, AMP), cries out like a woman in labor (Is. 42:14, AMP), hisses or whistles to the nations (Is. 5:26), and goes forth with the sound of the trumpet (Ps. 47:5).

This same God opened the sea for His people to walk through (Ex. 14); wrote on a wall with just a hand (Dan. 5:5); healed the sick (Matt. 14:14); walked on top of the sea (Matt. 14:25); forgave sinners (Lk. 5:24) and raised the dead (Jn. 11:43).

> The principle here is that our praise and worship should attempt to match its object. I say "attempt" because even an eternity of praise will never do justice to the attributes and character of God. ... Is there not, then, something desperately wrong if we get regularly bored in church? ... What kind of God do we think we have? Is He not endlessly creative, irrepressibly vital and alive, always doing "new things"? Indeed God is "the same yesterday, today and forever," but one of his unchanging characteristics is that He is always full of surprises![11]

It is simplistic to assume that we could all come to consensus regarding forms and styles of worship. However, clear biblical descriptions of worship transcend denominational culture. Diverse forms of worship should not divide Christians; rather, the reality of His presence in the Church should unite us and make us appreciate one another. As we encounter differences in worship, let it inspire us to greater devotion and deeper love for God.

I would like to assume that all the denominational fathers have given careful consideration to the great body of writings on praise and worship, both biblical and scholarly. Perhaps it is presumptuous of me to call for further study. But let us not hold on to our styles of worship for tradition's sake. Let us hold on to them only after careful and honest study of the Word of God proves them valid. Wardle calls the entire Church to openness in their forms of worship.

> I am not advocating change for the sake of change. What I am encouraging is flexibility and mobility in form and order. Our worship services should certainly be sensitive to tradition, but not completely determined by tradition. Forms of worship should not be institutionalized. Instead, they should be carefully designed, consistent with the moving of the Holy Spirit in this day—at this time and place in history.[12]

My desire in writing this book is not only to promote acceptance of denominational and cultural diversity in worship, but to prophetically call all people to transcend their denominational and cultural limitations so they can embrace the biblical model for prophetic worship. The simple truth is that the voice of God and manifestation of His presence should be found in every denominational setting. We must find how to fit our traditions and preferences into the plan of God for worship...rather than trying to fit God into our small worlds.

> *"Diverse forms of worship should not divide Christians; rather, the reality of His presence in the Church should unite us and make us appreciate one another."*

> Until we as pastors and worship leaders make it a point to "fill in our gaps" with the intentional, dedicated study of worship, church after church will be held hostage by our ignorance. Until we put worship back in its rightful place as the number one activity of the church, our churches will be malnourished and lacking in the spiritual power necessary to do God's work.[13]

What business do we have in confining God to our narrow and biased denominational boundaries or restricting the worship of His people to the meager expressions that we have claimed as our own? Let Him be praised in the dance! Let new and prophetic songs abound in the Church! Let every instrument prophesy and resound with impassioned praise! Let every man, woman, and child rejoice before Him with every ounce of their strength and every decibel of which they are capable!

Chapter Nineteen

The Impact of Culture on Worship

Culture... The harmonious development of all the (natural) powers and capabilities of man.
—Felix Perles

Culture greatly affects our attitudes toward worship. We need to be aware and careful that we do not allow culture to dictate our style and expressions of worship. It is popular today for churches to cater to the unchurched in their worship services. Some exclude or minimize expressions of worship that might "offend" visitors without thought as to the will of the Father or the biblical injunction for such expressions. Here we must tread carefully. After all, our primary objective as Christians is not to conduct worship services that will be pleasing to unbelievers, but to God. I agree with Schwanda when he says,

> An inherent danger in striving to be culturally relevant is that the church will instead become culturally driven. Indeed, in observing the push toward becoming all things to all men one might wonder whether some promoters of cultural sensitivity have not become imprisoned by the need to reach their market, regardless of how much their efforts might compromise the message of Jesus Christ.[1]

Having traveled to many nations, I have observed that churches of the same denomination often differ greatly from one country to another. Each may be experiencing worship in spirit and truth, yet

"Worship transcends culture."

cultural traditions lead some to more expressive forms of worship than others.

Even though worship *transcends* culture, it is expressed *through* culture. We must be careful to emphasize the aspects of our culture that release and enhance true worship while seeking to release ourselves from things that inhibit prophetic worship. Gustafson sums this up:

> For some reason, our own particular religious traditions and experiences tend to color our ideas of what God's preferences are and aren't. ... How quickly our preferences become biases. And how easily our biases become walls that keep us from the larger Body of Christ and from fuller expressions of worship. ... The sum total of these distinctives and preferences is termed *culture*. ... It is interesting that the root word for culture is *cult* which is, in its simplest definition, a system of worship or devotion. You could say our culture reflects our worship. We should neither despise nor deny our culture. ... When God says that His ways are higher than our ways (Isa. 55:9), He is saying that His divine culture is higher than our human culture.[2]

Worship leader and teacher Kent Henry states:

> In the past, churches have usually been opposed to this kind of activity (clapping, bowing and kneeling, dancing to the Lord, and the lifting up of hands). For the most part, this opposition has been based on cultural experience or style. Now, praise and worship services have returned to a more biblical precedent rather than following cultural orientation.[3]

The object of our worship is the same no matter what nation or culture we come from. The Lord's description of worship is outlined in the Word, which does not change from one nation to another. This is a great foundation for unity within the global Body of Christ and should be the chief influence of our worship traditions. Cornwall agrees. "Worship is the one religious activity that lends itself to such a delicate blending of different heritages, for worship is so Christ-centered and requires such a God-consciousness that participants must look away from themselves in order to worship."[4]

God desires that all people and nations worship Him. He is calling people from every tribe, tongue, and nation to worship before His throne (Rev. 7:9). God's call to enter into His presence with prophetic, abundant, and exuberant worship stands for all time and for all people.

I have seen this exhibited in practical ways many times and in many nations. For example, one of the words in Hebrew for "exalt" is *ruwm*—room (Strong's #H7311), meaning to *raise up*, or *to heave up*.[5] We tend to use the word "exalt" synonymously with "praise," but I believe that Strong's definition has opened up further meaning to us.

After studying the use of this word in scripture, I have come to realize that *the throwing of objects before the Lord in abandoned exaltation is quite appropriate and proper as a form of worship*. It is a valid way to honor the presence of our King. To some of you, this type of worship may seem shocking, but it is a natural human expression. We have all seen how adoring fans honor singers and actors by throwing flowers at their feet after a great performance or how sports fans toss their coats and hats when their team wins a victory.

In my travels, I have seen this type of worship occur spontaneously, time and again. Even people who are quite unaccustomed to such exuberant displays in their culture have eagerly heaved flowers, coats, paper, or other soft objects in the midst of unrestrained and passionate worship.

At a women's conference in Colombia, the ladies threw carnations and roses before the King and filled the room with a sweet perfume. I have witnessed normally undemonstrative Norwegians exalt the Lord by heaving things before Him. In Venezuela, thousands threw their coats into the air as they worshiped in an outdoor stadium.

In no way am I advocating inordinate excess just for the sake of change. But worship must become all that God intended it to be, not remain an expression inhibited by denomination or culture.

The Lord has hidden treasures of His glory in all the nations and peoples of the earth.[6] His voice can be heard and His hand can be seen in the sound and art of all peoples. When we become Christians, we bring these treasures and expressions of God's voice into our new nation—the Kingdom of God. The prophet Micah speaks of such treasures as he encourages Zion (the people who dwell in the presence of God, worshipers). "Arise and thresh, O daughter of Zion! For I will make your horn iron, and I will make your hoofs bronze; you shall beat in pieces many peoples, and I will devote their gain to the Lord, and their treasure to the Lord of all the earth" (Micah 4:13, AMP).

> "Worship must become all that God intended it to be, not remain an expression inhibited by denomination or culture."

Rhythmic styles of the African and Caribbean nations are full of life and great joy. The harmony of the Polynesian peoples and the melodies of the Celtic nations are exquisite. Instruments and songs from every country are now available to us. Their sounds can enhance the worship of any church.

I am very aware that many cultural traditions and musical sounds may not be appropriate for worship. The biggest challenge for the Body of Christ is to remain open and sensitive to the Lord in this matter.

In the past, we have "demonized" musical sounds merely because they were different or beyond our understanding and preference. We have made Christianity into a Western religion by forcing Western thought and culture upon our converts. An example can be seen in the way missionaries and Bible teachers promoted the singing of traditional Western hymns over the inclusion of indigenous music in worship. Local arts were impacted in most places Christianity was preached.

While this is a larger debate that lies beyond the scope of this book, I would like to suggest that musical forms and artistic styles may not be inherently evil. Rather, the heart of the worshiper and object of worship is what is good or evil. When Moses and Joshua were coming down from the mountain, they heard the sound of singing as the Israelites worshiped a golden calf (Ex. 32:17–18). It was not singing that offended the Lord, but the worship of a false god.

We must also be sure that we do not lump all unfamiliar cultural expressions into the category of the unregenerate and unusable. Our worship will be enriched by a genuine effort to redeem the arts from all nations. As we reclaim the treasures from the nations, a new sound and culture will emerge in the church which will entice and summon the unredeemed to the Kingdom of God.

> *"As we reclaim the treasures from the nations, a new sound and culture will emerge in the church which will entice and summon the unredeemed to the Kingdom of God."*

The first step in developing the worship music of the Kingdom of God is to foster respect for the distinct and ancient traditions handed down from generation to generation in all the nations of the earth. Ethnomusicologists King and Arthur have reported great strides in restoring artistic and cultural integrity to the worship of many nations.[7]

We must also identify things within our own culture that hinder worship. It is possible to use our culture and background as an excuse for rejecting intimate and ardent worship. For example, some people refuse to dance or shout in the presence of the Lord, claiming "cultural immunity" from such "imprudence". British and European people pride themselves on their reserve, yet these same people may be seen decked out in the colors of their home team, giving full- throated cheers at a ball game or political convention.

Sosene Le'au writes this testimony concerning the things the Lord showed him concerning his culture. God has:

- Called me to give up my culture so that I might be, before anything else, a citizen of His kingdom.
- Given my culture back to me with a fresh understanding of who I am in Christ, and who my people ought to be in Him.
- Shown me clearly that cultural diversity is one of God's great gifts to humankind.
- Shown me how He speaks through various cultures and peoples.[8]

The Lausanne Covenant of 1974 sums up this thought:

> Culture must always be tested and judged by scripture...
> The gospel does not presuppose the superiority of any culture to another but evaluates all cultures according to its own criteria of truth and righteousness. ...Churches have sometimes been in bondage to culture rather than to scripture.

To find the artistic treasures in any culture and break away from the confines of our cultural traditions, God's plan for His glory to cover the earth must be birthed in our hearts.

Culture and its effect on Art in Worship

Contemporary worship musicians and songwriters have begun to incorporate the sound, styles, and rhythms of the nations into their music. This is a powerful demonstration of prophetic intercession and the proclamation of our God, King over all peoples. When we hear the sounds of nations, our hearts are impacted by the global church.

In the secular world, there has also been a growing recognition of the dignity and worth of all peoples and cultures. The popularity of the indigenous music and art of the nations has increased markedly in recent years through music and movie trends.

It is possible to view secular folk music and other artistic expressions as the world's attempt at intercession because they communicate the heart of a nation. Performers and artists may not be aware of the full import of their declarations, but most folk music and art is a cry for:

- *Recognition*—as the story of the people is told;
- *Redemption*—as the heart's cry for all people is to be redeemed;
- *Restoration*—as all nations have suffered greatly, they are looking for the restoration of their history, culture, language and dignity.

Many worship ministers combine worship and intercession. They were made for each other. It is time they came together, and worship is the perfect setting. The band, "Caedmon's Call" dedicated an entire CD (*Share the Well*) to singing over India, Ecuador, and Brazil. While "Caedmon's Call" is not strictly a worship band, they highlight a definite trend. Rita Springer uses worship to open the door to powerful intercessory ministry. Also in the song, *Sons and Daughters,* Jason Upton is crying God's voice over young people in London. Israel Houghton also sings over the nations in the song, *We Speak to Nations.*

International sounds are readily available through recordings and Internet sites such as YouTube. The shrinking world, the Internet, and technology advancements make every computer and iPad a personal recording studio. Today it is much easier for international worship bands to share their music with the whole Body of Christ.

Recent years have brought international ministers of worship to the forefront. Worship leaders from South American countries (Marcos Witt, Marcos Barrientos), Australia (Hillsong), England (Graham Kendrick, Delirious, Martin Smith, Noel Richards, Tim Hughes and Matt Redman), Ireland (Robin Mark, Eoghan Heaslip), etc., have all received wide acclaim, and Paul Wilbur's album, *Lion of Judah,* is a powerful blend of many styles, including the sounds of Israel. Check out these worship recordings that highlight worship with very distinctive national sounds – not just Western worship songs translated into their language. These are just a few examples:

Caribbean: *Ketch A Fire* by Prodigal Son and Jason Mighty (https://youtu.be/32LH43LD1ao)

African: *All Around* by Israel Houghton (https://youtu.be/yKov_X5PwqE)

Celtic: *When It's All Been Said and Done* by Robin Mark (https://youtu.be/HkdaiSaiYEc)

Persian: *He is Lord* by Dariush (https://youtu.be/_SyrrpyOoJk)

Jewish: *How Great is our God // Gadol Eloha* by Joshua Aaron (https://youtu.be/sWSKtoURGAg)

Maori (NZ): *Cover Me* by Mark Naea and Lavina Williams (https://youtu.be/sWSKtoURGAg) OR *E Te Arikī*by by Tutevera & Tere (https://youtu.be/4tyMVnO_N3Y)

Russian: *Верую* (https://youtu.be/M0IQQ4v27VQ)

Spanish: Sumérgeme by Ezequiel Colon (https://youtu.be/qSBL6ikcnxM)

Peruvian: (https://youtu.be/XiABWws3Uos)

Cambodian: (https://youtu.be/ahdADxfOKlg)

Rural China: (https://youtu.be/HNbqEnSMHZY)

Indonesian: *Open the Sky* by Sidney Mohede and JPCC Worship (https://youtu.be/8idevGxTXNg)

Arabic: *Zeedo el-Maseeh Tasbeeh* (https://youtu.be/k8a6rfi-iWY)

Greek: *Με δέχθηκες!* by Averkios (https://youtu.be/mEpRDH4XhQE)

Pacific Islands: *Hakuna Mungu Kama Wewe* (https://youtu.be/iQpJ6YHNiQQ)

Native American: *Ride the Wind* by Broken Walls (https://youtu.be/VF7VvoM9Vwo)
Or this selection from Africa to South America:
Desire by Atta Boafo (https://youtu.be/GLFGaKNW6G8)

ALL NATIONS ARE CRYING AND GROANING FOR THE GLORY OF GOD

As the Church enters the last days here on the earth, we are looking for fulfillment of the promise in Habakkuk: "For the earth will be filled with the knowledge of the glory of the LORD, as the waters cover the sea" (2:14).

This glory is not some silver rain that suddenly appears in the heavens. It is the fullness of the character of God working in and through every believer, the supernatural weight of His manifest presence among us. It will be His likeness in our faces, His power in our prayers, His grace in our message, His holiness in our walk, and His numinousness[9] in our midst that will bring the display of His glory in the earth. When His character and nature flood our lives, then His glory will permeate the earth like an ocean.

We are entering a great, global revival where all nations and all people seek the one and only God who brings fullness and redemption.

Prophetic worship and intercession allows God to reveal His heart for the nations through dance and mime, or in spontaneous rhythms, harmonies, and melodies brought forth through the singers and instrumentalists. I have been in services where the Holy Spirit brought the sounds and dances of a particular nation into the service, and the whole congregation responded by lifting up their voices in intercession for that nation.

WORSHIP AND GOD'S ETERNAL PLAN FOR THE NATIONS

Kent Henry indicates the importance praise and worship have in the destiny of nations. "Praise and worship have the power to transform the hearts of men and women on such a large scale that an entire nation may be impacted."[10]

It is time for the Church to comprehend God's plan for the nations and become His voice of reconciliation and redemption to all peoples. It is impossible to say that we are worshipers and not hear God's intercession for the lost. Dutch Sheets speaks of the Church as being the "womb of God upon the earth where we release life through our prayers of intercession."[11]

Worship gives a correct worldview and a heart for the nations: "This call to the nations is both missionary zeal and prophetic insight. When one worships the true God fervently, the Holy Spirit reveals the heart of Father God to bring all peoples before Him in worship."[12] Our challenge, as the Church, is to become those who would birth and subsequently prepare for the multicultural song spoken of in Revelation 7:9:

> I looked, and behold, a great multitude which no one could number, of all nations, tribes, peoples, and tongues, standing before the throne and before the Lamb, clothed with white robes, with palm branches in their hands, and crying out with a loud voice, saying, "Salvation *belongs* to our God who sits on the throne, and unto the Lamb!"

It is interesting that the "great multitude" retain their ethnicity and language as they worship the Lord. Their nationality is evident and different languages noted. More remarkable are eight crucial areas of unity in this worship expression:

- Provision...........They are all wearing white robes of righteousness.
- Praise ....They are all singing the same words.
- Purpose ....They are all worshiping the Lamb.
- Pageantry ....They are all waving palm branches.
- Proclamation....They are all crying with loud voices.
- Perspective.......They are all beholding the Lamb.
- Place ....They are all before the throne.
- Posture ....They are all standing.

Through the provision of our salvation in Christ Jesus, the redeemed in this heavenly picture are all dressed the same and participate in the same worship service. All class, age, and cultural distinctions have been left behind.

Worship is the greatest unifying force in heaven and on earth. We must ensure that worship never separates us as believers. Not one of the great multitude is prepared to cite their nationality, denomination, or age, as a reason for doing something different in worship. From the description of this worship, we can assume it is thunderous, demonstrative, and spectacular. It is not divisive in any way as the sight and presence of the Lamb of God makes all this exuberance most appropriate. There is no greater tool for healing nations and repairing the breaches between us than worship. With our eyes fixed on Him, we will find no place for the pettiness that has separated us.

> *"Worship is the greatest unifying force in heaven and on earth."*

Multicultural neighborhoods are the norm in many cities today, yet many churches stubbornly remain closed and ethnically divided. We should commit to making our worship relevant for each generation and culture represented in our church family or local community. There are churches and organizations that model a refreshing multicultural atmosphere. These include Whole Life Ministries in Augusta, GA, and Glory of Zion in Corinth, TX, both of which have been multicultural since their inception. These churches are not only represented by ethnic groups from within the USA, but many other nations as well.

> Churches deceive themselves when they believe they are multicultural simply by the mere presence of one or more ethnic groups. ... Only when these folks are made equal partners in the faith mission of that congregation may we begin to call that congregation multicultural. ... The music ministry of the church may be a powerful means of establishing a strong foundation for building a multicultural congregation.[13]

The Lord is causing a new song to be birthed in the nations of the earth (Is. 42:10, 12). It is a song that transcends generations, nations, and denominations. It will be understood by young and old, strong and weak, rich and poor. The sound and style of the new song will be different than anything heard before. It is a sound from the heart of God. The prophetic realm and the sound of His voice in our worship are crucial. It will take a bending of our ears and hearts to hear and learn the song He is singing over us. We must commit to His perspective concerning the nations, participate in the sound, and spread His glory.

We begin with 1) the acceptance that all nations and peoples are equal and precious before God, and 2) the acceptance of artistic expressions of worship from other cultures. Then, we can move on to shared worship experiences.

We might think that this is the first time the Lord has summoned the nations to participate in prophetic worship together. Such is not the case. Some 3,000 years ago, King David established his tabernacle of worship on Mount Zion. He called for all nations to come and be born in Zion and worship with him there (Ps. 87). Surely, the Egyptians, Babylonians, Philistines, Ethiopians and other nations did not demand that their national sounds be played exclusively in the worship services. No, there was an understanding that the Lord had birthed a new and prophetic song relevant and acceptable for all nations. These were the songs of Zion spoken of in Ps. 137:3. "And the ransomed of the LORD shall return, and come to Zion with singing" (Is. 35:10).

We are in a day of renewal in worship. Every nation is called to Zion—to be birthed in worship, dwell in His courts, and run after His presence forever. This renewal of worship should carry with it new sounds and new songs. "He has put a new song in my mouth—Praise to our God; many will see it and fear, and will trust in the LORD" (Ps. 40:3)

> *"The prophetic realm and the sound of God's voice in our worship are crucial keys as we become ministers of His glory in all the earth."*

The particular word used in Psalm 40:3 is the word *tehillah*, which is a derivative of *halal*. Both of these words denote great boasting in the Lord and loud, exuberant praise. Whenever the word *tehillah* is used in scripture, there seems to be something supernatural happening.[14] It is as if God's manifest presence descends in the midst of the praises and He shows himself. His glory is seen as the worshipers sing, and sinners run to Him at the first glimpse of His beauty.

OUT OF ZION

There is a travail or intercession in Zion for a great nation to be born. This nation will affect all people on earth. God is birthing a new nation by assembling His people from the north, south, east and west. "Who has heard such a thing? Who has seen such things? Shall the earth be made to give birth in one day? *Or* shall a nation be born at once? For as soon as Zion was in labor ['travailed' KJV], she gave birth to her children" (Is. 66:8). (See also: Ps. 2:6; 110:2; Is. 2:2–3; 24:23; Micah 4.)

Zion is the name of the worshiping people or "nation" that will arise from the earth in the last days. This nation will consist of a great company of worshipers who display God's splendor and defeat His enemies (Ps. 48:2; Jer. 6:22–23; 50; Joel 3:16; Zech. 2:10–12).

Prophetic songs, sounds, and culture are found in the midst of Zion. As the Lord gathers us from all nations, we carry the treasures that He has hidden within each culture. The Church will look and sound like a melting pot of all nations.

Out of that melting pot will arise a prophetic sound coming from God himself. May the Lord tune our ears, eyes, and hands to heaven's sights and sounds. As we worship, may eternity overtake us. May God's supernatural culture be born in our hearts!

WORSHIP AND EVANGELISM

Conversion is a worship experience. It is also a prophetic encounter with God. Conversion takes place in our lives when the Holy Spirit reveals Christ to us, and our response is to abandon all of self to Him. There is no greater example of worship than this. My own personal salvation experience was accompanied by tremendous gratitude, love, and worship.

Worshipers make the best evangelists. As we commune with the Lord, He imparts His heart for the lost and for all nations to us. "The church has not yet fully realized the power of praise and worship to reach the lost. It can restore those Christians who have been hurt, and recover those that have fallen away from the Lord."[15]

Some may argue that we need to make our church services comfortable for unbelievers. They think that by patterning our worship after the worship of heaven, lost people will be offended by our extravagance. The God who dwells amongst us is awesome and irresistible. If He is in our midst, even the hardest of hearts will be overwhelmed by His love. There is no way that our worship services *can* be made "fit" for any and everyone—Christian or non-Christian alike. Webber puts it this way, "When worship planning is ... 'consumer-driven,' serious abuses of true worship may result."[16]

There are a few churches that have had great success in combining worship and genuine evangelism (Gateway Church in Dallas, TX, comes to mind), but churches need a mandate from the Lord in this area. Evangelism really should be the natural outflow of worship, the daily occupation of extravagant worshipers.

In First Corinthians 14, Paul gives the guidelines for prophetic worship. He encourages the use of the gifts of the Spirit when in the company of unbelievers, for he expects them to be transformed by the presence of the Lord. "He (the unbeliever) is convinced by all, he is convicted by all. And thus the secrets of his heart are revealed; and so, falling down on his face, he will worship God and report that God is truly among you" (1Cor. 14:24–25).

It is not the form of our service that is the key factor in bringing souls to Christ; it is an encounter with His presence. Where traditional worship might seek to make the unchurched person "comfortable," prophetic worship exposes them to the supernatural and to the questions everyone must answer:

"Who is this who even forgives sins?" (Lk. 7:49). "What shall I do to inherit eternal life?" (Lk. 18:18). "What must I do to be saved?" (Acts 16:30).

We are called upon to affect our surroundings and the people we work with through the fragrance of God. Every work of the church is an extension of the presence and voice of God that is heard in worship. Worship empowers and fuels evangelism.

> Rather than concentrating on being culturally sensitive, the church should become sensitive to the formative power worship exercises over people. It should re-evaluate its idea of who constitutes the object of worship—the worshiper or God. ... Let the church dedicate itself to discover anew the presence of God and to recognize that he alone is worthy of our worship. [17]

I close with Boschman's view on this matter. "Evangelism is a very important part of the mission of the church, but it is not the most important. Worship is. The church is first a worshiping community before it is anything else. ... It is the believer's utmost priority and highest occupation."[18]

Chapter Twenty
Music and Art in Worship

> *Religion is the everlasting dialogue*
> *between humanity and God.*
> *Art is its soliloquy.*
> —Franz Werfel

The Lord is calling the worshiping Church to take her place as a leader in the mountains of culture. Worship particularly involves the artistic world. Those who stand before the King of kings in worship should be able to declare His splendor in the most creative and excellent manner imaginable. All worshipers have the privilege of beholding Him, but artists have the privilege of describing Him. "Art is a collaboration between God and the artist, and the less the artist does the better."[1]

As much as we admire and enjoy great artistic achievements and talents, man's creations must never be elevated above God. It is possible to place art above the Lord and let it usurp the place of our deepest worship. Even Michelangelo repented of this fault as he wrote:

> . . . And where we all must haste to render up account
> Of every act committed—both ill and good.
> Wherefore I now can see, that by that love
> Which rendered Art my idol and my lord,
> I greatly erred. Vain are the loves of mortal man,
> And error lurks within his ev'ry thought.
> Lighthouses of my life, where are ye?
> When towards a twofold death I now draw nigh?
> One death well-known, the other threat'ning loud.
> Once-worshipped Art cannot now bring peace

> To him whose soul strives to that love divine,
> Whose arms shall raise him from the Cross to heaven. [2]

Sadly, it is also possible to lose respect for God's gift of the arts and to settle for a lack of excellence in the kingdom of God. As Allen and Borror state, many believers are not able to gain a correct perspective of art.

> Some Christians seem to believe that to be artistic is somehow unspiritual. They seem intentionally to avoid artistic pursuit and excellence so they will not fall into a possible trap of placing the art above God. We will see as we continue our thinking that true biblical spirituality and true artistic integrity are not mutually exclusive. [3]

Over the centuries, various Protestant churches have feared the arts and misunderstood this great gift from the Lord. The arts were primarily imparted to us as a tool for greater worship. Instead, large portions of the church have rejected the arts. Creativity should be a reflection of God's character. "God has revealed himself in the way that humankind can best understand: through His Son Jesus. But there is still much to be learnt about him through human creativity, which is at its most truthful when it reflects God's own creative nature." [4]

The Lord is the consummate artist. He is a:

- Sculptor (Gen. 1-2)
- Potter who made His own clay (Jer. 18:1-6)
- Painter who created all the colors (Gen. 1–2)
- Musician who formed every sound and gave us ears to hear (Rev. 1:10, 15)
- Dancer (Ps. 68:24; Zeph. 3:17 "He rejoices over you with joyful songs and dances.")
- Singer (Zeph. 3:17; Rev. 1:10). Everything He created sings back to Him
- Poet (Job 38–41) So much of the Bible is beautiful poetry inspired by the Lord

- Writer who has written the greatest best seller of all time—the Bible (2Tim. 3:16)
- Story-teller and actor (Jesus used parables in the Gospels to convey mysteries–Hos. 12:10, AMP)
- Architect (Ps. 90:2; Is. 44:24)
- Tailor and worker of needle and thread—He has woven a garment of light for himself (Ps. 104:2), and has provided a golden wedding garment for His bride (Ps. 45:9, 13–14)
- Master Chef and Creator of culinary delights (Ex. 16:31; Num. 11:7–8; Ps. 34:8; 119:103; Song 2:3)
- Perfumer (Ps. 45:8; 3:6; 5:1; 5:13). Even His name is a delightful perfume (Song of Sol. 1:3.
- Landscape Gardener and flower arranger (Lu. 12:27)
- Engraver (Is. 49:16)
- Master Carpenter (Matt. 13:55; Mk. 6:3).

In all of these, He is without compare. There is none who can match His artistry, excellence, and genius. The Shulamite sums it up in the Song of Solomon, "Yes, he is altogether lovely—the whole of him delights and is precious" (Song of S. 5:16, AMP).

Other artists describe His brilliance and expertise as an artist.

- "Christ was the greatest of all artists."[5]
- "God is the perfect poet, who in His person acts His own creations."[6]
- "God is the supreme artist. He loves to have things beautiful. Look at the sunset and the flowers and the snow-capped mountains and the stars. They are beautiful because they have come from God. God loves to have things beautiful in church, too."[7]
- "Music strikes in me a profound contemplation of the first Composer."[8]

Although every art form is appropriate for use as an expression of worship, some are easier to apply in a public setting.

These include music, song, drama, dance, mime, poetry, painting, pottery, calligraphy, sewing, and handiwork as used in banner making. I have seen other forms of art such as sculpting, stained glass work, and architecture skillfully used as instruments of worship—even prophetically— but for ease of writing and giving examples, I will refer to those previously listed.

There are three reasons for the Lord's use of His art and creation. They apply to our artistic expression as well:

1. To reveal His glory and nature to all mankind: "The heavens declare the glory of God; and the firmament shows His handiwork" (Ps. 19:1).
2. To communicate with His people and show us His ways and thoughts (Gen. 1–2). "We give praise *and* thanks to You, O God, we praise *and* give thanks; Your wondrous works declare that Your Name is near *and* they who invoke Your Name rehearse Your wonders" (Ps. 75:1, AMP).
3. To give and receive pleasure: "For You created all things, and by Your will they exist and were created" (Rev. 4:11).

THE FIRST REASON FOR ART—TO REVEAL THE GLORY AND NATURE OF GOD

"The first and primary use for all art is to show the glory and nature of God."

The first and primary use for all art is to show the glory and nature of God. "Good painting is nothing but a copy of the perfections of God."[9]

Anointing in any art form uncovers something of God's character and nature. The worship arena is the first place we should find the Christian artist. For example, a banner has the potential to be more than a colorful decoration in the sanctuary—it is a point of faith that lifts our eyes and hearts to the Lord. The psalmist speaks about setting up banners with the names of God on them in order to remember what He has done and put our trust in Him (Ps. 20:1, 5, 7). A skilled banner-maker draws us to God in worship time and again as we see and are reminded of His great exploits.

British writer and composer, Andrew Wilson-Dickson says that music can be judged as true or false according to the accuracy with which it reflects the nature of God's creation.[10] He goes on to quote the poet, Ezra Pound,

> Bad art is inaccurate art. It is art that makes false reports. ... If an artist falsifies his report as to the nature of ... god ... of good and evil ... of the force with which he believes or disbelieves this, that, or the other. ... If the artist falsifies his reports on these matters ... then that artist lies. By good art I mean art that bears true witness, I mean art that is most precise.[11]

Artists can participate in worship as they declare the glory of God, make His praises glorious (Ps. 66:2), and beautify the place of His presence. When Moses was commanded by God to make a tabernacle that would show His glory, he called upon skillful artists of all kinds to craft the beauty and splendor that was due Him. This task was headed up by Bezalel, the master craftsman (Ex. 31:1-11). He is the first person in the Bible to be filled with the Spirit and wisdom. Four chapters in Exodus (25–28) are used by the Lord to describe the elaborate and artistic beauty of the tabernacle that was to be constructed. Bezalel's name means "in the shadow or protection of God." Prophetic artists are those who live in the shadow and secret place of God (Ps. 91:1).

When David built the tabernacle on Mount Zion, he consecrated it with skillful music, song, and dance (1Chron. 15–16). His most skillful musicians were left before the ark to offer prophetic praises to the Lord day and night. Solomon called for workmen and artisans by the thousands to build a magnificent temple to display the glory of the Lord (2Chron. 2-4).

Similarly, Christian artists should devote their talents to the description of God's unsearchable glories and manifest presence. I say 'unsearchable,' because all eternity will not afford us the time needed to complete the description of His wonders.

Giorgio Vasari (1511–1574), recognized as the first historian of art, says of Michelangelo's statue *Moses*,

> You seem, while you gaze upon it, [the marble statue of Moses], to wish to demand from him [Michelangelo] the veil wherewith to cover that face, so resplendent and so dazzling it appears to you, and so well has Michelangelo [sic] expressed the divinity that God infused in that most holy countenance. In addition, there are draperies carved out and finished with most beautiful curves of the borders; while the arms with their muscles, and the hands with their bones and nerves, are carried to such a pitch of beauty and perfection, and the legs, knees, and feet are covered with buskins so beautifully fashioned, and every part of the work is so finished, that Moses may be called now more than ever the friend of God, seeing that he has deigned to assemble together and prepare his body for the Resurrection before that of any other, by the hands of Michelangelo.[12]
>
> Michelangelo used his rare genius to show us the glory of God lying beyond the figures he carved from stone. The stunning "David" was sculpted out of a discarded, inferior block of marble. This is so much like the Lord, who takes our once useless and inadequate lives and forms the most priceless treasures in us. He assists us and provides the tools and inspiration as we create masterful praises for our Creator. He equips us to chisel songs of praise out of our most desperate days.[13]

Christian artists are those who have rivers of living water coming from their innermost beings (John 7:38). With a talent dedicated to God and the glory of God flowing like a river from our lives, Christian artists should blaze the trail of distinction, beauty, and excellence above all other artists.

I once saw a harpist from the Chicago symphony play during some special worship meetings. The Lord began to speak of the new day that was coming to the Church. The harpist (a Chinese woman) stood in front of her harp and began to slowly beat the bass strings with the palm of her hand. It sounded like the chiming of a gong or a clock, the Lord was declaring the hour of His glory over the nations. Some flute players joined in by playing unusual sounds on their instruments, using a pentatonic scale. We were playing the sounds of the Chinese people. The congregation lifted their voices in intercession for China and other nations as the evening progressed.

On another occasion at the Karitos conference in Chicago, there was an altar call for young people who had been sexually abused. During the altar call, prophetic artist, Linda Iorio, was painting a beautiful picture of a lion—the Lion of Judah—ministering to a young woman. When the painting was finished, Linda came and asked me if she could hold up the picture so everyone could see it. God spoke to her and said that the woman in the painting was too afraid to come forward for prayer, but He was waiting for her, to bless her, and to heal her. When she held up the painting, a young woman came forward. I gasped, as she was exactly like the woman in the painting. This could have been a photograph. The prophetic ministry that came through the painting was profound. That beautiful young woman was deeply affected by the painting, and her life was changed. She now has the painting that so clearly spoke to her about God's specific love for her.

Such prophetic clarity is needed in Christian artists today. To prophesy with instruments, dance, or song requires more than artistic ability. The church must not become a place for "jam sessions." Rather, it is the setting for the most profound unfolding of God's character and purposes.

> *"Art, in a prophetic sense, makes a highway to God Himself."*

THE SECOND REASON FOR ART—COMMUNICATION BETWEEN GOD AND HIS PEOPLE

The second use of art is to promote and enhance communication between God and His people. It is the role of every artist to declare the heart cries and needs of the people before God. Likewise, the artist must "speak" for God and communicate His thoughts and ways to the people. When we look at all that He has created, the sheer magnificence of His handiwork speaks to us of His awesome power, unfathomable greatness, and infinite mercy.

My former husband, Michael, has always been an excellent singer of prophetic songs. I have seen him bear the burdens of hurting people before the throne of God when they were unable to verbalize the prayers themselves. As a prophet, he was able to "hear" their sorrows and sing a life-changing song of comfort and deliverance from the heart of God.

> *"Art connects mankind with each other and with God."*

THE THIRD REASON FOR ART—GOD CREATES FOR PLEASURE

God was and is creative for the sake of His pleasure. There is nothing wrong with the concept of art as entertainment. After creating a most spectacular and remarkable universe, the Lord stood back and said, "It is good!" He took pleasure in His handiwork.

We can delight in multitudes of exquisite things crafted by God and man. Such joy is a gift from God. Unfortunately, most artists (including Christians) see no more use for their skills than this. Art becomes an end in itself, and the highest goal of an artist, merely to achieve excellence.

As worshipers, the first two reasons for art must always be considered, or we will fall into the trap of limiting our art to worldly concepts of performance, entertainment, and accompaniment. Too many churches have music programs that are founded on these limited principles.

The church organist or choir member, musicians and singers for example, should not view their role as providing entertainment for the people as they enter and exit the church, or mere accompaniment for the congregation as they sing. There is a higher calling upon these artists to declare the very manifest presence of God and His work among His people.

Art makes a highway to God. Our goal is His presence. Even children can function prophetically as able ministers in God's presence, if they have hearts that are dedicated to God and sensitive to His prophetic anointing.

This does not mean that we should abandon all pursuit of excellence and professionalism in our artistic ministries. Quite the contrary. Christian artists should strive to offer God nothing short of their best. The more excellent an artist is, the more tools he/she has to describe the glory and voice of God. If I tried to hold a conversation in Spanish, I would be extremely limited in conversation, because my abilities in Spanish are sadly lacking. If, however, I was able to converse fluently in that language, I could accomplish much. The same applies to the language of arts. When an artist has great skill and applies it to the prophetic realm, magnificent things take place in the presence of God.

I am grateful for churches over the centuries that have made room for the very best of music, art, sculpture, and architecture. Handel, Bach, Michelangelo and countless others were primarily church artists. Their talents spilled from the church into the world so millions could appreciate and cherish their handiwork.

> *"After creating a most spectacular and remarkable universe, the Lord stood back and said, 'It is good!' He took pleasure in his handiwork."*

Many churches today include accomplished artists on staff and in their services.

Art must never become the primary object of our attention in worship. It is not an end in itself, no matter how exceptional it is. Perfect performance will never be the primary goal of the prophetic artist. Rather, he will always set his heart upon uncovering and declaring the glory of God.

While artists need to renew their vision and commitment to

worship, churches must also reassess their theology on how we view the arts. I really appreciate Webber's perspective on the subject:

> One of the great problems within the evangelical culture is a repudiation of the arts in general, and more specifically the failure to employ the arts in worship. This disdain toward the arts is deeply rooted in a view that consigns material things to the devil. The pietistic and fundamentalist backgrounds of modern evangelicalism are addicted to this erroneous view, a dualism that sets the material against the spiritual. ... The visible arts as well as theater, the dance, color, and tangible symbols have historically had a functional role in worship.[14]

It is time for the worshiping Church to pursue excellence in all the arts for the purpose of proclaiming and revealing the glory of God in the earth. God is restoring and redeeming art to its intended place as a prophetic tool of His glorious plan. Let us shout with the psalmists and the prophets: "Make a joyful shout to God, all the earth! Sing out the honor of His name; make His praise glorious" (Ps. 66:1–2).

> Let them praise His name in chorus *and* choir *and* with the [single or group] dance, let them sing praises to Him with the tambourine and lyre! For the Lord takes pleasure in His people; He will beautify the humble with salvation *and* adorn the wretched with victory. Let the saints be joyful in the glory *and* beauty [which God confers upon them] (Ps. 149:3–5, AMP).

A re-defining of arts ministries is in order. For example, if we continue to speak of church musicians as "musicians," then their expectation will be to provide music. Their full prophetic role and potential is so much more. I prefer to think of them as "keepers of the sounds of God," as this is closer to what he/she does. The Lord desires to sing and speak to His Church through His prophetic sounds played on instruments – not just through music. Musicians who have given their spiritual ears to hearing and learning the sounds and songs of God are keepers of the sounds of God. When He shouts, they will know exactly what sound and instrument is needed. When He whispers into the hearts of His people, they will know the tune that carries His gentle voice.

Singers are "keepers of the songs and words of God." Their most important tool is the Word of God since this is where the framework for the songs of God comes from. Those who lead the singing should always have their Bibles handy.

Poets and readers are "keepers of the words of God." Dancers are "keepers of the goings of God." All other visual artists are "keepers of the sight of God." Their job is to describe Him in a way that we can "see" Him.

Again, all artists have the enormous privilege of describing Him in such a way that we can "taste and see that the Lord is good." We carry on our lives the sound and sight of God. Our worship can be smelled by the Lord (Gen. 8:15-22) and should perfume the whole sanctuary and the communities we live in. Music, dances, paintings, poems, songs, and sculptures should carry with them the very hand of God, so that we feel His touch and hear His voice deep in our souls. That is how the arts are prophetic.

I want to list some of the individuals and churches that are ministering with innovative, creative and prophetic worship in these days:

Aaron Strumple - *Coming After You*
(https://youtu.be/842arIaqqBw)
Groups such as **Stikyard** are doing incredibly innovative things with rhythm instruments (https://youtu.be/nBru-sU3apc).
Vertical Church Band – *If I Have You*
(https://youtu.be/ADWchFE0RrE)
Phil Wickham – *This is Amazing Grace / At Your Name / You're Beautiful / The Stand* (https://youtu.be/9adcHWb6IUU)
Samuel Lane – *Look to Jesus*
(https://youtu.be/T5KDd8iFD7A)
SisterBrother – *Be of Good Faith*
(https://youtu.be/ylT18c4s5U0)

Planet Shakers – *Only Way* (https://youtu.be/YcLyvFmIlUs)
Bethel – *Raise a Hallelujah* (https://youtu.be/awkO61T6iok)
Jesus Culture – *One Thing Remains* (https://youtu.be/6_KXsMCJgBQ)
Hillsong United – *King of Kings* (https://youtu.be/dQl4izxPeNU)
Passion – *It is Finished* (https://youtu.be/QkxcGLID3Y8)
Urban and hip-hop worship – (https://youtu.be/bU3W-e-tq5g) or
Lecrae – *Blessings* (https://youtu.be/gu59YLVTfV0)
Gateway Worship – All He Says I Am (https://youtu.be/ra8xwPVNLEw)

Rick Pino – http://rickpino.com
Jason Upton – https://jasonupton.com
Psalmist Raine – https://www.berefresh.com
Joann McFatter – https://joannmcfatter.com
Jason Keith and Sanna Luker – http://www.keithluker.com
Lily Band – www.lilybandmusic.com
Rita Springer – https://www.ritaspringer.com
Don Potter – whttps://www.facebook.com/therealdonpotter/
Ruth Fazel – https://ruthfazal.com
Stephen Roach – https://www.stephenroach.org
Leon Timbo – https://www.leontimbolove.com
Leonard Jones – https://leonardjonesmusic.com
Kim Walker-Smith – https://jesusculture.com/artists/kim-walker-smith/
Misty Edwards – https://www.facebook.com/Misty-Edwards-138391694729/
Jonathan David and Melissa Helser – https://www.jonathanhelser.com
David Ruis – http://rickpino.com
Israel Hougton – https://www.israelhoughton.net
Kimberly and Alberto Rivera – https://kimberlyandalbertorivera.com
Chandler Moore – http://www.chandlerdmoore.com
Matt Gilman – https://en.wikipedia.org/wiki/Matt_Gilman
Cory Asbury – https://bethelmusic.com/artists/cory-asbury/

Kari Jobe – https://www.karijobe.com

Unique and distinct prophetic worship can be found in many churches and worship events, including: Bethel (Redding, CA), Living Waters and the Worship Symposiums (Pasadena, CA), Glory of Zion (Corinth, TX), Whole Life Ministries (Augusta, GA), IHOP and One Thing events (Kansas City, MO and around the world), Living Water (Ashdown, AR), Gathering of Artisans (Ashville, NC), The Mission (Vacaville, CA), Karitos Worship Arts Conferences (Chicago, IL), The Fellowship (Sandy, UT), Throne Zone Conferences, Dance Camp (Charlotte, NC), Morning Star (Charlotte, NC), La Casa (Bogotá, Colombia), and Communidad Cristiana de Fe (Colombia).

I hate to even make lists like these because there are literally thousands more artists and churches where you can find prophetic worship around the world. Prophetic musicians, singers, dancers, artists abound in every nation. Just do an Internet search or go on YouTube, and you will find a plethora of prophetic services and artists. I could never compile an adequate list of prophetic artists. Every style of music can carry God's song over His people and nations.

I must say however, that I am really impressed with the prophetic young worship ministers coming out of IHOP, Bethel, Resound, YWAM, Worship Together, Hillsong, etc.

As you do your own searches, remember that just because someone labels his or her worship as "prophetic" doesn't make it so. Prophetic worship must include the voice, presence, and character of God.

> *"Perfect performance will never be the primary goal of the prophetic artist. Rather, he will always set his eyes upon the ultimate goal of uncovering and declaring the glory of God."*

CHAPTER TWENTY-ONE
RECOGNIZING THE PROPHETIC SOUND IN MUSIC

*Music is a principal means of glorifying
our merciful Creator.*
—Henry Peacham

*Hear attentively the thunder (roar) of His voice,
And the rumbling (sound) that comes from His mouth.*
Job 37:2

The prophetic sound in music is the sound of heaven in our midst. The Lord is fully present in our services whenever we gather, but also, He wants to fill our sanctuaries with the sounds of heaven. He can undoubtedly speak directly with His voice, but regularly, He brings heaven's sounds through the skillful ministry of music, song, dance, flags, etc. He also uses prophets and people in the congregation.

I don't know if you have ever noticed, but God is very noisy, and He is surrounded by the thunderous voices of angels and other heavenly beings. In chapter 24, you can see a comprehensive list of how God's voice is described in the Word. But also:

– Adam and Eve could hear the sound of God walking in the garden (Gen. 3:8).
– God is surrounded by thunder, lightning and earthquakes (Ex. 19:16, 18, 20; Job 37:4-5; Rev. 4:5; 6:1; 14:2).
– When He goes before us into battle, He sounds like a company marching in the tops of the trees (1Chron. 14:15).
– He sounds like a great waterfall (Ps. 42:7).
– God ascends with the sounds of trumpets and shouting (Ps.

- The earth shook when God went before His people in the wilderness (Ps. 68:7-8).
- His glory sounds like the roar of rushing water (Ex. 37:7)
- God sings joyfully over us (Zeph. 3:17).
- Jesus is going to return with power and glory...the heavens will shake, and the sea will roar (Mk. 13:24-27. Lu. 21:25-28).
- The Holy Spirit came on the Day of Pentecost as a mighty rushing wind (Acts 2:2).

Blessed are the people who know the joyful sound
(call to worship)!
They walk, O lord, in the light of Your countenance.
Ps. 89:15

In prophetic worship, we must make way for the sounds of heaven and the sounds of God's voice. As Psalm 89:15 says, we need to discern and know what God is saying and flow with His sound. We hear where He is going in the worship and play the sound of His voice and footsteps. There will be plenty of occasions when the sounds and music are unlike anything you have heard in your church before. The point is that the Lord wants to make Himself known, understood, and heard. During these times He often comes among us as a sound or a song.

THE SOUND OF HEAVEN

Job 36:29 *Indeed, can anyone understand the spreading of clouds, The thunder from His canopy? (The noise from His Tabernacle?)*

Job's friend, Elihu, poses a great question: does anyone understand the thunderous sound of God's voice as he roars from His tabernacle? Can we fathom the purpose for His voice in the earth? God's voice is heard from the thunder of the skies to the tranquility of dawn. The entire universe has been upheld by His voice ever since He spoke and said, "Let there be light." Now His voice and the sounds of His presence continue today, especially in worship.

Through each of us, God's sons, we resound (re-sound) His voice throughout the earth. When musicians, singers, dancers, etc. function as prophetic ministers and not just accompanists of worship, then we will hear the sounds of heaven flowing through them. There is a sound of kingdom dominion that is present when we worship. As the Lord is exalted, His kingdom becomes established in that place.

> *"Through each of us, God's sons, we resound (re-sound) His voice throughout the earth."*

The Word is filled with supernatural songs and sounds that caused a shift in the atmosphere and defiance of natural law to such an extent that magnificent miracles occurred:

- Josh. 6 – Joshua received detailed instructions from God on the use of trumpets and shouts of praise that amazingly brought down an enormous wall around the city of Jericho.
- 1Sam. 16:14-23 – David played the harp when Saul was troubled by a spirit, and Saul was made whole.
- 2Chron. 20:21-22 – King Jehoshaphat appointed singers to go out before the army in battle. Their supernatural songs of praise confused the enemy and resulted in Judah completing a resounding victory in the face of overwhelming odds.
- Ps. 32:7 – God surrounds us with songs of deliverance. Every singer in God's house needs to know how to sing these songs.
- Ps. 40:3 – The Lord filled David's mouth with a new song that caused many to fear and put their trust in the Lord.
- Ps. 42:7-8 – After crying out to the deep waterfalls of God's love, the psalmist sings about the supernatural comfort of God's song that is with us through the night or dark seasons

of our lives. (See also Ps. 77:6).
- Song of Sol. 2:11-12 – The Shulamite tells us of the song that our Bridegroom King sings to turn the season from winter to spring.
- Is. 42:10 – Isaiah calls for worshipers to sing a song "such as has never been heard in the heathen world." (Amp.)
- Hos. 2:14-15 – Hosea spoke of God filling us with songs that turn our wilderness into a vineyard and our trouble into doors of hope. (See also Is. 35:1-2; 51:3).
- Hab. 3:17-19 The Prophet Habakkuk sang a song that took him from despair over Judah's judgment and bad fortune to rejoicing in the Lord and leaping upon the mountains.
- Zeph. 3:17 The last song in the Old Testament is a song of God over His people
- Acts 16:25-26 – Paul and Silas sang hymns while they were in prison. These songs caused a mighty earthquake, and their chains fell off.
- Revelation – This book is filled with supernatural sounds of heaven as elders and angels sing new songs, cry out with loud voices, and use trumpet blasts to unseal the decrees of heaven over the earth.

Singers and musicians have a call to go beyond the song and step into the realm of the supernatural with their music. We are keepers of the sounds of God and keepers of the songs/words of God. Through our worship ministry we bring His songs and sounds into the earth's atmosphere.

I bring a variety of different instruments into worship – not because I want to look clever, but because the unique sounds of each one can carry aspects of God's voice into the earth. I see myself as a priest and intercessor – delivering the prayers and cries of God's people before His throne and then taking God's breath and song and blowing them into the hearts and lives of the listeners.

Wherever we have fought and won victories in our personal lives; and encountered God on a deeply personal level, we now minister with authority and anointing – functioning as supernatural musicians and singers. Out of our victories and encounters with God, we qualify to bring the sound of heaven into the earth and shift the atmosphere over families, cities, and nations.

The Church needs another reformation of worship. Years of tradition have threatened to hold us back from the possibilities of presence-filled music. We seem bound to the sounds and styles of past generations while the secular music and arts progress with each generation.

I go to a lot of different churches around the world and one thing is universal—churches tend to get stuck in major ruts of musical style. Tradition dictates artistic style and greets every degree of change with reluctance and skepticism. Each generation has fought for their music to be heard in the church while previous generations faithfully cling to the musical styles of their teenage years. Some even continue the endless debate, which attempts to confer God's blessing or Satan's inspiration on music.

> As far back as Pope Gregory, the Roman Catholic Church tried to "canonize" music. There are still orders of the Church which wholeheartedly subscribe to the Gregorian chant. ... Other attempts have been made to canonize music.
> ... History indicates that the body which canonizes musical form and style begins to fossilize right there. The very nature of music, which has brought the church much good, demands that it will continue to develop and change. Sometimes we wish it would stop, but it will not.[1]

The end result for every generation is that the worship music and styles of our young people are always soundly condemned and censured, and the prophetic people who attempt to bridge the gap stylistically are silenced. No wonder the Church lags behind the world by about 10 to 15 years in all areas of artistic expression.

It is irrational for us to settle on one particular style and deem others particularly favored by the Almighty himself. Considering how music has changed over the centuries, it is a wonder that we can let ourselves get away with this nonsense. Take King David, for example. Apparently, the Lord approved of his music, and yet it would have sounded nothing like the music of the Early Church, of our grandparent's generation, or the music today. Neither the major nor the minor keys were in use until the 16th Century, so David's songs of praise would have been vastly different from our own. He would have used a melodic scale that would be foreign to our ears, and still the Lord said He loved David, and accepted his praises because he was a man after God's own heart (Acts 13:22).

I have seen massive changes in music over the last 45 years. Most churches did not have worship teams, guitars, drums, video projection systems, dancers, flags, or anything that resembles contemporary worship back in those days. Choruses were simple songs without verses, and the lyrics were usually taken directly from the *King James Bible*. These simple choruses were repeated multiple times. Who knew that this would be a major and difficult change for some people?

In the 70's, the time of singing was referred to as "the song service," and if there was a leader, they were called "song leaders." There was no understanding of worship leaders and teams. Songs had no copyright, and only a few made money on the songs they wrote for the Body of Christ. I remember people leaving churches because pianos were used instead of organs, and drums, guitars, and other instruments made it onto the platform.

Now all of this has changed, and people have a new set of complaints for contemporary worship ministers. Songs often have multiple sections: verses, bridge 1, bridge 2, chorus and a couple of different endings. On a whole, I would say worship is louder than in previous generations; guitarists and keyboardists are more inclined to use effects on their instruments. Unconventional instruments are sometimes used and longer instrumental introductions and interludes are common. Melody lines are more complex, and the lyrics are much more conversational and informal.

Apart from all that, there are huge changes to the worship

atmosphere where lighting, smoke, video screens, staging and backdrops have become an important part of the service. Many churches invest heavily in these areas.

This only goes to show that the worship in our hearts is vastly more important to the Lord than the style of music. Focusing on instruments and style is a complete deviation from the real issues of worship.

There are only a few things the Bible has to say about the style of worship music. According to the book of Psalms, the two most common stylistic recommendations are that music should be: *joyful* (Ps. 5:11; 27:6; 32:11; 35:9; 40:16; 63:5; 66:1; 67:4; 68:3; 81:1; 95:1–2; 98:4, 6; 100:1; 149:5) and *loud* (Ps. 32:11; 33:3; 47:1; 98:4; 150:5). Perhaps an ageless innocence is captured in the simplicity and naiveté of music that is loud and joyous. Certainly, every generation is able to comply with such an unmistakable bidding.

Isaac Watts (17 July 1674 – 25 November 1748) wrote approximately 750 Hymns. He is regarded as the "Father of English Hymnody." Watts wrote some of the most beloved hymns in Christendom. However, in his day, there were many who regarded his work as outrageous. During this time, churches mainly sang out of the Psalms. Watt's famous and much-loved hymn, "When I Survey the Wondrous Cross," was the first introduction to lyrics that used the pronoun "I" from a subjective point of view. Now the *individual* singer of the hymn (as opposed to the congregation) could consider the weight and value of the cross of Jesus Christ. Frank Trotter quotes music historian William Studwell as saying, "This literary license did not please everyone and some felt his hymns were 'too worldly' for the church as they were not based on the Psalms."[2] Trotter goes on:

> There is no doubt that the "popularity of Isaac Watts" hymns caused a tempest in his day...Singing verses that were of 'human composure' (such as "When I Survey the Wondrous Cross") caused great controversy. One man complained, 'Christian congregations have shut out divinely inspired Psalms and taken in Watts' flights of

fancy.' The issue split churches, including one in Bedford, England, that was once pastored by John Bunyan.[3]

If we are to embrace prophetic worship, we must get ready for some dramatic changes in the styles of music we are prepared to include in worship services. The issue of style has the potential to bridge the gap between generations, bring the presence of God and the spirit of revival to the youth of our communities, and extend healing and reconciliation to diverse ethnic groups within our society.

Even more than that, we get to participate in heaven's sounds and watch the impact this has in the earth. All it takes are ears that will become tuned to Heaven's sounds and God songs.

Each move of God in the earth births songs and artistic expressions trumpeting the voice of God. Prophetic artists will pick up new sounds, styles, and messages of God and reinforce His summons to the Church through the arts. When determining the style of worship music, we should not be consumed with our own national, denominational, and generational preferences. We must make room for the voice of the Lord to exceed each of these. As Norm Frederick says, "There is no generation gap in the finishing generation."[4]

There is an age-old debate in the world as to whether art should be a reflection of society or a statement concerning where society is going. A similar debate is needed in the Church, where artists have lingered years behind current trends, "cutting edge" expressions, and the voice of God. This debate relates primarily to prophetic worship.

Consider this question in the light of your church's music and songs: Do we only sing of what He has done in the past, or are our songs a prophetic proclamation of what He is revealing of himself today? The skillful worship leader incorporates songs and musical styles reflecting God's present message without rejecting the rich volume of hymns and songs held dear by his or her congregation.

It is quite possible that some secular artists have tapped into a type of prophetic flow that enables them to express their art in a cutting-edge way. The song, *Yesterday*, written by Beatle, Paul McCartney, has been recorded by over 2200 different artists. McCartney, billed as the most successful songwriter of all time, received this song in a dream.[5]

How much more should anointed Christian artists mark their work with excellence and impact the Church and the world we live in? We must become a reflection of all that Christ has done over the centuries and also give voice to His present work and future glory in the earth.

Churches bound by tradition are content with the same songs year after year. Their understanding of God will not change. I am not advocating that we relinquish all the outstanding Christian music of the past centuries and give ourselves over to a free-for-all in the worship service. But I am calling for us to listen with a prophetic sensitivity to the music of all generations and nations, and more particularly to the sounds of heaven.

Songs and hymns that reinforce what God is saying in the church should remain, but not suppress the voice of God as He draws us on through the sounds of the next generation. We need to be open to the things that God is saying and encourage diversity of expression and musical style to include *all* the generations of our church body.

We must also be open to other art forms in worship such as dance, drama, and mime. There is no reason for ignoring cultural and artistic expressions that have already proven to be powerful tools in the prophetic worship of many churches today. In the end, the arts we use must be those that best reflect what the Lord is saying among us and where He is leading us in this season.

THE POWER OF PRAISE

The Psalms of David and his musicians teach us about the awesome power of praise. There is a prophetic sound of praise that affects every area of our lives – especially when the enemy's torments confront us. Look at this list of the effects of powerful praise. As we fill the atmosphere with the sounds of mighty worship, heaven invades the earth; His kingdom is revealed, and His glory is unleashed upon the earth:

- Praise defeats evil kings and vanquishes ungodly empires—Ps. 2
- Praise delivers nations into our hands and lost peoples into God's Kingdom—Ps. 2:8; 47
- Praise pours trouble and shame upon our enemies—Ps. 6:9-10; 44:4-8; Ps. 132:18
- Praise saves and delivers us from all our enemies—Ps. 7:1-6
- Praise causes strength to arise—Ps. 8:2
- Praise silences the enemy—Ps. 8:2; Matt. 21:16
- Praise makes my enemies fall down and perish—Ps. 9:1-3
- Praise makes a place of refuge and defense in times of trouble—Ps. 9:9-10; 59:16-17; 91:1-2; 94:22
- Praise destroys evil nations and brings justice to the fatherless and oppressed—Ps. 10:16-18
- Praise releases the captives—Ps. 14:7
- Praise unleashes hope—Ps. 16:8-9
- Praise fuels complete and abundant joy in times of suffering—Ps. 16:10-11
- Praise steers us away from the path of the destroyer and keeps our feet from stumbling—Ps. 17:4-5
- Praise brings salvation from all my enemies—Ps. 18:3
- Praise makes sure our voice is heard by the Lord in times of distress—Ps. 18:6
- Praise ensures our deliverance from strong enemies because He delights in us—Ps. 18:16-19
- Praise arms us with strength for the battle—Ps. 18:32, 39; 37:39

> *"There is a prophetic sound of praise that affects every area of our lives – especially when the enemy's torments confront us."*

Recognizing the Prophetic Sound in Music

- Praise lifts us to God's high places and makes our feet as swift and sure as the deer—Ps. 18:33
- Praise equips our hands for battle—Ps. 18:34
- Praise grants us victory over the enemy and makes our feet trample his neck—Ps. 18:37-40
- Praise shows us how the Lord deals with those who try to harm us—Ps. 18:47
- Praise is our source of strength and help—Ps. 20:1-3
- Praise lays the foundation for our total restoration—Ps. 23:3; 80:3, 7, 19
- Praise guards us from shame—Ps. 25:1-3
- Praise vindicates us (proves us to be correct or free from blame)—Ps. 26:1; 54:1-7
- Praise drives out fear - replaces it with confidence—Ps. 27:1-3; 56:11; 91:5-8
- Praise creates a secret hiding place in times of trouble—Ps. 27:5
- Praise lifts up our heads above our enemies—Ps. 27:6
- Praise keeps us on God's path and brings us confidence—Ps. 27:11-13
- Praise forms God's strength and shield inside our hearts—Ps. 28:7
- Praise nullifies the wisdom and counsel of the wicked—Ps. 33:190
- Praise cuts off the authority and power of evildoers and brings us into our inheritance—Ps. 37:9; 69:35-36
- Praise leads the ungodly into relationship with the Lord—Ps. 40:3
- Praise picks us up from discouragement and replaces it with hope—Ps. 43:5
- Praise leads us out of captivity—Ps. 53:6; 68:18
- Praise brings God's salvation and peace in the midst of battle—Ps. 55:16-18
- Praise sustains us—Ps. 55:22

- Praise turns back our enemies—Ps. 56:9
- Praise creates a place of refuge under His wings—Ps. 57:1
- Praise permits us to hear God laughing at our enemies, and see His victories on our behalf—Ps. 59:8-10
- Praise supplies us with valor—Ps. 60:12; Ps. 108:13
- Praise provides us with a shelter and strong tower of safety from our enemy—Ps. 61; 62:5-8; 91:1-2; 144:2
- Praise preserves our lives from fear, secret plots, and the sharpened tongues of the wicked—Ps. 64:1-9
- Praise accompanies God as He arises and scatters His enemies—Ps. 68:1
- Praise shows us the complete destruction of the enemy—Ps. 73:17-19
- Praise reveals God's mighty arm and powerful right hand that strengthens us—Ps. 89:13, 20-23; 98:1
- Praise stands us up against evil—Ps. 91:10; 140:1-8
- Praise releases God's angels to guard and protect us—Ps. 91:11-12
- Praise places God's authority in our feet to trample upon the enemy—Ps. 91:13
- Praise brings our voice before the Lord and opens our ears for His reply—Ps. 91:15
- Praise assures us of God's presence and deliverance in times of trouble—Ps. 91:15
- Praise causes the fear of God to fill the earth, and the nations to tremble before Him—Ps. 96:1, 7
- Praise increases us and makes us stronger than our enemies—Ps. 105:24
- Praise redeems us from the hand of the enemy and gathers us from far away—Ps. 107:1-3
- Praise brings us out of darkness and death, and breaks our chains—Ps. 107:14
- Praise ushers the Lord to the right hand of the poor and saves them from their accusers—Ps. 109:30-31

- Praise prepares us to rule our enemies—Ps. 110:1-2
- Praise turns us into overcomers despite overwhelming odds—Ps. 118:1-14
- Praise lifts our eyes to the Lord who is our help—Ps. 121:1-2
- Praise preserves our going out and coming in forever—Ps. 121:7-8
- Praise turns back our captivity and fills our mouths with laughter and singing—Ps. 126:1-3
- Praise assembles our children as warriors of the Lord—Ps. 127:3-5
- Praise revives us in the midst of trouble—Ps. 138:7
- Praise covers our heads in the day of battle—Ps. 140:7
- Praise opens the way for justice to be ministered to the poor and afflicted—Ps. 140:12
- Praise opens up the path of safety when we are overwhelmed—Ps. 142:1-6
- Praise releases us from prison—Ps. 142:7
- Praise revives us after the enemy has persecuted, crushed and overwhelmed us—Ps. 143
- Praise trains our hands for war and our fingers for battle—Ps. 144:1
- Praise rescues us from liars—Ps. 144:9-11
- Praise gives us authority and dominion in the nations – Ps. 149:6-9
- Praise delivers us from our enemies and lifts us up above those who are against us—Ps. 18:48-50; 143:9
- Praise delivers us from all fear, all trouble, all afflictions—Ps. 34:4, 17, 19; 38:40; 41:1; 50:15; 59:1; 56:3-4
- Praise delivers us from injustice—Ps. 43
- Praise delivers us from death and keeps us from falling—Ps. 56:13
- Praise delivers us from cruel, and murderous sinners—Ps. 59:1-2, 16-17; 71:4
- Praise delivers us from poverty and oppression—Ps. 72:12-

15; 76:9; 82:4
- Praise delivers us from every trap and plague—Ps. 91:3; 140:4-5
- Praise delivers us from false accusation; lies and deceit—Ps. 120; 144:1-11
- Praise delivers us from trouble and distress—Ps. 107:6, 13
- Praise delivers us from destruction—Ps. 107:20

Chapter Twenty-Two

The Maturity of Worshipers

*Worship is a vital key to personal change.
It is the very essence of maturation.
Worship is not simply human activity,
but rather an encounter with a living God.*
—Sam Sasser

Worship is one of the most exposing things we engage in. To truly worship, we must pour out our hearts before the Lord with vulnerability, honesty, and transparency. It is an act of spiritual maturity. Immature Christians will be more comfortable with the same routine in worship week by week where they know what is going to happen from beginning to end with little required of them.

> *"Although we are servants and sons of God, we are also His Bride. It is time for us to act like a bride and not children who must have everything done for us." It is the bride who must make herself ready."*

Time to Grow Up

The Holy Spirit calls us to grow up and experience greater degrees of victory over our enemies, greater intimacy with Christ, death to self, and service to one another. This maturity is for the entire Body of Christ.

Mature Christians read the Bible rather than seek blessings; find God in prayer rather than through endless prophetic words; lay hold of God rather than always wanting hands laid on them;

pursue His presence rather than preachers; and follow the Lord's will rather than their own.

THE ROYAL BRIDE PREPARES HERSELF

Many believers agree that we are in the final hours of the Church Age here on earth. Exactly how many months or years will pass before Christ's return is uncertain, but the reality of His coming seems to be near. One sign of His return will be the maturity and promotion of the Church to the position of His bride. Although we are servants and children of God, we are also His bride. It is time for us to act like a bride and not children who must have everything done for us. It is the bride who must make *herself* ready, "Let us be glad and rejoice and give Him glory, for the marriage of the Lamb has come, and His wife has made herself ready" (Rev. 19:7).

We must become an Esther Church, clothed in royal robes and found standing in the inner court of the king's palace (Es. 5:1–3). Esther knew that she lived a life of destiny—that she was in the kingdom "for such a time as this" (Es. 4:14). He is waiting for us to appear before Him in our royal apparel. Garments of self must be peeled off, and we must be clothed with Christ and His nature (Col. 3:8–14).

Recall how Ruth prepared herself for Boaz (Ruth 3:3–8). She washed, anointed, and clothed herself, then lay down at his feet. At midnight, Boaz stirred himself and found a woman lying at his feet.

I would like to suggest that Ruth here represents the Church who waits for her Kinsman-Redeemer (Christ) to recognize her. Each of us pays the price for our own washing, anointing, and clothing. Christ has provided a way for us to be formed into His likeness while we wait before Him as a mature woman ready for her Boaz.

THE BRIDE AND THE BRIDEGROOM

The bride of Christ can recognize His voice, know how to

respond appropriately in worship, look and act like a mature woman, die to self, and be ready for greater depths of intimacy. We only need to read the Song of Solomon to see the extent of God's purposes for those who profess to love Him. He has every intention of drawing the Church into the most intimate of all relationships: marriage. We will rule with Him throughout eternity as those who have overcome and entered into a marriage relationship with Him.

The song of the bride and the Bridegroom constitutes one of the great themes of worship. More and more songs are being written about this aspect of our encounter with Him. But the Lord is calling us to push past sentimental feelings to the full maturity of bridal love. I love the chorus to *10,000 Reasons, (Bless the Lord)* by Jonas Myrin and Matt Redman.[1] Check out these verses:

> The sun comes up, it's a new day dawning
> It's time to sing Your song again
> Whatever may pass, and whatever lies before me
> Let me be singing when the evening comes.
>
> And on that day when my strength is failing
> The end draws near and my time has come
> Still my soul will sing Your praise unending
> Ten thousand years and then forevermore.

It takes maturity to walk in the truths of this song. If we want to worship with words like this, we need to live them throughout the week. Eternal worship begins with consistent and unshakable worship today.

> *"Worship is one of the most exposing things we can every engage in as humans."*

ENCOUNTERING GOD

Worship is an encounter with the awesome and holy God who reveals himself to His people. Prophetic worship provokes us to continued death, change, spiritual growth, and maturity. Prophetic worship is not possible unless the congregation is committed to such advancement. Otherwise, worship will remain a ritual rather than an encounter.

An encounter with God is crucial to the worship experience. Believers should come to the worship service with the expectation that the Lord will meet them personally. As we have seen in previous chapters, Paul speaks of this when he says, "But *we all*, with open face, beholding as in a mirror the glory of the Lord, are being transformed into the same image from glory to glory, just as by the Spirit of the Lord." (2Cor. 3:18). Wardle comments on this passage:

> People often do not encounter God in worship. This problem is by far the most devastating. Sunday after Sunday, people leave church without sensing the presence of God in worship. The entire experience becomes an exercise in human effort. Where and when this is true, people leave the service much as they entered. They are unchanged, uninspired, and unprepared to serve Christ in the marketplace of daily living.[2]

The mature believer understands that we do not come to church to *get* the presence of God—we come to church *carrying* the presence of God. When we live and move in Him (Acts 17:28), we become "people of the Presence." We are those willing to make the costly and meaningful changes true relationship brings. Mature worshipers know that beholding Him will result in the death of self, which produces His likeness.

> *"The sight of ourselves in the light of His glory and holiness can truly be devastating."*

The "beholding" is for all of us, but the costly aspect is that the sight of God often involves the sight of self—and the sight of ourselves in the light of His glory and holiness can be devastating.

When we behold Him, we have the opportunity to glimpse

something of ourselves that we may never have seen or understood before—or been willing to face. But if we face the truth steadfastly, not turning away, we will find Him again— standing at the end of all our ugliness and failures, ready to redeem and restore every dark and broken place within. The final outcome of this holy encounter is that we are changed from glory to glory.

Despite the glorious transformation offered us, change is still difficult and often frightening. One reason is that the Lord seems to zero in on deeply held personal problems and our sinful solutions to the devastations of our lives. I lost my mother when I was a young baby. This resulted in deep, inner brokenness and behavior in my life that violated my personal code of ethics. I don't believe in blaming everything on past hurts. I am personally responsible for the choices I made. But as we look deep within, we can find some answers to issues we face. I maintain that a personal encounter with God can bring profound healing and lasting restoration. This is exactly what happened to me as I sought the Lord over my inner struggles. He visited me in a type of vision as I was worshiping. The Lord showed me the moment of my conception, and how He had formed me in my mother's womb. I immediately knew that He had determined that I should exist, and that He had an eternal purpose for my life. I will never forget this encounter and the ongoing healing that I experienced in worship.

Only with the knowledge and experience of grace can the process of change become a joy, and only when we are prepared to mature will we offer ourselves for this difficult course. This is not to say that prophetic worship leaves a congregation in a place of insecurity and uncertainty—quite the opposite. There is nothing more secure than to have our eyes fixed upon the Almighty as we rest under His shadow.

Physical maturity is not necessarily related to spiritual maturity. For six years, I had the privilege of leading weekly chapel services for kindergarten to sixth grade students at a Christian Academy. These young people became skilled in ministering prophetically. They learned to sing prophetic songs, pray for the sick, receive words of knowledge, and prophesy.

When a wind of revival blew through our church in the spring, it was the children who first received God's outpouring. Many were "caught up" into heaven in visions; some began to quote scriptures they had never learned. They waited upon the Lord for hours in worship and intercession, saw miraculous answers to prayer, and allowed the Lord to convict them of sin and hypocrisies.

This is a valuable lesson. It is not our youthfulness, inexperience, or lack of Bible knowledge that preempts the work of God in our lives, but stubborn resistance and hard-heartedness to His Spirit. May each of us be as bold as these children as we encounter the Lord Almighty.

A Pastoral Dilemma

Former American President Calvin Coolidge said, "It is only when men begin to worship that they begin to grow."[3] Pastors are faced with the responsibility of bringing their congregation to the place of mature worship. We may have experienced services where immature believers have "prophesied" crazy things, or the expressions of worship have been inappropriate in some way. For fear of these things, some pastors are tempted to curb opportunities for participation, restricting all worship expressions and exercise of the spiritual gifts to the religious professionals. Or they may prefer to opt out of any congregational participation in public ministry altogether. "Many believers have accepted the power of God in theory but have rejected it in practice. Fearing wild fire, congregations have opted for no fire at all."[4]

However, with regular teaching and practical training, God's people can quickly come to a place of proficiency and confidence in all aspects of prophetic worship. The Lord doesn't intend for His presence to be an unsolvable puzzle. Rather, He invites us all into the joy and simplicity of personal and corporate communion. In order for the saints to be adequately equipped to minister effectively and prophetically in worship (Eph. 4:11–12), the following needs to occur:

- Time needs to be given to regular training in worship.
- Opportunities must be opened up in every service for the people to actively participate in worship.
- We must make provision for believers to make mistakes from time to time without "shaming" them into non-participation.
- Experienced leaders must occasionally step aside and allow others to lead and exercise their giftings. People will rise only to the level of their leaders' expectations.
- Loving and constructive correction and encouragement must be given to those who minister in any capacity during the service.

It may be helpful for a microphone to be placed near the front of the congregational seating, where all are invited to contribute to the service what they feel the Lord has given them. Each must first consult with one of the pastors/elders stationed there as to the content of their message and the best time to give it. At the appropriate time in the service, they are invited to share their scripture, testimony, song, prophecy, or other leading. This is beautifully modeled by *The Fellowship* in Salt Lake City, Utah.

This model would be easy for any church to adapt for congregational participation. If someone makes a mistake and, undoubtedly, there will be mistakes, this also becomes part of the maturing process. Our standard for maturity must be measured by the scripture, which I used previously. "How is it then, brethren? Whenever you come together, each of you has a psalm, has a teaching, has a tongue, has a revelation, has an interpretation. Let all things be done for edification" (1Cor. 14:26).

> *"Every pastor is faced with the responsibility of bringing his or her congregation to the place of maturity in worship."*

Every pastor is faced with this choice: *Should I do all the work myself—preaching, prophesying, controlling the worship service, organizing the music ministry, doing the announcements, and so on? Or, should I invest my time in training each member of the church to serve the body and flow maturely, correctly, and deeply in prophetic worship?*

My conclusion—voiced with great sadness—is that most pastors have chosen the former route, either doing everything themselves or giving over control of their services entirely to a group of paid professionals.

THE WORSHIP TEAM MUST COME TO MATURITY

The worship leader(s), the singers, musicians, dancers, and any other worship artists must pay the price for maturity. Prophetic worship is impossible unless these ministers become students of the presence of God as well as of their craft.

They can learn to embrace the prophetic anointing that comes with their artistic gifting and yield to the full cost of prophetic responsibility. There is much more to being an able minister of the presence of God than having ability in music and the arts. It costs our time and effort to develop any artistic skill, but it costs our lives if we want to be adept at communing with God and ministering His voice or song prophetically in the midst of the congregation (Ex. 20:19).

In the Hebraic tradition, all worship ministers, from the reign of King David on, were trained in prophetic worship. Young men and women were trained under their fathers to prophesy both in song and with their instruments. Thus, they were able to minister prophetically at the command of the king (1Chron. 25:1–8). It appears that there was no such thing as a temple musician who was not skilled in both music and the prophetic realm. This should serve as an example to those of us who would minister in worship.

Maturity is born out of our private place of devotion to God, the place of His presence created in our hearts. It is a place of continual communion. "We are mobile temples of worship."[5]

The Maturity of Worshipers

There are a few things that the worship team can do to prepare themselves for prophetic worship:

- Practice flowing in prophetic music and song during your rehearsal times. David's teams were trained by their fathers for ministry before the Lord (1Chron. 25:6). They were expected to be skillful *and* prophetic. We tend to focus on the "skillful" part of the equation and forget to prepare ourselves for prophetic ministry.
- Come to every service prepared to minister the sounds and songs of God.
- Study the Word of God and allow the Word to be a foundation for all of your ministry. Take the Word with you when you stand in your place of ministry.
- Make room in the service for the presence and voice of God. Don't fill the entire worship segment of the service with songs; learn how to linger in His presence. Practice waiting in the presence of God—stay longer than is expected.
- Become a life-long student of the presence of God. Imagine what worship would be like if we were as diligent at studying the character of God as we are at studying our music and arts.

We do not have to be perfect in order to lead others in worship "It is the simplicity and purity of devotion to Christ that must be the springboard for everything that we do."[6]

Christian maturity must be gauged by the depth and reality of our personal relationship with the Lord and our obedience to His claims upon our hearts. Our Christianity is expressed more in our everyday lives than it is in our public performances. We must begin to see ourselves as living temples of His presence and ministers of His glory in the earth.

Let me summarize this way...in order for any church to move forward in prophetic worship, three groups of people *must* move forward together and mature in worship:

1. The pastor(s) and leaders who are responsible for birthing and releasing prophetic worship Biblically and theologically.
2. The worship team who are responsible for releasing prophetic worship musically, artistically and experientially.
3. The congregation who are responsible for embracing prophetic worship and unleashing its full potential upon their lives and communities.

Only when these three groups combine can prophetic worship reach its full potential and transform individuals, cities, states and nations; shift atmospheres; release the roar of God into multi-generational, multi-cultural situations; prepare the Church for full-blown revival and transport her into the uncompromising, pervasive hospitality of God on a regular basis.

Chapter Twenty-Three
Individual Experience vs. a Corporate Journey

*A church breathes through its worship system!
The vitality of a local church is linked to its devotion.*
—Ernest Gentile

There is a difference between our personal worship experience with the Lord and our corporate worship experience. In our personal worship, the communication is one-to-One. He speaks to us and deals with us on an individual level. When we gather for corporate worship, we are going before the Lord as a group—a family. We need the other members of the Body of Christ as much as our physical bodies need their many parts. His glory is seen, and His voice is heard through our brothers and sisters. They become His hands moving in ministry among us.

In corporate worship, we cannot hold to a personal agenda or remain a separate entity, worshiping in our own way. For we are a spiritual house made up of living stones (1Pet. 2:4– 5); *one* Church made up of *many* dynamic individuals.

The usual layout of church sanctuaries is understandable. We seat people in rows so that more can fit into our buildings. This fosters an audience mentality, making it possible for individuals to hide and scarcely participate in the worship. I love the way my present church (Living Water of Ashdown, Arkansas) has put all the most comfortable chairs they can find into a circle so that everyone can feel like a part of the whole.

Foster encourages corporate submission:

> The language of the gathered fellowship is not "I," but "we." There is a submission to the ways of God. There is a submission to one another in the Christian fellowship. There is a desire for God's life to rise up in the group, not just within the individual.[1]

Kendrick bemoans the imbalance of individuality within community.

> Worship has become tailored to individuality rather than community, and instead we have diplomatically learned to avoid anything that might upset the *status quo* of separation. We sit in rows facing the front of the building and stare at each other's heads as if to watch a performance or a show.[2]

CORPORATE WORSHIP AND THE PROPHETIC ANOINTING

Because of the relationship of commitment and covenant that we have with one another, our encounter with God is strengthened when we gather. As we participate in worship, the Holy Spirit delights in drawing upon each individual, as a master conductor directs a symphony. Each person must function in their gifting in order for congregational worship to journey into the knowledge of Him. "Worship generally reaches higher levels of expression when a body of believers is worshipping together."[3]

> "Because of the relationship of commitment and covenant that we have with one another, our encounter with God is strengthened when we gather."

The Lord stands in the midst of the congregation (Ps. 82:1) and calls. We relate and respond to Him as one. Observe the following examples where we see the Lord treating a body of people as if they were one man, where we see God's call upon us to become one and flow in worship as a unified people.

- The children of Israel went through the wilderness together as one group, not individual tribes. They were delivered (Ex. 12, 14); blessed (Gen. 12:3); fed (Ex. 16:10–36); visited by God (Ex. 19–20); and punished (Joshua 7) as one.
- The Book of Psalms calls for unified praise and worship from the whole congregation: Ps. 47:1; 67:3; 97:6; 106:48; 107:32; 111:1; 149:1.
- In Paul's instructions on congregational worship (1Cor. 11–14), he calls for us to consider ourselves as one, each one taking part in the service (1Cor. 14:26).

I am not saying that all worship is *exclusively* a congregational journey. Certainly, the Lord ministers in a dramatic way to individuals during a service. Our focus includes a broader perspective. Wherever the Lord takes us in worship, we must go together.

Many Christians get offended with worship leaders who ask for congregational participation and response such as the clapping or lifting of hands. If we allow this attitude to continue and grow, the congregation will become just an assembly of individuals, experiencing God (or not) in different ways and on different levels throughout the service. They will never see themselves as parts of a whole.

Although this situation is prevalent today, it is not God's best for His people. Corporate worship with true prophetic anointing becomes difficult to achieve only when our rebellious human nature stands in the way, not because of any barriers God has raised. We are a people who insist on having things our own way. The rights of individuals reign supreme in our Western world.

For example, in our personal devotional time with the Lord, He might be dealing with us about things in our lives that need to be changed, or we may be enduring a time of sadness or struggle. But when we join our congregation for worship, these intensely personal experiences need to be put aside, lest they hinder us from entering into the fullness of His presence and working.

It is always amazing to me to look out on a congregation—no matter what its size—and see how the Lord has melded individuals together. There are often folk from many different socio-economic, ethnic, generational, and intellectual groups joined together as one. We might not even choose one another as friends in another setting, but as Christians, the Lord has made us family. What joy it is to see unity grow in a corporate prophetic anointing.

I refer to corporate worship as a "journey into God," because the Lord actually invites us to enter His presence and go somewhere with Him. For example, He might speak to the congregation through an individual that He is the Lion of Judah who leads us into battle. The musicians may be inspired to play the sounds of the war using drums, trumpets, violent rhythms, etc. Someone might step to the front and share a scripture revealing God's call to war (Ps. 18:31-43; 149:5-9; 2Chron. 20:14-17; Rev. 1:13-16). A singer may follow with a song based on one of these scriptures and include further revelation they have received as they have known the warrior King in their personal lives.

The journey continues as dancer(s) or mime(s) depict the Lord battling on our behalf. A pastor may then invite those who are facing trials to the front for prayer. Maybe the Lord will have the congregation go to war on behalf of nations, cities, individuals, families, etc. Prophetic intercession begins, and great things are accomplished in the Kingdom.

By the end of such a service, every member of the congregation can feel like they have contributed to the revelation of God. Each believer should leave the service strengthened with more of God in their heart. The effects of such an encounter ring in our hearts forever.

Personal Devotion

In emphasizing corporate worship, I do not mean to diminish the need for a growing depth of personal worship and relationship with God. Individual devotion enhances corporate worship, and our corporate worship encourages our personal relationship with God. We are worshipers every day of our lives, in every situation.

Our individual communion with the Lord should strengthen others. The stronger we are in our daily walk with Christ, the more we will be able to build up the rest of the Church and those who do not know Christ.

Any extreme is wrong. Forsaking the Church community and corporate worship is dangerous for any believer, while a lack of personal devotion to God will ultimately produce spiritual death.

The idea in worship is that we see ourselves as a group of people who are on a journey into God. Each one important and each one, from the youngest to the oldest, has a vital part to play. The Lord often draws from the wealth of our personal communion with Him to speak into the corporate worship service. "Social religion is perfected when private religion is purified."[4]

The success of corporate worship depends upon the authentic devotion of individuals and their ability to grow together as a sincere, worshiping community.

> *"Our public worship must always flow out of our personal devotion."*

Chapter Twenty-Four
Hearing The Voice of God in Worship

We don't ever need to be afraid of the voice of God, unless we have already decided to disobey Him.
—Anonymous

It is unthinkable to have prophetic worship without regularly hearing the voice of God. His voice is sweet, and for those who have taken time to know Him, it is easily heard. "My sheep hear my voice, and I know them, and they follow me" (John 10:27). God's voice must be obeyed (Ex. 19:5; 23:22; Deut. 13:4) especially in worship. Every prompting and whisper of the Lord in worship leads us into the knowledge of God.

Hearing the voice of God is part of what we describe as *an encounter with God.* Prophetic worship is dependent upon such an encounter, upon hearing and knowing His voice. I wonder, on how many occasions does God desire to speak to us, but our ears are deaf and our eyes dull to His prophetic presence? "God often visits us, but most of the time we are not at home."[1]

> "It is not possible to have prophetic worship without hearing the Voice of God."

One reason we fail to hear God's voice is that we do not recognize it. There are nearly 1,000 references in Scripture referring to God speaking in some way to His people. The following scriptures describe the variety of sounds that God's voice makes. As you read these scriptures, consider the volume and quality of God's voice.

- He was heard by Adam and Eve. (Gen. 3:10 is the first mention of the word "voice" in the Bible.) Numerous people in the Old and New Testaments heard God's audible voice.
- He creates with His voice (Gen. 1:3–26; Ps. 29:4–9; 33:6, 9; Jer. 10:13; 51:16).
- He spoke face to face with Moses (Ex. 19:19; 33:11; Acts 7:31) – Also accompanied by a long, loud trumpet (Ex. 19:16).
- He has a voice that is preceded by a loud trumpet (Ex. 20:19).
- He has a voice that can cause death (Ex. 19:19; Deut. 5:25-26; 18:16).
- He speaks with His voice from above the Mercy Seat (Num. 7:89).
- He speaks in fire (Deut. 4:12, 15, 33, 36; 5:22, 24 26; Mk. 12:26).
- He speaks out of thick darkness (Deut. 5:22-23).
- He has a still, small voice (1Ki. 19:12)
- He spoke audibly to Samuel (1Sam. 3)
- He thunders with His voice (2Sam. 22:14; Job 37:2, 4–5; 40:9; Ps. 18:13; 29:3; 77:18; 104:7; Rev. 14:2).
- He shouts and cries out loudly (Ps. 47:5; Is. 42:13).
- He has a powerful voice (Ps. 29:4).
- He has a majestic voice (Ps. 29:4.)
- He has a voice that shatters trees (Ps. 29:5).
- He has a voice that divides flames (Ps. 29:7).
- He has a voice that shakes the wilderness (Ps. 29:8).
- He has a voice that causes the deer to give birth (Ps. 29:9).

- He has a voice that strips everything off the trees (Ps. 29:9).
- He has a voice that melts the earth (Ps. 46:6).
- He has a mighty voice (Ps. 68:33).
- He has a voice that came out of the cloudy pillar (Ps. 99:7).
- He has a voice that spoke and plagues came to His enemies (Ps. 105:31, 34).
- He has a voice that commands the waters (Ps. 104 7).
- He has a voice that comes over the mountains (Song of Sol. 2:8).
- He has a sweet voice (Song of Sol. 2:14).
- He has a voice that comes knocking and calling for us as we sleep (Song of Sol. 5:2).
- He has a glorious voice (Is. 30:30).
- He has a voice that can destroy the enemy (Is. 30:31).
- He utters His voice and there is a tumult (multitude) of waters in the heavens (Jer. 10:13).
- He roars with His voice (Job 37:4; Is. 42:13; Jer. 25:30; Hos. 11:10; Joel 3:16; Amos 1:2).
- He shouts with His voice (Jer. 25:30).
- He has a voice like many waters (Ez. 1:24; 43:2; Rev. 14:2).
- He has a voice like the noise of an army (Ez. 1:24).
- He has a loud voice (Ez. 9:1).
- He has a voice that sounds like the wings of the cherubim (Ez. 10:5).
- He has a voice like the sound of a multitude (Dan. 10:6).
- He roars with His voice through His people (Joel 3:16; Amos 1:2).
- He spoke to the fish and made it spit Jonah out (Jonah 1:10).
- He cries with His voice over a city (Micah 6:9).
- He has a terrifying voice (Hab. 3:16).
- He sings and rejoices over us (Zeph. 3:17).

- He spoke audibly to the prophets throughout the Old Testament.
- He spoke audibly to Jesus and all who were with Him (Matt. 3:17; 17:5; Mk. 1:11; 9:7; Lk. 3:22; 9:35; Jn. 12:28-30).
- He spoke audibly out of a cloud (Mk. 9:7).
- He spoke audibly to Saul of Tarsus (Acts 9:5, 7; 22:7-8; 26:14).
- He spoke audibly to Peter (Acts 10:13-15; 2Pet. 1:18).
- He spoke audibly to John (Rev. 1:10).
- He has a voice that will be heard by the dead (Jn. 5:25, 28; 11:43).
- He has a shouting voice (1 Thess. 4:16).
- He shakes the earth with His voice (Heb. 12:26).
- He has a voice that cries out and knocks at the door of our hearts (Rev. 3:20).
- He has a voice like a trumpet (Rev. 4:1).

God's Voice is Heard in Many different Ways

It is clear from Scripture that God spoke often to His people and His prophets by way of an audible voice (for example, see: 1Sam. 3:4, 6, 10; 1Ki. 8:15; Ezek. 37:3). I have listed below some of the other ways that God speaks to us:

- Personal prayer and communion with God—2Chron. 7:12–16; 2Cor. 13:14: Ps. 141:2; Matt. 6:9–13; Lk. 3:21; 11:2–4; Acts 4:31; 16:25; 1Cor. 14:15; Jas. 5:13, 16; 1Pet. 3:12; Jude 20.
- Spirit of the Lord—2Sam. 23:2
- Out of a whirlwind—Job 38:1; Job 40:6
- Angels—Gen. 31:11; Num. 22:31:35; Jud. 6:12; Zech. 1:14; Lk. 1:13, 19, 28; Acts 8:26; 27:23
- A heavenly voice—Jn. 12:28; Acts 10:13, 15

- Dreams—Gen. 31:11, 24; 37:5, 40:8-41:39; 1Sam. 28:6; Dan. 2; Matt. 1:20
- Visions—Gen. 46:2; Is. 1:1; Jer. 1:2–4; Ez. 1:1; Am. 3:7; Hab. 2:2; Acts 9:10; 10:3; 11:5; 16:9-10; 18:9; 1Cor. 14:3; Heb. 1:1
- Signs—Ex. 10:2; Jud. 6:17, 36-40; John 3:2
- A face to face encounter—Ex. 33:11
- Through the Urim—Num. 27:21; 1Sam. 28:6
- Mouth to mouth—Num. 12:8
- Words which are seen—Amos 1:1
- Unusual manifestations: A donkey and a hand—Num. 22:28–30; Dan. 5:5, 24-28. The main thing we can learn from these two instances is that the Lord can use anything to convey His message to us.
- Prophets—1Sam. 9:9; 28:6; 2Kgs. 3:11; 2Kgs. 21:10; Matt. 1:22; 2:15; 3:3; 1Cor. 14:3–5; Heb. 1:1; James 5:10
- Seers—1Chron. 21:9; 25:5
- Various Arts
    - Prophetic songs—1Chron. 25:1–7; Eph. 5:19; Col. 3:16; 1Cor. 14:15
    - Musical instruments—1Chron. 25:1-7
    - Mime/drama/storytelling/poetry: Ez. 37:1-15; Psalms and other poetry books: Lk. 15
    - The arts that beautify the house of God and reveal His nature there: Ex. 25:8-9; 35:4-19, 35:30-39
    - Dance: 2 Sam. 6:14; Ps. 149:3; 150:4
- The Word— Ex. 24:7; Neh. 8:1–12; Ps. 19:7; 119:24, 162; Jer. 30:2; Matt. 3:1–3; Mk. 1:14; Acts 4:4, 31; 10:44; 24:14; Rom. 10:15, 17; 1Cor. 1:17, 23; Col. 3:16; 1Tim. 4:13; 2Tim. 2:15; 4:2; Heb. 4:12; 1 Jn. 2:14; 5:7; Rev. 1:3
    - The preached Word of God
    - The written Word of God

- The prophesied word of God
- Wise counsel—Prov. 1:5; 2:6; 3:13; 11:14; 19:21; Acts 20:27
- Symbolic acts—Hos. 1-3; Ez. 3:15; 4:1-3; 4:4-8; 4:9-17; 5:1-4
- Symbolic events:
  - Baptism, Matt. 3:13–17; Mk. 1:9–11; Lk. 3:21–22; Jn. 1:31–34; Acts 2:38; 19:5
  - Laying on of hands, Acts 8:17; 19:6
  - Processions, 1Chron. 13:5_8; Ps. 68:24-27; Matt. 21:1-9; Mk. 11:1-10; Jn. 12:12-15; Rev. 14:1-4; 19:11-14
- The service (liturgy), communion, and the body ministry or fellowship that follows—Acts 2:42-47; 4:32-35; 20:7, 11; 1 Cor. 10:16; 11:23-26; 14:26. Sacraments—Lk. 24:35
- Tongues, interpretation, prophecy and other gifts of the Holy Spirit—Acts 2:11; 19:6; 1Cor. 12:8, 14; 14:3–5; 22–31. These gifts help us to see, hear, and interact with the Lord.
- Praise and worship—1Cor. 14:24-25; Ps. 95:6; 138:2; Jn. 4:23; 1Cor. 14:24-25
- Preaching, parables and stories—Acts 4:29, 31; Rom. 16:25; 1Thess. 2:13; Titus 1:3
- Parables and mysteries—Mk. 2:2; 4:33; Lk. 8:11; 1Cor. 2:7
- Creation—Matt. 2:1-2; Rom. 1:20
- Silence—Ps. 65:1 (Amp); Hab. 2:20; Acts 11:18; Rev 8:1.
- Acts or services of dedication and repentance—2Chron. 7:1–11; Lk. 15:10; Acts 2:38; 3:19; 2Cor. 7:10–11.
  - Altar calls
  - Special public prayers, such as healing prayer

You know you are hearing the voice of God when you hear these things:

- He gives instruction in righteousness (2Tim. 3:16).
- He gives correction in righteousness (2Tim. 3:16; Prov. 3:11-12).
- He causes you to profit in Christ (2Tim. 3:16; Jn. 15:16).
- He brings to your remembrance the Word of God (Jn. 14:26).
- He guides you into Truth, (Jn. 16:13)
- He exhorts you, (Jude 3; Rom. 12:1)
- He comforts you, (Jn. 14:16; Ps. 23:4)
- He rebukes and reproves you (Titus 1:13; 2Tim. 4:2).
- He convicts you of sin (Rom. 6:1-23).
- He leads you to salvation (Rom. 10:9-10; 2Tim. 3:15).
- He assures you of the Father's love toward you (1Jn. 3:1; Jer. 31:3).
- He admonishes and warns you (Eph. 6:4; Acts 21:4,10-14).
- He edifies you (Eph. 4:12).
- He increases your faith (Rom. 10:17).
- He causes you to triumph in life through Christ (2Cor. 2:14).

> *"In prophetic worship we must learn to be open to the present voice of God as He is seen and heard among His people."*

Strangely enough, some Christians are content with the reports of what others have studied, heard, and learned about the Lord. Some are satisfied with reading His written Word, claiming to never hear Him personally.

The Word of God must always be our basis for hearing the voice of God. In prophetic worship, God's voice is freely available to us. What better place is there to receive His thoughts about today and the future than in worship?

There are countless instances where the Word of God was used in worship to bring direction and insight to the congregation. I heard a singer prophetically singing over a congregation that the Lord was calling broken and backslidden people to His arms on one particular day. At that very moment, a woman was standing at the congregation microphone ready to read the story of the prodigal son to the congregation (Lk. 15:11-32). Clearly, these two people had independently received the same direction for the service—the Lord wanted to bless His people through song and through His Word. Several people made their way to the altar that day and received the healing and comfort of God.

THE PROGRESSION OF THE VOICE OF GOD IN WORSHIP

There are many ways to enter the presence of God, many pathways in worship that lead into His courts. Griffing spoke often of these different phases of communication with the Lord in worship:[2]

- We minister to one another
- We minister to God
- God ministers to us
- We minister to the world

We minister to one another: As we enter into the presence of God, we need to be in one accord. The worship leader should choose songs that gather the people and unite their hearts. This gathering experience often takes place naturally before the service begins. Some churches make a place for such fellowship at the beginning of the service. Worship unites a congregation in ways that nothing else can. Once we have experienced His presence together, there comes a unity that time and interpersonal difficulties can scarcely mar.

We minister to God: The second phase is setting our attention upon the Lord. It is here that our priestly ministry to the Lord begins. He is the focus of our worship, the central theme of our songs, and our chief goal. We must never allow other things to tempt us to forsake our focus.

During this phase, there is a sense of *ascension* in our songs and communication with the Lord. Worship leaders can compile their song list according to theme and key signatures in such a way that we "lift" the congregation before the throne of God; lead the people to His face so they can commune with Him. The goal at this stage is to bring the congregation into a place of speaking or singing *to* God. It is here that the Lord is enthroned in praise. He inhabits our songs and shows himself to us (Ps. 22:3).

> "Worship unites a congregation in ways that nothing else can."

God ministers to us: Waiting on the Lord for His response and voice is the third phase. It takes a prophetic, listening heart to hear and the death of self to enter in.

We must believe that the Lord manifests himself to His people. It is the manifest presence of the Lord that sets us apart from all other religions on earth. Our God is real and present at all times, and He "shows" us His face in our midst. "Man's spirit and God's Spirit are never more uniquely blended than when we are in worship ... for worship is a love experience which, for one moment, blends two as though they are one."[3]

The children of Israel were invited to commune with the Lord as priests, and they eagerly accepted this honorable national office (Ex. 19:5–9). But it was at the very moment when God spoke to His people and displayed His awesome presence that they ran from Him and asked Moses to speak for Him instead. They were not prepared to pay the price that was required of all who desire to speak face to face with a holy God. Speaking with Him meant that they would die. Then they said to Moses, "You speak with us, and we will hear; but let not God speak with us lest we die" (Ex. 20:18–19).

Unfortunately, many of us are still running from God today. We say to our pastors, "You pay the price to go and talk with God, then come and tell us what He says and we will listen to you; but don't let God speak with us or we will die."

> "We must believe that the Lord manifests Himself to His people. It is this manifest presence of the Lord that sets us apart from all the other religions on earth."

Every believer has been invited to commune with God as a priest, but the price remains the same—death. The death to self we experience is not the same death that Old Testament saints endured, but it is the price for intimate fellowship.

The flow of this conversation with the Lord should have a theme and definite subject. We must allow the Lord to impart knowledge of himself and His thoughts concerning our personal lives. Consider carefully what He is saying and be cautious in the meeting place of God with His people.

I have noticed three subjects that the Lord engages in:

1. God's first and favorite subject seems to be himself. What I mean by this is that as He manifests himself, the most appropriate and constant subject is the declaration of His person, character, and attributes. There are angels around His throne for one purpose—they cry out what they see in His presence. Day and night they proclaim, "Holy, holy, holy is the Lord of hosts. The whole earth is full of His glory!" (Is. 6:3). "Holy, holy, holy, Lord God Almighty, who was and is and is to come!" (Rev. 4:8; 5:12-13).

   These are just some of the unceasing cries that surround

His presence and make a display of His glory to all who look and hear. These statements are not just mere words, but are the infusion of His glory into the atmosphere, the display of His person into the universe. It would be impossible to describe His holiness in such a way as to exhaust the subject. Angels will never complete this song. The layers of His holiness never come to an end. It is impossible to complete the description of His beauty. Every attribute is unending in scope and magnitude. After a thousand years of contemplation, they might look again and fall before Him in amazement as one more layer of holiness is revealed. Day and night, year after year, century after century throughout eternity, there will be no end to the description of this one attribute alone.

We can sing, "Holy, holy, holy!" three times and be ready for the next song because we are simply singing a song. If we go through the song to the God who is holy; if we would meet Him and commune in this place of worship; if we would behold His holiness and be changed, then we can say we have met Him and heard His voice in worship. He is ready to speak into our lives as we contemplate His glory, majesty, wisdom, power, love and peace! This first subject is the primary subject surrounding God's voice and revelation. The second and third subjects flow out of this one.

2. God's second subject surrounds the words He has for His children. This is usually *our* favorite subject. We like to hear Him describing His love for us and all the wonderful things He is doing, and is going to do, on our behalf. I think this has been the focus of the majority of our prophetic words and worship over the years. He brings comfort, guidance, wisdom, peace, revelation, etc. This is a most necessary part of God's voice among us, but it should not prevail over the subject of God himself. I don't

want to diminish the importance of God's voice in our lives. He has a lot to say to us.

3. God's third subject draws us to His kingdom matters. Once we see Him and are changed into His likeness, we are ready to work alongside Him and partner with Him as He floods the earth with His glory. We get to make decrees over cities and nations (Job 22:28, AMP) as we speak and declare the will of God into situations (Eph. 6a, 20). We administer God's kingdom justice; participate in prophetic intercession on behalf of all peoples; play a crucial role in shifting the atmosphere over nations and cities and call nations and generations into the kingdom of God. We are His royal ambassadors – this is just one of the holy callings and privileges that worshipers engage in: Now then, "we are ambassadors for Christ, as though God were pleading through us: we implore you on Christ's behalf, be reconciled to God" (2Cor. 5:20).

When we worship, we stand before His throne and minister His blessing and kingdom life into whatever nation He has assigned us to. God has given us a mandate to govern the earth that He has made – to minister to it and in it on His behalf Genesis 1:28: "Fill the earth and govern it..." (NLT)

We see this again in Psalm 8 – all the earth is in submission to God's people.

Psalm 8:5-8

Yet what honor you have given to men,
created only a little lower than Elohim,
crowned like kings and queens with glory and magnificence.
6 You have delegated to them
mastery over all you have made,

> making everything subservient to their authority,
> placing earth itself under the feet of your image-bearers.
> 7-8 All the created order and every living thing
> of the earth, sky, and sea—
> the wildest beasts and all the sea creatures—
> everything is in submission to Adam's sons.

Not only is the earth in submission to the Church, but all Kings and nations are in complete submission to the rule of God through Christ the Son of God and the Church – the Bride of Christ.

Psalm 2:7-9

> "I will reveal the eternal purpose of God.
> For he has decreed over me, 'You are my favored Son.
> And as your Father I have crowned you as my King Eternal.
> Today I became your Father.
> 8 Ask me to give you the nations and I will do it,
> and they shall become your legacy.
> Your domain will stretch to the ends of the earth.
> 9 And you will shepherd them with unlimited authority,
> crushing their rebellion as an iron rod smashes jars of clay!'"

These verses come to life in worship. As this third subject is unwrapped in any given service, we can expect to see kingdom work being accomplished. We need to be ready for the day when it is on the heart of God to unleash His Ambassadors of Hope into nations and generations – right there in your sanctuary, wherever you meet. Your congregation has the authority to affect nations as you worship. Your focus moves into dynamic worship intercession and warfare – taking on the subject(s) on the heart of God. Each member of the congregation must step into their role as Royal Ambassadors before God's throne, and lift their voices on behalf of cities, nations and peoples.

We can compare what Ambassadorial duties might involve and prepare ourselves to accomplish similar work in an even greater spiritual sense. As Christ's Ambassadors, we represent our King on a number of official occasions. We have standing before the throne of God and authority to speak on His behalf in the nations. We have power to affect the spiritual atmosphere and change events here on earth through effective intercession, mighty warfare and the formidable work we can do as ambassadors.

An ambassador:
- Attends official and important functions as a representative of his/her government (Dan. 3:2).

    Every time we gather, we are in attendance as Christ's Ambassadors to administrate His Priestly prayer in the earth "...May Your kingdom come...may Your will be done on earth as it is in heaven." Not only do we gather to worship God, but we gather to call His kingdom into this earthly realm (Matt. 6:10). Official gatherings of our churches are occasions for the King to reveal his plans and purposes.

- Carries messages from their king or leader to other leaders (Esther 3:12).

    As Royal Ambassadors, we carry the greatest message of all (the Gospel) and the mandate of our King into the nations of the earth.

- Contracts alliances and treaties (Gen. 26:26-31; Josh. 9:4).

  We gather to forge an alliance between our King of kings and the cities and nations of the earth. God's plan is to bless and restore cities and nations to their true destiny – not those depraved and sad stories that our nations and cities have come to be known for. God will see His glory cover your land, and alliances with heaven will bring that about. There will be times in worship where decrees need to be spoken and/or written over your city and nation.

  You shall also decide and decree a thing, and it shall be established for you; and the light [of God's favor] shall shine upon your ways. Job 22:28

- Solicits favors (Num. 20:14).

  In worship and intercession, we are asking for favor for our nations and cities. As ambassadors we have authority to call the favor of heaven into our nation.

- Argues or protests when wrong is done (Jud. 11:12).

  Just as ambassadors stand up for individuals or situations when injustice is occurring, we also can become ministers of God's kingdom justice. When politicians run out of ideas, when nations and people lose hope, it is time for the Church to arise and to wash the hopeless, poor and destitute with God's justice. He has ideas and plans beyond your imagination; He has miracles or restoration and justice that armies and politicians have never conceived of. We need to access heaven's court and lift our voices as true Ambassadors of the King's earthly realm. Be prepared for the Lord to download unusual ideas and solutions to long-standing and difficult problems. Don't be afraid to confront leaders and powers of darkness with God's justice.

- Extends congratulations and condolences for significant events in the name of their government. Speaks blessings from the king (2Sam. 10:2).

  On behalf of our King, we get to speak His official blessing to all leaders of our cities, states and nations. Not all significant events are natural events. At times, there may be natural and historical markers that have huge spiritual significance. These are times to remember God's blessings and call upon Him to wash the nations and pour out His glory and fire.

- Congratulates a king or queen (leaders) on his/her accession to the throne (1Ki. 5:1).

  Ambassadors are invited to attend important State events such as coronations, inaugurations, weddings, funerals, etc. Let the Church assemble for the joyous and solemn occasions of our nations. Our voices should be heard in the highest courts, palaces and halls of government.

- Grants access to the king's kingdom.

  Embassies and consulates grant visas and access to nations. This is one of our greatest privileges – we have the authority to open the doors of heaven and grant "whoever calls on the name of the Lord" (Acts 2:21) entrance into this great kingdom that we represent.

  Now then, we are ambassadors for Christ, as though God were pleading through us: we implore you on Christ's behalf, be reconciled to God. 2Cor. 5:20

  And God has...given us the ministry of reconciling others to God. 2Cor. 5:18 (TPT)

- Brings healing between fractured and wounded nations and peoples (Prov. 13:17).

  Where covenants have been broken, blood has been spilled, evil has been committed, idolatry has taken place etc. Kingdom Ambassadors are needed to wash and heal the land.

An undependable messenger causes a lot of trouble, but the trustworthy and wise messengers release healing wherever they go. Prov. 13:17 (TPT)

- Promotes peace and diplomatic relationships between nations and peoples. (1Ki. 20:31-34; Prov. 15:1; 25:15).

Through God's wisdom and grace, we build bridges and soften hearts. Worshipers should be known as the wisest and most gracious people in the land. Our lives are filled with God's favor as we cry out: *"So wake up, you living gateways! Lift up your heads, you ageless doors of destiny! Welcome the King of Glory, for he is about to come through you."* Psalm 24:7 (The Passion Translation). We are living gateways...ageless doors of destiny that unite our earthly nation with heaven's coming King. What a privilege! We work alongside our Father to bind our land to its true call and destiny and we open doors of opportunity for our people to impact the entire world. Every nation has a global directive to assume her place in the family of nations and fulfill her most important function. Every nation carries treasures of God's eternal plan – every nation carries huge importance in God's courts

As Ambassadors, we have the Kingdom mandate of bringing "Peace on earth and goodwill to all men" (Lu. 2:14).

- Works on trade deals (Acts 7:10).

Wherever Joseph went, the people around him prospered and were blessed. Whether he was in Potiphar's house, the prison, or in Pharaoh's courts – they were all made more prosperous because of God's favor on Joseph's life.

As Ambassadors of the Kingdom of God, we open

heaven's door to entrepreneurs and business; release Kingdom finances into the body of Christ; participate in international trade negotiations through prayer and worship; bless the economy of cities and nations.

- Protects citizens and sometimes works on military issues (2Cor. 10:4).

Whenever citizens of the Ambassador's home nation are in trouble, the Ambassador fights on their behalf for their safety and protection. In these days we see a rise in human, sexual and drug trafficking. Many of our Kingdom citizens are in trouble around the world due to religious extremism, terrorism, persecution, and political turmoil. We have a lot of work to do in realms of spiritual warfare to shut down these evils and see God arise (Ps. 68:1). Verse two of Psalm 68 says that the wicked flee at the presence of God. When the worshipers arise...when we lift God's presence in the nations, every enemy is defeated.

The possibilities are endless. This makes church the most exciting place to be on any given Sunday. We are partnering with our Father and King on official business through prophetic worship and prayer. We can see in this glorious work of worship that the congregation is a long way from being an "audience."

We may not necessarily see all three of these subjects in a service. However, there is one worship service in the Bible where we do see all three subjects, but this is unusual:

Isaiah 6:

V1-4 Subject One:

The Lord speaks of himself, allows His attributes to be made known. His holiness and glory are described.

V5-7 Subject Two:

The Lord ministered to Isaiah after allowing him to see his own heart. Isaiah was "undone" in the presence of the

Lord, but He received forgiveness and cleansing.

V8-9 Subject Three:
> The Lord's voice was heard asking if someone could go out on His behalf. Isaiah, the one who now had a cleansed mouth, volunteered to go and do the Lord's work.

We minister to the world: In the fourth phase of worship, we go from communion with the Lord to being living witnesses of His excellence. In the Book of Acts the boldness of Christians who had been face to face with the Lord caused unbelievers to recognize Christ in them (Acts 4:13).

Worship is not intended to keep us away from the world, but to propel us into becoming dynamic examples of the holiness, power, grace, and love of God. Worship was never intended to become a separate experience from the wider community of fellow human beings. Whatever God shows us of himself must now be modeled in our lives.

Prophetic worship is not for the few who come to our services, but it signals a time of blessing for all the earth. When we commune with the Lord, we gain His heart for the lost, His love for the nations, and His perspective for every situation. Worship releases us from the walls of our churches as more able ministers of God's glory. Hopefully, a new day of supernatural evangelism awaits the world as the Church learns how to enter the most supernatural and life-changing encounter known to man, "prophetic worship."

> *"Worship releases us from the walls of our churches as more able ministers of God's glory."*

TUNE YOUR EAR TO THE VOICE OF GOD

We live in an age of media. There are so many words and

opinions coming at us from so many different sources. Let us still our hearts, linger in his presence, and tune our ears to the voice of God. Allow Him to break in upon your news, TV, radio, movies, e-mail, cyberspace, video games, iPhones and iPads, Kindles, newspapers, magazines, and advertising billboards, and fill your life with His voice and perspective.

The voice of the Lord, powerful and full of majesty, is able to break the cedars, divide the flames of fire, shake the wilderness and cause the deer to give birth (Ps. 29). Surely, if we would allow His voice to be heard in our churches, we would see the evidence of His transforming power on a regular basis. I adjure you to let the mighty voice of the Lord be heard in your worship.

Chapter Twenty-Five

Conclusion

*Christian worship is the most momentous,
the most urgent,
the most glorious action
that can take place in human life.*
--Karl Barth

If the things I have said here about prophetic worship are true and theologically correct, then they must be able to apply to all denominations, generations, people groups, and personalities. Any church can flow in prophetic worship if they desire. It must be able to work within the framework of any liturgy or service that is Bible-based. It must be simple enough for children to participate in and profound enough for the seeker to run after forever. It must apply to any culture willing to submit to Christ, and no individual should feel excluded.

> "When He reveals himself to us, we will be shaken to the core—we will be ruined for ordinary things forever."

In order for prophetic worship to flow in every church and in the lives of all believers, we need to be willing and brave enough to face God in the most honest way, at the deepest level. When He reveals himself to us, we *will* be shaken to the core—we will be ruined for ordinary things forever. Church will never be the same again. Self will be forced out of our hearts again and again and will suffer a glorious death.

God's kingdom and the concept of relationship with Him must make sense to all mankind at a deep level of our being, since His foremost priority in creating us was to enjoy intimacy with us in worship. We were created for this. Gentile says, "Every religion finds its highest expression in worship."[1] The real question is, do we make sense to Him? Are there areas of our belief systems and lifestyles that must change in order to enjoy His manifest and prophetic presence? Is there room in your worship for God's manifest presence?

> "Is there room in your worship for God's manifest presence?"

We will never be able to fully grasp God's love and desire for us. Since the creation of man, the Lord has been forming, wooing, and waiting for His people to delight in His presence and have intimate fellowship with Him. The passionate song He sings over us must resound to every corner of our hearts until we are conquered by love and devoted to His Kingdom forever.

"My dove in the clefts of the rock, in the hiding places on the mountainside, show me your face, let me hear your voice; for your voice is sweet, and your face is lovely" (Song of S. 2:14, NIV).

"I will betroth you to Me forever; yes, I will betroth you to Me in righteousness and justice, in lovingkindness and mercy; I will betroth you to Me in faithfulness, and you shall know the Lord" (Hos. 2:19–20).

May each of us respond to Him with renewed vision for prophetic worship, which is the only way to know Him in extravagant intimacy. I praise God for those individuals and churches that contend for His presence and delight in hosting Him.

Time For Change

For many, entering into prophetic worship will involve great change, which is difficult and unsettling to us. It is easier to maintain the status quo. I entreat the Church, *regardless of your denomination or tradition, will you prayerfully consider making gentle and appropriate changes to your worship based on the principles outlined in the previous chapters?*

We must press through. Those in opposition may be strong and quite persuasive as people have programmed God out of their lives and religious services since the beginning of time.

Let God have His way with you.

"He desires to break in upon us, fill our hungry hearts with His presence, and transform us by His glory. It is hard to be told that one is not worshipping properly. Nobody likes to hear that; however, the Spirit of God wants to adjust us so that He can break into our churches in all His fullness."[2] Please note that as soon as you make headway into this worship, you will need to stay in prayer, or your church will easily slip back into the old status quo. It will be so much easier to default into the ways of worship that have been practiced in your church for decades.

Prophetic Worship

As I said in chapter one, prophetic worship is not necessarily loud, long, spontaneous, unusual, etc. These are not the factors that determine if worship is prophetic. God's voice and presence in the worship are the keys to understanding true worship. Worship is true, or authentic when our hearts are poured out before Him, and His voice and character are found among us. As heaven is unleashed upon your corporate worship, glory will be in your midst.

You can tell if you really worshiped—you will be changed. It is impossible to worship and stay the same. It is not the music or the songs that change you, the presence of God changes you. True worship will always bring glorious change.

The Lord Calls us to Intimate Worship

We also need to give time to the place of private devotion. Foster speaks of "the sanctuary of the heart," meaning that a place of inner devotion must be set aside for personal and intimate communion with the Lord. Our corporate expressions of worship are an extension of private worship. If any congregation has ardent and faithful worshipers in attendance, their corporate worship will have a greater chance of being vital and prophetic.

The worship I have described in this book is biblical and ultimately fulfilling for every man, woman, and child, regardless of denomination and culture. Such worship is born out of a deep reverence and fear of God and a respect for the traditions and integrity of every church and nation. The Psalmist asks a pertinent question: "Who may ascend into the hill of the LORD? Or who may stand in his holy place? He who has clean hands and a pure heart, who has not lifted up his soul to an idol" (Ps. 24:3–4).

In the end, it comes down to the purity of our love, passion and devotion to Christ, our Lord and King. Our worship of Him is induced by His passion for us. In the Song of Solomon, the bride pleads with her Lord that He wear her on His heart and hand as a sign of His devotion to her. The love between Christ and His Church is a holy love described here as fire: "Wear me as a seal close to your heart, wear me like a ring upon your hand; Love burns like a blazing fire; a most vehement flame (Song of S. 8:6, compilation of various translations).

Songwriter and friend, Mimi Ribble, wrote a beautiful song some years ago. These words express my final prayer for the Church in these days, that we allow the flame of our devotion to be exposed to the winds of the Holy Spirit; that this flame would grow in our hearts; and it would draw us to new depths in worship.

Keeper of the Flame

Keeper of the flame,
the flame within my heart.
The flame of my desire to know You and worship You more.
Blow upon the embers, let the flame grow brighter
'til all I do honors You, O Keeper of the Flame.[3]

The New Testament responds to this cry, "Let us therefore come boldly to the throne of grace" (Heb. 4:16a).

Teach people how to seek God— When they encounter Him,
They will worship.

ENDNOTES

Chapter One

[1] Bob Sorge, *Exploring Worship,* 126.
[2] Judson Cornwall, *Meeting God,* 154.
[3] Ralph P. Martin, *The Worship of God,* 10.
[4] Bob Sorge, *Exploring Worship,* 125.
[5] Ibid., 142.
[6] Ronald F. Youngblood, ed., *Nelson's New Illustrated Dictionary,* 1033.
[7] Robert E. Webber, ed., *The Complete Library of Christian Worship,* vol. 2, 346.
[8] A. W. Tozer, *The Pursuit of God,* 36.
[9] Ibid., 33.
[10] Ibid., 34–35.

Chapter Two

[1] Tom Schwanda, *Library,* vol. 2, 402.
[2] Michael Coleman, jacket notes from CD *Because We Believe,* ©1997, Hosanna! Music.
[3] Ibid., 20.
[4] *Life Application Bible,* notes on 1Chron. 16:25, 696.
[5] *The Oxford English Dictionary,* vol. 12, V–Z, 1933, 320–321.
[6] Judson Cornwall, *Elements of Worship,* 1.
[7] Sally Morgenthaler, *Worship Evangelism,* 48.
[8] Martin, *Worship of God,* 29.
[9] Sammy Tippit, *Worthy of Worship,* 13.
[10] David Peterson, *Engaging With God—A Biblical Theology of Worship,* 70.
[11] Paul Sarchet-Waller, *Praise and Worship,* p. 8.
[12] Sorge, 1.
[13] Gerhard Tersteegen, source unknown.

14 Cornwall, *Elements*, 45.

Chapter Three

1 J. Daane, *The International Standard Bible Encyclopedia,* vol. 4, pp. 826- 827.
2 Webber, *Library,* vol. 2, 291.
3 James Empereur, *Library,* vol. 2, 262.
4 G. Thomas Halbrooks, *Library,* vol.2, 293.
5 Henry Jauhiainen, *Library,* vol. 2, 338.
6 LaMar Boschman, *A Heart of Worship,* 52.
7 Morgenthaler, 49.
8 Jauhiainen, 338.
9 Richard Foster, *Celebration of Discipline,* 158-159.
10 Kevin Conner, *The Tabernacle of David,* 103.
11 This paragraph is based on the author's notes of a sermon preached by Olen Griffing, entitled, *"The Praise Life of Jesus."*
12 Jauhiainen, *Library,* "A Pentecostal/Charismatic Manifesto," 338.
13 Gerrit Gustafson, *Library,* vol. 2, 310-312.
14 Gregory Wilde, *Library,* vol. 2, 276.
15 G. W. Bromiley, *ISBE,* vol. 3, 596.
16 Cornwall, *Meeting*, 149
17 From the Greek word, *epiclesis,* the 'calling down' of the Holy Spirit during the Eucharistic prayer to make Christ present in the Eucharist—in the elements of bread and wine and in the gathered community of worshipers.
18 Wilde, 278.

Chapter Four

1 Andrew Wilson-Dickson, *The Story of Christian Music*, 11.
2 Peterson, 56.
3 Ernest B. Gentile, "Worship God," in *Restoring Praise and Worship to the Church—An Anthology of Articles,* ed. Bob Sorge, 241.

4 Terry Law, *The Power of Praise and Worship,* 135.
5 Gentile, "Worship God," 242.
6 Ronald B. Allen, *Lord of Song,* 150.
7 Andrew Hill, *Enter His Courts With Praise!,* 6.
8 Carroll E. Simcox, *A Treasury of Quotations on Christian Themes,* n.p.
9 Francis J. Hall, source unknown.
10 Richard C. Leonard, *Library,* vol. 1, 21.

Section 2: Introduction
1 Herbert Lockyer, *All the 3's of the Bible,* 20.
2 Ibid., 25.

Chapter Five
1 Michael Marshall, *Library,* vol. 2, 375.
2 Webber, *Library,* vol. 2, 374.
3 Graham Kendrick, *Worship,* 183–184.

Chapter Six
1 Charles H. Spurgeon, *Evening by Evening,* 54.
2 Tozer, 41.
3 These points originated in a sermon preached by Olen Griffing, Senior Pastor of Shady Grove Church in Grand Prairie, Texas in the 1990s.

Chapter Seven
1 Cornwall, *Elements,* 45.
2 W. E. Vine, *An Expository Dictionary of New Testament Words,* pp. 64–65. Each of the definitions for the Greek words in this row come from Vine's dictionary.
3 F. W. Danker, *ISBE,* vol. 3, 382.
4 Adam Clarke, *The New Testament of our Lord and Saviour Jesus Christ,*

3261 –3327.

[5] Tippit, 69–70.

[6] David Blomgren, "The Prophetic Spirit in Worship," in *Restoring Praise and Worship to the Church—An Anthology of Articles*, 129–130.

Chapter Eight

[1] Cornwall, *Meeting*, 155.

[2] E. F. Harrison, *ISBE,* vol. 2, 479.

[3] Clarke, *NT,* 326.

[4] Leonard, 72.

[5] Spurgeon, *Treasury of David,* vol. 1, 318–319.

[6] I heard this through the teaching of Charlotte Baker. She insists, however, that Paul Wilbur (formerly from *Israel's Hope*) shared this with her.

[7] LaMar Boschman, *Pathways*—LaMar Boschman Ministries newsletter June 1998, vol. 1, Number One.

[8] Leonard, *Library,* vol. 1, 71.

[9] Foster, 160.

[10] Spurgeon, *Treasury,* 219.

Chapter Nine

[1] John Dryden, source unknown.

[2] Morgenthaler, 47.

[3] George MacDonald, source unknown.

[4] John W. Stevenson, *The 2nd Flood—the Discipline of Worship,* 46.

[5] Foster, 173.

[6] W.E Vine, Merrill F. Unger, William White, Jr., *Vine's Complete Expository Dictionary of Old and New Testament Words,* 639.

[7] *Random House Webster's Dictionary,* 415.

[8] William Morris, Editor, *Young Students Intermediate Dictionary,* 455.

[9] Foster, 173.

[10] Tozer, 94.
[11] *The Jerome Biblical Commentary*, 279.
[12] Foster, 173.
[13] Tozer, 36.
[14] Law, 136.

Chapter Ten

[1] St. John of Damascus lived during the years of c. 700–c. 760. This was the most frequently quoted definition of God used during the Middle Ages.
[2] Bernard of Clairvaux 1090-1153. [3] Alan W. Watts, source unknown. [4] Peterson, *Message,* 423.
[5] Martin, *Worship of God,* 210. The information from this chart was first taken from the writing of Stephen S. Smalley—"The Christ-Christian Relationship in Paul and John," in *Pauline Studies,* (Grand Rapids: Eerdmans; Exeter: Paternoster Press, 1980), 95–105.
[6] Peterson, *Message,* 373.
[7] Judson Cornwall, *Let Us Worship,* 137.

Chapter Eleven

[1] Cornwall, *Let Us Worship,* 96.
[2] Tozer, 17.
[3] Foster, 158.
[4] Clarke, *NT,* 326.
[5] *The Voice Bible*
[6] Eugene H. Peterson, *The Message.*
[7] *The Amplified Bible*

Chapter Twelve

[1] Jack Hayford, *Worship His Majesty,* 24.

[2] Webber, *Library,* vol. 2, 343.

[3] Tippit, 64.

[4] Jaroslav Pelikan, "The Vindication of Tradition": The 1983 Jefferson Lecture in the Humanities.

[5] Matsuo Basho. Born 1644, Basho was a famous Japanese poet and haiku master.

[6] Ambrose Bierce, *The Devil's Dictionary.*

[7] Hill, 52. The first sentence of this quote comes from C. D. Erickson, *Participating in Worship: History, Theory and Practice,* 16.

[8] Paul Waitman Hoon, *Library,* vol. 2, 403.

Chapter Thirteen

[1] Tippit, 43.

[2] Matthew Henry, *The Bethany Parallel Commentary on the New Testament,* 526.

[3] Ibid., 526.

[4] Ibid.

[5] Adam Clarke, *The Bethany Parallel Commentary on the New Testament,* 526.

[6] Tozer, 33.

[7] Foster, 165.

[8] Ronald Allen and Gordon Borror, *Worship: Rediscovering the Missing Jewel,* 39.

[9] Cornwall, *Elements,* 45.

Chapter Fourteen

[1] Foster, 165.

[2] Morgenthaler, 67.

Chapter Fifteen
[1] Robert Webber *Worship Is a Verb*, 12.
[2] Tom Schwanda, *Library*, vol. 2, 400.
[3] Martin, 228.
[4] Tippit, 96-97.
[5] Cornwall, *Elements*, 109.
[6] Tenney was speaking at a workshop on Friday May 8th, 1998, entitled "Touching the Face of God: Changing the Face of Your City."

Chapter Sixteen
[1] Anonymous quote by an Employment Counselor.
[2] Vine, Unger, and White, 542–543.
[3] Hill, 106.
[4] A. W. Tozer, quoted in *Worthy of Worship*, by Sammy Tippit, 18.
[5] Ladislaus Boros, source unknown.
[6] Herbert Van Zeller, source unknown.
[7] Charlotte Baker – from private conversations

Chapter Seventeen
[1] Edgar Watson Howe, source unknown.
[2] Webber, *Library*, 344.
[3] Notes on worship by Dr. Sam Sasser.
[4] Bob Sorge, "The Full Purpose of Worship," in *Restoring Praise and Worship to the Church—An Anthology of Articles*, 35.
[5] Allen, 151.

Chapter Eighteen
[1] Tozer, 35.
[2] Ibid., 36.
[3] Cornwall, *Let Us Worship*, 116.

[4] Cornwall, *Elements,* 47.
[5] Allen and Borror, 75.
[6] Ernest Gentile, *"Worship—Are We Making Any Mistakes?,"* in *RestoringPraise and Worship,* ed. Bob Sorge*, 21.*
[7] Webber, *Library,* 344–345.
[8] Ibid., 347.
[9] Foster, 169.
[10] Boschman, *Heart,* 55.
[11] Graham Kendrick, *Worship,* 17–18.
[12] Terry Howard Wardle, *Library,* vol. 2, 405.
[13] Morgenthaler, 50.

Chapter Nineteen

[1] Schwanda, 399.
[2] Gerrit Gustafson, *Library,* vol. 4, 181.
[3] Kent Henry, *Library,* vol.2, 351.
[4] Cornwall, *Elements,* 108.
[5] James Strong, *Strong's Exhaustive Concordance,* (Appendix: Dictionary of the Hebrew Bible), 107.
[6] Sosene Le'au offers an interesting and helpful list of the strengths of various people groups in his 1997 book, *Called to Honor Him,* 97–99.
[7] I attended a Promise Keepers Worship Summit in Denver, Colorado, in March 11–12, 1997, with Roberta King, Appianda Arthur, Sosene Le'au and other ministers in the area of worship, where they gave a report on their work in several nations.
[8] Le'au, 29–30.
[9] See pp 94–95 for an explanation of the numinous aspect of God's presence.
[10] Henry, 352.
[11] Dutch Sheets, *Intercessory Prayer,* 116.
[12] Gentile, "Worship God," 242.
[13] Anton E. Armstrong, *Library,* vol. 4, 180-181.

[14] Ibid., 36–40.
[15] Henry, 351.
[16] Webber, 399.
[17] Schwanda, 402.
[18] Boschman, *Heart*, 31.

Chapter Twenty

[1] André Gide, source unknown.
[2] Michelangelo quoted by Giorgio Vasar, *The Great Masters*, 301-302.
[3] Allen and Borror, 22.
[4] Wilson-Dickson, 11.
[5] Vincent Van Gogh in c 1880, quoted in Uhde, *Vincent Van Gogh*, 1947.
[6] Robert Browning, "Paracelsus," 1835.
[7] John S. Baldwin, source unknown.
[8] Thomas Browne, source unknown.
[9] Michelangelo Buonarroti quoted in *Holland De Pintura Antigua*, (16th C).
[10] Wilson-Dickson, 12.
[11] Ibid., p. 12. Quoting from T.S. Eliot, ed., *Literary Essays,* by Ezra Pound, London, 1960, 43, 45.
[12] Giorgio Vasari, *The Great Masters*, 235–236.
[13] Vivien Hibbert, *Praise Him*, 12.
[14] Webber, *Library,* vol. 2, 348.

Chapter Twenty-One

[1] Source unknown.
[2] Dr. Frank Trotter:
   http://www.fumcpasadena.org/sermons/2009/3.29.09.pdf
[3] Ibid.
[4] Norm Frederick, Elder/Pastor at Shady Grove Church, Grand Prairie, Texas, Feb. 24, 1998.

[5] Paul McCartney speaking to Oprah Winfrey—*Oprah Winfrey Show,* December 19, 1997.

Chapter Twenty-Two
[1] Words and music by David Ruis, © 1994 Mercy/Vineyard Publishing.
[2] Terry Howard Wardle, *Library,* vol. 2, 405.
[3] Calvin Coolidge, quoted in: *12,000 Religious Quotations,* 479.
[4] Wardle, 406.
[5] Boschman, *Heart,* 18.
[6] Sheets, 143.

Chapter Twenty-Three
[1] Foster, *Celebration,* 171.
[2] Graham Kendrick, *Worship,* 44–45.
[3] Cornwall, *Elements,* 111.
[4] Tozer, 87-88.

Chapter Twenty-Four
[1] Anonymous.
[2] Olen Griffing is the Apostolic Elder of Gateway Church in Dallas, TX. These four phases were first spoken of by Ralph Nabors in relationship to cell ministry. Pastor Griffing applies them to worship.
[3] Cornwall, *Elements,* 119.

Chapter Twenty-Five
[1] Gentile, "Worship God," 242.
[2] Gentile, "Worship—Are We Making Any Mistakes?," 20–21.
[3] Words and Music by Mimi Ribble, © 1991 Mastersong Music.

BIBLIOGRAPHY

Allen, Ronald, *Lord of Song,* Portland, OR: Multnomah Press, 1982.

Allen, Ronald and Gordon Borror, *Worship; Rediscovering the Missing Jewel,* Portland, OR: Multnomah Press, 1982.

Alsobrook, David, *True Worship,* Paducah, KY: Anointed Bible Study Fellowship, Inc., 1983.

Baker, Dr. E. Charlotte, *On Eagle's Wings,* Seattle, WA, 1979.

_____, *The Eye of the Needle and Other Prophetic Parables,* Hagerstown, MD: Parable Publications, 1997.

Blomgren, David K., Douglas Christoffel, and Dean Smith, *Restoring Praise and Worship to the Church—An Anthology of Articles,* Shippensburg, PA: Revival Press, 1989.

Blomgren, David K., *The Song of the Lord,* Portland, OR: Bible Temple Publications, 1978.

Boschman, LaMar, *A Heart of Worship.* Orlando, FL: Creation House, 1994.

_____, *The Prophetic Song,* Bedford, TX: Revival Press, 1986.

_____, *The Rebirth of Music,* Shippensburg, PA: Destiny Image Publication, 1986.

Bromiley, Geoffrey W., General Editor, *The International Standard Bible Encyclopedia,* Volumes One—Four, Grand Rapids, MI: William B. Eerdmans Publishing Company, 1986.

Clarke, Adam, *The New Testament of our Lord and Saviour Jesus Christ,* Volume Five, Nashville, TN: Abingdon, from text written C. 1624.

Conner, Kevin J., *The Tabernacle of David,* Portland, OR: Bible Temple Publishing, 1976.

Cornill, Carl Heinrich, *Music in the Old Testament,* Chicago, Chicago, IL: The Open Court Publishing Company, 1909.

Cornwall, Judson, *David Worshiped a Living God,* Shippensburg, PA: Revival Press, 1989.

_____, *David Worshiped With a Fervent Faith,* Shippensburg, PA: Revival Press, 1993.

_____, *Elements of Worship,* South Plainfield, NJ, Bridge Publishing, Inc., 1985.

_____, *Let Us Draw Near,* Plainfield, NJ: Logos International, 1977.

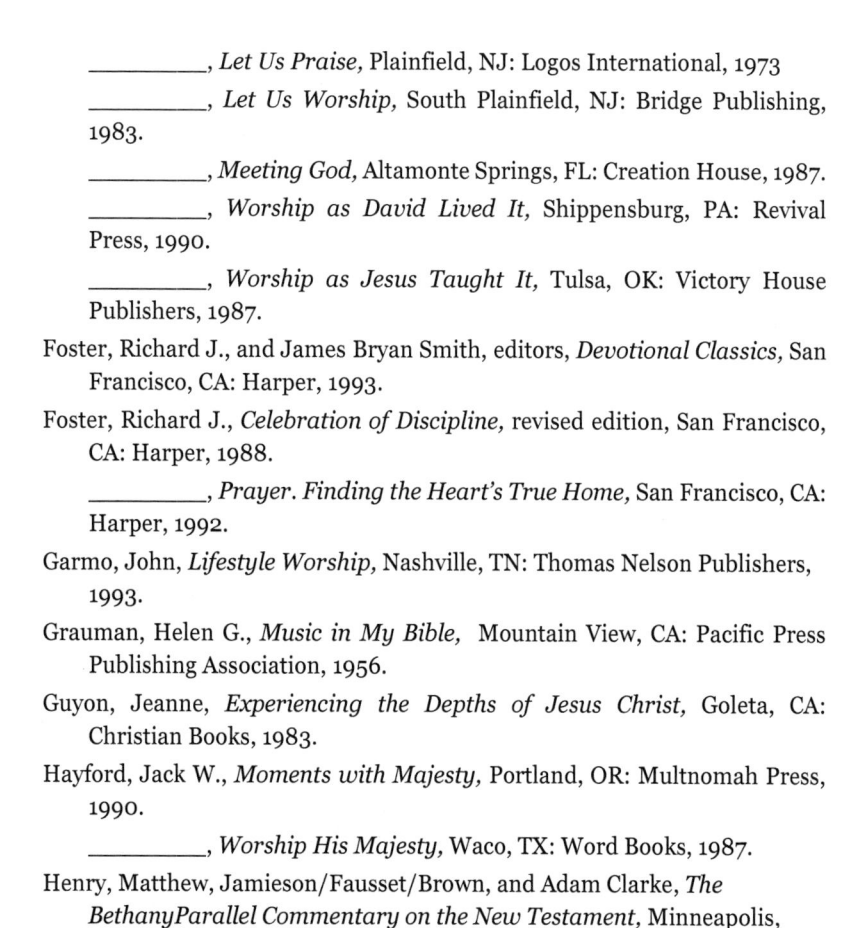

>   _____, *Let Us Praise,* Plainfield, NJ: Logos International, 1973
>
>   _____, *Let Us Worship,* South Plainfield, NJ: Bridge Publishing, 1983.
>
>   _____, *Meeting God,* Altamonte Springs, FL: Creation House, 1987.
>
>   _____, *Worship as David Lived It,* Shippensburg, PA: Revival Press, 1990.
>
>   _____, *Worship as Jesus Taught It,* Tulsa, OK: Victory House Publishers, 1987.

Foster, Richard J., and James Bryan Smith, editors, *Devotional Classics,* San Francisco, CA: Harper, 1993.

Foster, Richard J., *Celebration of Discipline,* revised edition, San Francisco, CA: Harper, 1988.

>   _____, *Prayer. Finding the Heart's True Home,* San Francisco, CA: Harper, 1992.

Garmo, John, *Lifestyle Worship,* Nashville, TN: Thomas Nelson Publishers, 1993.

Grauman, Helen G., *Music in My Bible,* Mountain View, CA: Pacific Press Publishing Association, 1956.

Guyon, Jeanne, *Experiencing the Depths of Jesus Christ,* Goleta, CA: Christian Books, 1983.

Hayford, Jack W., *Moments with Majesty,* Portland, OR: Multnomah Press, 1990.

>   _____, *Worship His Majesty,* Waco, TX: Word Books, 1987.

Henry, Matthew, Jamieson/Fausset/Brown, and Adam Clarke, *The BethanyParallel Commentary on the New Testament,* Minneapolis, MN:Bethany House Publishers, 1983.

Hibbert, Mike, and Vivien Hibbert, *Music Ministry,* Christchurch, New Zealand, 1982.

Hibbert, Vivien, *Praise Him,* Texarkana, AR: A division of Phao Books, 2006, 2007, 2014.

Hill, Andrew E., *Enter His Courts With Praise!,* Grand Rapids, MI: Baker Books, 1985.

The Jerome Biblical Commentary, Englewood Cliffs, NJ: Prentice-Hall Inc., 1968.

Kempis, Thomas à, *Of the Imitation of Christ,* Springdale, PA: Whitaker House, 1981.

Kendrick, Graham, *Learning to Worship as a Way of Life,* Minneapolis, MN: Bethany House Publications, 1984.

_____, *Worship,* Sussex, Great Britain: Kingsway Publications Ltd., 1984.

Kraeuter, Tom, *Developing an Effective Worship Ministry,* Hillsboro, MO: Training Resources, 1993.

Law, Terry, *The Power of Praise and Worship,* Tulsa, OK: Victory House Publishers, 1985.

Lockyer, Herbert, *All the 3s of the Bible,* Grand Rapids, MI: Fleming H. Revell, 1973.

Le'au, Sosene, *Called to Honor Him.* Tampa, FL: Culture Com Press, Inc., 1997.

Martin, Ralph P., *The Worship of God,* Grand Rapids, MI: Eerdmans, 1982.

_____, *Worship in the Early Church,* Grand Rapids, MI: Eerdmans, 1974.

Morris, William, Editor in Chief, *Young Students Intermediate Dictionary,* Middletown, CT: Field Publications, 1973.

Morgenthaler, Sally, *Worship Evangelism,* Grand Rapids, MI: Zondervan Publishing House, 1995.

Peterson, David, *Engaging With God—A Biblical Theology of Worship,* Grand Rapids, MI: Wm. B. Eerdmans Publishing Co., 1992.

Peterson, Eugene, H., *The Message,* Colorado Springs, CO: Alive Communications, 1993.

Pettis, Ashley, *Music: Now and Then,* New York, NY: Coleman-Ross Company, Inc., 1955.

Roberts, Debby, *Rejoice: A Biblical Study of the Dance,* Little Rock, AR: Revival Press, 1982.

Sarchet-Waller, Paul, *Praise and Worship,* Hong Kong: Elim Full Gospel Publications, 1986.

Sendry, Mildred, and Alfred N., *David's Harp,* New York, NY: Philosophical Library, 1969.

Sendry, Alfred, *Music in Ancient Israel,* New York, NY: Philosophical Library, 1969.

Simcox, Carroll E., *A Treasury of Quotations on Christian Themes,* New York, NY: The Seabury Press, 1975.

Sheets, Dutch, *Intercessory Prayer,* Ventura, CA: Regal Books, 1996.

Sorge, Bob, *Exploring Worship: A Practical Guide to Praise and Worship,* New Wilmington, PA: Son-Rise Publication, 1987.

Spurgeon, Charles H., *Evening by Evening,* Pittsburgh, PA: Whitaker House, 1984.

_____, *The Treasury of David,* Vols. 1 & 2. MI: Byron Center, Associated Publishers and Authors, Inc., reprinted 1970.

Stevenson, John W., *The 2nd Flood,* Shippensburg, PA: Destiny Image Publishers, 1990.

Strong, James, *The Exhaustive Concordance of the Bible,* Grand Rapids, MI: Baker Book House, 1980.

_____, *The New Strong's Complete Dictionary of Bible Words,* Nashville, TN: Thomas Nelson Publishers, 1996.

Tame, David, *The Secret Power of Music,* New York, NY: Destiny Books, 1984.

Tenney, Merrill C., *The Zondervan Pictorial Encyclopedia of the Bible,* Grand Rapids, MI: Zondervan Corporation, 1976.

Tippit, Sammy, *Worthy of Worship,* Chicago, IL: The Moody Bible Institute, 1989.

Tomkins, Iverna, *If It Please the King,* Decatur, GA: Iverna Tomkins Ministry, no date.

_____, *The Ravished Heart,* Decatur, GA: Iverna Tomkins Ministry, no date.

Tozer, A. W., *The Pursuit of God,* Camp Hill, PA: Christian Publications, 1993.

_____, *Signposts,* Compiled by Harry Verploegh, Wheaton, IL: Victor Books, 1988.

Truscott, Graham, *The Power of His Presence,* Burbank, CA: World Map, 1972.

Unger, Merrill F., *Unger's Bible Dictionary,* Chicago, IL: Moody Press, 1966.

Vine, W. E., Merrill F. Unger, and William White, Jr., *Vine's Complete Expository Dictionary of Old and New Testament Words,* Nashville, TN: Thomas Nelson, Inc., 1985.

Vine, W. E., *An Expository Dictionary of New Testament Words*, Westwood, NJ: Fleming H. Revell Co., 1940.

Vasarai, Giorgio, *The Great Masters*, Translated by Gaston Du C. de Vere, edited by Michael Sonino, Hong Kong: Hugh Lauter Levin Associates, Inc. 1986.

Venolia, Jan, *Write Right!*, third edition, Berkeley, CA: Ten Speed Press, 1995

Wilson-Dickson, *The Story of Christian Music,* original ed., Oxford, England: Lion Publishing, 1992. This ed., Minneapolis, MN: Fortress Press, 1996.

Webber, Robert E., ed., *The Complete Library of Christian Worship,* Volumes One to Seven, Nashville, TN: Star Song Publishing Group, 1993.

_____, *Worship Old and New,* Grand Rapids, MI: Zondervan Publishing Co., 1982.

Wiersbe, Warren W., *Classic Sermons on Worship,* Grand Rapids, MI: Hendrickson Publishers, Inc., 1988.

Wiley, Lulu Rumsey, *Bible Music,* New York, NY: The Paebar Company, 1945.

Yancey, Philip, *Reality and the Vision,* Dallas, TX: Word Publishing, 1990.

Resources available through Vivien's Website:
www.vivienhibbert.com

OTHER BOOKS BY VIVIEN HIBBERT:
• *Praise Him* - This book includes hundreds of lists that describe the Lord and why He is worthy of praise. This is a helpful resource for prayer and meditation, or for worship leaders, songwriters, writers, poets, and all students of God's presence who love to worship.

SPIRAL BOOKLETS:
• The Role of the Congregation in Worship
• Secrets and Mysteries of God
• Prophetic Song
• The Fragrance of God
• David's Tabernacle – God's Plan for Glory
• The Anointing
• The Courts of the Lord
• Hiding Places
• Keys for Worship renewal
• Taste and See
• Hearing God's Voice

CD'S BY VIVIEN HIBBERT:
• *Shepherd's Suite* - is based on Psalm 23. It is an instrumental CD that takes you on a journey through each verse of this Psalm. Vivien is playing mandolin, flutes, hammered dulcimer, mountain dulcimer and an Australian didgeridoo.

• *Songs From The Father's Heart* - is an instrumental soaking CD. It focuses on the songs that the Lord sings over us to bring comfort and healing in our lives. Vivien is playing mandolin and flutes and is joined by several excellent musicians from Norway.

About Vivien Hibbert

Author, teacher, musician and worship leader, Vivien Hibbert was born in New Zealand and began full time ministry in 1977 as a teacher of praise and worship. In 1985, Vivien immigrated to the U.S. and has served in full-time pastoral and/or music ministry until today.

In Vivien co-founded the Worship Arts Conservatory, the first online school of worship. Currently, she is the instructor of the online School of Worship and School of Prophetic Worship Teams at the Eagles international Training Institute in Dallas.

Vivien is a regular faculty member of several worship conferences in the United States and overseas and has taught extensively at Youth With A Mission both domestically and abroad. She has ministered in over twenty nations and is a member of ICE (International Council of Ethnodoxologists).

Vivien has many years of experience in a wide variety of ministries including teaching in church services, bible schools, prisons, hospitals, conferences, retreats, women's conferences, youth meetings in many nations and denominations.

Vivien has written numerous books, recorded four albums/Cds, and made numerous radio and television appearances.

She now lives in Texarkana Arkansas, where she is working with her home church, Waterwaze, to equip local ministries. Waterwaze conducts regular nights of prophetic worship for the cities of Texarkana and Ashdown and they periodically send worship teams into various prayer and worship events in Arkansas and beyond.

Contact Information: www.vivienhibbert.com
Blog: www.theheartoftheworshiper.blogspot.com
YouTube: Vivien Hibbert